THE MAKING OF 12 WESTERNS:
Or How I Made a Dozen Movies in One Year During a Global Pandemic and Survived

By Travis Mills

Table of Contents

INTRODUCTION

By Gus Edwards

I'd like to say without fear of hyperbole or exaggeration that for the film student or aspiring filmmaker this might possibly be the most important book you will ever read about the practical art of getting films made. Saying that I know there are many, many books about making movies in all kinds of ways. I know that for sure, I've read a good number of those books during the twenty odd years I taught film as Arizona State University. The problem for me with those books is that most of them glamorize and romanticize the filmmaking process to the extent that it inspires an inordinate number of young people, who really don't know what they're getting into, to enroll and sometimes even go through several years of film school training only to realize at the end what an often frustrating, heart breaking, dream destroying endeavor it can be. And once realizing that they drop out and move on to other things often regretting the time (and money) spent. This is the first book I've read that gets down to the nuts and bolts business of what the filmmaking process is all about when you don't have a major studio or a rich family behind you as a funding source. This book tells you what to do, and how to go about things when you're just a lone filmmaker with a dream and a genuine as well as a tenacious desire to see that dream realized. A dream that doesn't rely on some mythical Hollywood producer coming out of the shadows at the last minute with a bag full of money to help you to make it happen. What this book does tell you is how you can make that dream a practical reality through sheer will power and an incredible amount of hard work. Of course some training and talent is also necessary. But the most important ingredients, as far as I can tell, is a hard core vision that cannot be shaken or compromised and the passionate and stubborn will to see it through to the bitter end. And that is what you have with Travis Mills and his *12 Westerns in 12 Months.* Who does this? Who would even dream of this? Only a madman or a visionary. And I could make an argument that they are more often than not, one and the same.

I remember when he first came to me with the idea, I thought it was absolute lunacy. Twelve westerns in twelve months. Why twelve and why westerns? Now I have to say that I was used to Travis' madness because prior to this, a few years earlier he had spoken to me about a project he was considering. And that was *52 short films in 52 weeks.* I thought he was mad then but then he went on to do exactly what he proposed. He made 52 quite respectable short films adapted from classic short stories that were in the public domain. I remember the work he put into reading hundreds of short stories before deciding which ones to adapt. And after that pulling a flexible cast and crew together in order to get it all done while staying on a schedule he had set for himself. All with not much money that he solicited from crowd funding sources. It was all a tightrope act watching him get to the end and then presenting all 52 films in a weekend long premiere in Phoenix that turned out to be one of the best films viewing events I have ever attended. When it was all over we all breathed a heavy sigh of relief because it was over. The mountain had been climbed and now it was time to just smile and relax and bask in the warm, sunlit feeling of mission accomplished. Now, here he was a few years later telling me about wanting to do not 12 shorts but 12 feature length films in as many months. And not just films but westerns. I think I might've even understood 12 films placed in contemporary times. But westerns? That meant costumes, guns, horses, period locations and a whole host of other problems one wouldn't have to deal with if the setting were contemporary. But it had to be westerns he insisted. He was enamored with the genre, which hadn't been in favor for quite a while. I suppose his intent was to try and revive it in some way. I am a great fan of westerns so I could understand his great affection for it. But twelve films and again without money? The man was not only mad but suicidal as well.

The first thing he needed were stories to tell. In other words, scripts. And since he had no money to purchase any he had to write them himself. Most of them anyway. Periodically he would send them to me for comment or just an outside opinion. I would give it and he would go on. Along with writing the scripts he was once again looking for funding, collecting crew members, scouting locations, making deals with horse owners and wranglers and in general doing all the preproduction work that every film requires. Particularly fiction films. With documentaries you can sometimes go in without much preparation or a plan. But with fictional narrative it all has to be preplanned down to the minutest detail. Especially if you're working with an extremely limited budget. And so he did, driving to and fro, hither and yonder meeting with potential investors, costume providers, union representatives, lawyers, actors, banking personnel and the myriad of people directly and indirectly involved in the filmmaking process. On productions with any kind of budget most of these tasks are done by a dozen or more specialists. But here it was Travis and Travis alone. Travis in person, Travis on the phone, Travis via texts and email, Travis trying to do as much as one could in the course of a working day, Travis trying to be everywhere at once. I know and I can attest to this because I witnessed much of this activity first hand.

I've known Travis for nearly twenty years. We met when he took several of my film classes at ASU. He was a young man interested in literature and film. We talked often after class and would sometimes meet for lunch just to talk films from just about every perspective from the practical to the theoretical. He was obviously passionate about the subject. All aspects of it. And when ASU officially inaugurated its film school, he was a member of its first graduating class. After that our get- togethers went beyond talking about films to actually making them. But in an informal way. Get a few people together, work on a project that would take a day or at most two to complete and then move on from there. But Travis wanted more. He wanted to make filmmaking his fulltime profession. Somewhere during that time we started *Running Wild Films*. But I was fully retired so that meant that Travis would have to take the reins and carry the burden if the company was going to be more than a plaything for a retired film professor. He did, planning and executing ambitious projects like *Durant's Never Closes (2016)* and the *52 shorts* previously mentioned, among many, many other films. His output was prolific. And with each new film I could see his mastery over his craft becoming more and more pronounced. As a director he was learning how to tell his story with grace and dynamism. Added to that he had become not only a good director of actors but a good film actor himself.

12 films in 12 months. What's the reason? Where's the logic? What's the rationale? I have no idea. Some have even suggested that it was a stunt to draw attention to him as a filmmaker. If it was it's quite a daring one and as previously mentioned crazy as well. But I don't think so. I think he did it because for his own private reasons he felt he had to; felt he was compelled to. Again, I'm just speculating. I just know that he decided to give this challenge to himself and I accepted it because I know there is no sensible answer as to why. It's like the men who climb Everest. Their answer is always the same: "Because it's there." For his own reasons, growth and to challenge himself Travis decided to embark on this journey accompanied by friends, co-workers and hired hands. Many came and went but he was the one there from beginning to end.

He clearly knew he was venturing into uncharted territory and so like the great explorers Lewis and Clark he kept a journal. I was fortunate enough to receive his entries on a weekly or bi-weekly basis which meant that from the comfortable confines of my home I was vicariously experiencing the journey along with him. And it was quite a trip I have to say. A trip filled with just about every human emotion possible: love, anger, frustration, confusion, joy, sorrow, suspense and desperation. Even death enters in the equation. It wasn't anything I was prepared for and I am still a little shaken by the experience. But also enlightened in a variety of ways especially in the art of making motion pictures for public consumption and the price one has to pay for the privilege. It's all in there. Reading this book and the immediacy of its style reminded of the war journals I'd read. Books like Richard Tregaskis' *Guadalcanal Diary* and Tim O'Brien's *The Things They Carried*. So what I guess I'm saying is that beyond its ability to teach and inform it is also a damn good read.

But going back to my original point I really believe that this book is indispensable for most filmmakers but particularly the independent ones as well as the aspirants. Because by going on this journey of making twelve films in as many months one will learn all the multiple and unforeseen obstacles that can be encountered in the process of making a film. Everything from dealing with unreliable crew members, difficult and moody actors, rigid and recalcitrant union representatives, unreliable prop and location situations along with trying maintain equanimity with the disparate number of people that make up a film crew. And finding that possibly, the most perplexing item of all is discovering how difficult communicating with a vast number of people can be even when you are all supposedly speaking the same language. Another lesson that can be learned in going through this process is the one known as patience. As a Producer/Director one learns to embrace this as a virtue. Perhaps the highest virtue of all.

I said Producer/Director but Travis is actually more than that. He is a "complete filmmaker" in the French meaning of the term. By that they are referring to one who is capable of executing just about every aspect of the filmmaking process from conception to cinematography, lighting, directing, scoring and editing it all into its final form. Travis has done all that and goes even a step further. He creates his own film trailers, plans its publicity and negotiates its distribution. The only other filmmaker I know of who was so totally involved with the creation and fate of his films was the now legendary African American filmmaker Oscar Micheaux, who like Travis has to do it out of financial necessity. And it is the wealth of this knowledge that he brings to this book/journal of making 12 westerns in 12 months. Read it and see if you don't agree with me about its importance as an invaluable resource to anyone who wants to or thinks about becoming a filmmaker in the near or distant future.

FOREWORD

by Travis Mills

My friend and mentor Gus Edwards has always encouraged me to write, whether it be scripts, short stories, or journal entries. As I approached the 12 Westerns, he encouraged me more than ever to record my thoughts. Never a good diary keeper, it helped to have an audience to write for and therefore these entries were sent to Gus every couple weeks throughout 2020. It was also Gus who inspired this book. "You should collect these into a book when you're done," he suggested, saying that it would not only be interesting for some readers but would also serve as a manual to future filmmakers.

Those expecting a conventional narrative will be disappointed. This book was never intended to tell the full story of what happened last year and to be honest, I have neither the time or perspective to write that kind of piece right now. Instead, what you have here are my thoughts and feelings from the moment. I have tried to edit and change as little as possible to preserve the authenticity of this experience. Some names have been changed. Gus wisely suggested that the more personal aspects of my adventures be left out. Otherwise, this is a raw glimpse at what it was like to make twelve feature films in twelve months in what might be the worst year I could have ever picked to do so.

Some may say this book focuses too much on the problems and not enough on the positive aspects of what happened but in the end, making movies is all about problems and how you solve them.

PRE-PRODUCTION

Highlights from the Months Before 2020

The 12 Westerns project was born at the end of 2013. I'd completed another crazy endeavor, 52 short films in 52 weeks, and wondered what challenge might come next. 12 features in 12 months? But they couldn't just be any kind of movie. After all, I could make 12 movies in a hotel room, or 12 movies with just two actors sitting and talking. The Western genre came to mind. What would it be like to explore the Western in twelve different movies? I fell in love with the idea and made a hasty announcement, claiming we'd start production during 2015.

The writing process began immediately but I soon learned that mounting a Western production was easier said than done. Soon, I had a handful of scripts but found myself distracted with other projects. Flash forward a few years, I remember telling my friend and mentor Gus Edwards that I needed to commit to making the 12 Westerns or admit that it would never happen. I decided this crazy project would occur during 2020 no matter what… even if I ended up just filming myself walking through the desert with my dog Bandit. I have always been one to make a decision and dive straight in, head-on.

I have included some short journal entries before filming began to share insight into a filmmaker's preparation and struggles through pre-production.

NOVEMBER 24, 2018

Yesterday I wrote an option agreement for Don Simonton, author of the *Texas Red* book. So far he's very cool and no drama. I hope we make good collaborators.

DECEMBER 4, 2018

The meeting with Nick Fornwalt (Director of Photography) ended up being more about reconnecting than talking about *Heart of the Gun*. I was hoping he'd have more criticisms of the script but it was still nice to have him as a sounding board for some of the recent ideas I've had. We both feel there's something missing in the script.

While re-reading it I was really struck by the idea of this infertile hero. I don't know if that was consciously a big part of how I felt about him originally but it is now.

The more I discuss these Westerns with collaborators, the more real the project becomes, sometimes in scary ways. Nick asked if we'd shoot this in 20 days and I said yes, that's the max I could do while still having a break before the next Western. Then he said, well you wouldn't even have a break if you did 20 days. I was confused but he's right: usually we shoot five days on with two days off then five days on and so forth. That makes 28 days. So my turn around would be 2-3 days max before I start filming again. Therefore some of the Westerns may have to be 15 days of filming instead of 20 and some may have to bleed over into a second month.

DECEMBER 17, 2018

For a moment I thought the *Texas Red* Western was going to be no more but Don and I agreed on a deal. I am waiting to start work on it till our contract has been signed. Too many times I've done even a day's too much work on a project that I shouldn't have.

I got a call from a man who asked for Jason Phelps. At first I thought it was a wrong number and almost hung up, but turns out it was a potential location for our Colorado western.

Jason is supposed to scout it soon and I'm crossing my fingers that it's an early breakthrough.

Tomorrow I'm going to meet a potential investor. We'll see. There's more to write now but I don't have the energy to describe it. Maybe tomorrow.

JANUARY 2, 2019

There have been some developments. A person, to remain unnamed, contacted me with a western script and potential funding. The story has promise and I agreed to pursue it if the writer is willing to make changes. The writer is. Let's see what happens.

FEBRUARY 18, 2019

I have also added the challenge of contacting one person per day from now till 2020 who might be able to help with the Westerns. These could be people to help with funding, scouting, resources, or even actors (some far fetched tries but what do I have to lose). Some of these people I've worked with before, others I've only spoken to in the past, and still some are complete strangers.

FEBRUARY 22, 2019

Yesterday, I contacted Ward Emling, retired film commissioner here in Mississippi, hoping that he'll help me make some new connections.

I announced the *Texas Red* project publicly yesterday and was pleased that it seemed to get some attention.

The stakes feel high for *Son of a Gun* being a success since I know every dollar we make on it will effect funding for the Westerns.

FEBRUARY 26, 2019

Contacted Nicholas Barton today, a director of two Westerns who influenced my current self-distribution model in theaters.

I'm waiting to meet Ward now in the library bar. There's 10k now sitting in the bank waiting to be help make a Western... that feels good.

MARCH 1, 2019

Today, I met for a few hours with Don Simonton, writer of the *Texas Red* book. We talked about a lot of things from William Friedkin to his background to my background and of course the subject of our movie. We argued some about the beginning, how to open the film, but eventually decided to see what would come in the writing.

Now I'm in Natchez, worn out. I imagine there will be days next year when I'm so tired I'll fall down or fall asleep wherever I'm sitting.

MARCH 3, 2019

Today I'm going to hang out with a girl and make her watch a Western. Even when having fun, I need to make progress on the Westerns.

MARCH 7, 2019

Today has been underlined with frustration, personal and professional.

I wrote eight pages of the *Texas Red* script. I'm waiting to see what Don thinks of them, hoping we won't go through this script process in conflict of vision.

I am now revising the *Deputy's Wife* script based on notes from Mario and I. A few pages in.

Contacted a person who might be an investor but I feel they've already been sucked up by some others in the industry, some people who've been assholes to me. Time will tell.

MARCH 9, 2019

Rewriting *Deputy's Wife* is fun. I'm trying to have more fun with the characters and dialog than I did before. It was controlled before. I want it to have more color now. More flavor. Something I want to discuss with Mario is casting this film with a bunch of ethnicities but having no reason behind these choices. Giving it no historical explanation. Example. The deputy is black. His wife is white. Or vice versa. Jonathan is Mexican or Chinese. But doing it in a way that is never addressed by the film. Don't explain it. Don't justify it. Because it justifies itself. Why not do this? Why not ?

MARCH 11, 2019

Every day is like a ticking clock on a time bomb... I only have so many days.

Yesterday I contacted Erin. Today, a location in Louisiana. Waiting for a call back. I also contacted an investor on *Blood Country* to see if they wanted to reinvest.

I'm at page 20 in my revision of *Deputy's Wife*. And we received 250 dollars in donations the last day and a half. A nice little roll. Maybe we're gaining momentum.

MARCH 12, 2019

Today I contacted another western town location in Texas.

Whereas yesterday more than 10 pages flowed with ease for *Deputy's Wife*, today I struggled to even write three. I'll never know why that is.

Last night I finished the shootout scene for the *Texas Red* story. I feel good about it. We'll see.

Since the writing wouldn't flow today, I turned to research for the Natchez Trace reading the first part of the Outlaw Years book. This minor detail was my favorite part: Page 30: "In those days men rose at dawn or earlier and went to bed at dusk: their lives followed the sun"

MARCH 15, 2019

Some people wonder why I don't get excited about the promise of funding. Well, here's an example of why:

A couple months ago in Arizona I met with a guy who approached me about investing. We went to lunch and he was ecstatic about it, saying he'd put 20 to 30k into one. Maybe more. He was a Midwest guy too, someone who'd made their living in farming, and he assured me that when someone from where he was from said they'd do something, they followed through. He offered helicopter location scouting rides, a four wheel drive vehicle for me to use, and much more. I insisted we focus on the investment first. He even invited me to Christmas with his family where I met many characters.

But when I sent him the contract (the same deal memo I use with all my investors) and followed up about it, he said it was far from okay with him, that it had issues. I asked what the issues were, that I could speak with his lawyer(s) about alterations. We scheduled a call for a couple days later. That day... nothing. No answer. No text back. No response. I figured I'd lost him. A couple weeks later I get a random text. No, he's still interested he says. I ask when can we talk? No response. None. The other day I decide to text one more time as a last ditch effort. I get a call from his number hours later but can't answer so it goes to voicemail. It's a woman, his accountant, saying that I should call her on his phone and she'll help me out. Finally, progress. No. I call her. She asks if I'm some random LLC that's charging his account. No I'm not. Well, my client can't help you, she says. End of story. That's why I don't get excited.

MARCH 16, 2019

The meeting with Joe today went well. It's amazing how much can be accomplished just by talking a story out. We should be going to Meridian sometime to see if there's interest there for the rodeo movie.

MARCH 21, 2019

I've fallen behind on contacts but can't let that happen.

Yesterday Don and I went scouting in Franklin County and other spots in Mississippi for the *Texas Red* story. We saw many things, some useful, and spoke at length. I think filming a good portion of the chase in the Homochitto Forest may be a good idea. The rolling hill landscape is great, mixed with the swamps.

I'm determined to finish the script and have a table read with actors before the end of April.

At the same time, I must push hard to finish the *Deputy's Wife* script and to really make progress on the Natchez Trace. I think with that one, I may aim for a detailed treatment/outline to start location scouting/casting first and then tinker with the dialog as we go.

My sleeping seems to have already changed. I can stay up later than usual. Perhaps my body can feel it coming.

MARCH 27, 2019

Last night while thinking of what might make a good "cheap" western to start with in January if I'm struggling to get funding to get things going, I went back to my notes from years back in this phone and discovered all kinds of story ideas I'd forgotten about. One was called *Ride Across the Water* and I'd actually come up with two completely different plots for this same title. The first was geared towards the Australian investor we had for a bit and the second one I found very interesting now. It may be perfect for the Sabine Crossing movie set in Louisiana. I can also see it being a good vehicle to work with Chris Bosarge again.

MARCH 29, 2019

I contacted Roger Corman and Lloyd Kaufman.

Texas Red is up to 23 pages and *Deputy's Wife* is around 68.

MARCH 30, 2019

I finished the revised *Deputy's Wife* today. 47 pages to 83 pages. A lot more character. A lot more depth. I don't want to touch it for a while. Let it sit till we start working with the actors.

APRIL 2, 2019

Once again, someone contacted me who has promised "funded projects" before, promising them again. The first time I told him to email me details. He said he would and it never came. This second time I said again, let's get the details going. He said he was writing the email as we spoke. That was days ago and it still has not come.

A good way to separate these characters from the serious ones is that they always want to talk about more projects than one. They won't zero in. It's always a "package" or "let's make six Westerns together!" Every flake I've encountered dreams big and delivers nothing.

APRIL 8, 2019

Today I learned that the Guinness world records thing is pretty much a big money scheme. You have to pay to even submit an application. If they reject it, you don't get your money back. The fee for a business, which I'd be considered, is 1000 dollars to submit. What a crock of shit.

I spoke with a female producer today who has read one of the Westerns to potentially come on board. She read it three times and provided great notes. She's right about a lot of its weaknesses but she also likes it enough to come on board. I'm trying not to get my hopes up but she seems like a good person to work with.

Five more pages of *Texas Red* written today.

APRIL 10, 2019

I contacted Michael Biehn.

APRIL 11, 2019

Yesterday I almost wrote five more pages of *Texas Red*. Close. The script is getting more scattered as I go but I have to reach the end so that the process can continue.

Both John Maxwell and Shannon Williams are interested in the table read. That excites me.

This Georgia trip does not yet. It worries me. I'm carving out 16 hours of drive time and who knows how much more while being there. I hope these guys are sincere and serious. Time will tell. If they're not, this will probably be the last time I will consider something like this and from then on rely completely on myself.

APRIL 12, 2019

I'm sitting in my car about to fall asleep in a parking lot in Meridian. Bandit is in the back. I'd drive more but why push it. I have a 6.5 hour trip tomorrow.

The meeting with the barrel racing women and men went well tonight. I like a lot of them already and felt the same excitement here that I did in Brookhaven when I first started there and Monticello when I came with *Blood Country*.

APRIL 15, 2019

The meeting from this weekend has left me hopeful. It would be a great relief to not have to find funding for five of these, regardless of losing some control. I find myself thinking, foolishly, of which five already.

APRIL 16, 2019

I left messages at the History Channel and Icon.

I finished the *Texas Red* script. Now I'm tired.

APRIL 17, 2019

I spoke with Cedric Burnside this morning. The prospect of casting him in the Texas Red project or even having him as Red makes me more excited than I've been in a long time.

I received an email back from Thomas Jane asking how I was going to pull this off and what the budgets were. I doubt I'll hear again but who knows.

APRIL 24, 2019

I could pull my hair out or punch a couple people in the goddamn face for not knowing how to listen the last couple days. It's an epidemic, bad listening. I hate it. Believe it might be the number one human issue that prevents us from accomplishing more, from solving our troubles on a small and large scale. I may retire from movies and commit my life to listening and trying to help others listen.

APRIL 28, 2019

It looks like a couple more weeks before I hear anything either way from my Georgia funding connections.

I am excited for the table read tomorrow night since it is the most "real" thing to happen for the Westerns yet.

APRIL 30, 2019

The best part of last night's reading was when I concluded the event, telling the actors they could all go but they didn't! Normally they would flee the scene but in this case, they stayed and discussed the film at length... a good sign I think.

MAY 2, 2019

I'm in a Walmart parking lot waiting to pick my mom up from the airport watching *Johnny Guitar* on my phone.

MAY 9, 2019

In the past few days, I've crossed most of the country. I've seen two western towns, one near Austin and one in New Mexico. I've arrived where I'll be living for a month: Superior, Arizona.

I made the mistake of listing all the things in my head that I needed to do on arrival only to discover that I have barely any cell service here and that without WiFi, I'm highly limited. Also, the first day there was no water, working toilet/shower, or fridge. Still there was a roof over our heads, the roof of an RV to be specific and that's what matters. It felt more important than ever to be next to Bandit, reminded more than ever of our closeness when surrounded by less.

Since then, some of the issues have been fixed and I am still waiting on WiFi, doing what I can without it while making trips to the local bar and library to email people.

I started revising *Texas Red* today as best as I can. Don's notes are hard to read at times, which is another argument for writing notes digitally instead of by hand.

In terms of the towns, they each have their strengths and weaknesses but that is just going to be the case with these movie sets. Unless I write a movie specifically for one of these places, changes will need to be made to any existing script to fit.

MAY 10, 2019

I met with Butterfly today. It's my natural inclination now to be skeptical about partners since other producers have turned out so poorly but I like her. She seems to be no funny business and practical, though I don't think we've quite figured out how to listen to each other yet.

I also met with Gus today. He shared thoughts on *Deputy's Wife* and the *Natchez Trace*. He felt the *Trace* should wait till after the 12 and be given more time to make, like a whole year. I know what he's saying but fuck it, I have to go for it.

MAY 15, 2019

Yesterday I signed the deal with this new investor, which is great progress. I decided that Bandit and I should celebrate so we walked down to a local restaurant with patio seating. We waited 15 mins while the waitress served everyone but us. Finally I gave up and left, ordered a pizza. Then we tried to finish watching the *Cowboys* and the disc wouldn't stop skipping... sometimes celebrating is a bust.

MAY 16, 2019

Had a great meeting with Wendy last night, revising the *Guide* script. She was very open to my thoughts and we came up with some good changes together.

Part of me thinks that I should abandon any form of a social/dating life I'm trying to have till this project is over. It leaves me tired and rarely fulfilled.

MAY 17, 2019

We may have 15k for *Deputy's Wife* to start, which would be a huge step forward. Fingers crossed. Another funded western would be incredible...

MAY 19, 2019

The auditions went mostly well yesterday. The first four hours flew by and then the rest went on at a crawl. But I can't complain much. We saw good people. It's amazing how few people tried out for the lead roles. Young people must just be lazy or not understand being proactive. Perhaps most of the "serious" ones are starving for roles in LA. They could be in Tucson auditioning for a paying lead...

MAY 20, 2019

As soon as you're up, you're down... the 15k for *Deputy's Wife* that sounded like such a sure thing a couple days ago is now gone. Why? I don't know. Mario sent me the text from his contact today saying that he's "reluctantly" passing and to let him know when he works with a different company... I may be reading into something that isn't there but different company? Did he see something about me he didn't like? It all seems so odd and of course discouraging but what the hell, we'll get the money somewhere. I don't even have time to let this or things like it bother me. I have no time.

MAY 21, 2019

I have a new way of working. I have these tasks listed in my calendar and they keep getting longer and longer. From 20-25 a day that involve everything from writing to editing and other things. The problem has been on what to approach first and how long. I will spend too long on one and not enough on another. Some days I'll want to do one task and not another but they are all equal in worth. So... this new way. I set a timer for 30 mins and pick a task. I have only those thirty mins to work on it and as soon as they're up, I'm done and have to move that task (if not complete) to the next day. Then I go onto the next task and set the timer again. It's working.

MAY 24, 2019

The scout with Butterfly went well. We spoke from Tempe to Prescott without much of a break. It was funny because I said, "This is good. I think we're getting a better sense of each other which will help on set." Sometimes when I say things, she doesn't respond which is something I haven't gotten a sense for yet or figured out about her. I'm not sure if she's processing it or doesn't agree or perhaps there's another option. Regardless, I like her directness. She's no funny business when it comes to work but can joke around. My fingers are constantly crossed that this collaboration works out.

We met with Patrick and Mark of the C-Bar series and shot the shit for a while. They're doing pretty much the same thing as me and unlike a lot of filmmakers out there seem to have no petty animosity towards me. They realize we can help each other and we can. I like Mark. Like me, he doesn't mind cutting someone out of the work process if they're a pain in the ass.

Speaking of process, working with Wendy more on the script revision has been fun. We're coming up with new ideas and sharpening what's there. I am curious to see what this next draft looks like.

MAY 25, 2019

This has turned into a rough week. I was crossing my fingers for nothing and have lost another collaborator. It felt lonely to read the words that came via email, claiming that though the person's experience with me has been nothing but good, they must no longer work with me... if everyone whose experience with me was good actually stood up with me and for me, there wouldn't be a problem. The issue isn't the enemies. It's the friends who are quiet...

I struggled most of the day to not feel sorry for myself. The DH Lawrence quote that I try to live by didn't do any damn good at getting my head back on track. Finally only one thing did:

The realization that if an Academy Award winning filmmaker (who has directed many actresses to awards and nominations, who has made tons of classics and worked with the best of the best) can be treated like shit after all these years and tossed out into the cold without a shred of evidence, then why of course would I not be fighting this bullshit as well.

My friend James said I would persevere through it. That also helped. I have no choice but to work and let my work be the weapon.

MAY 27, 2019

I had coffee with Nick today. Told him the "bad news" but it didn't seem to phase him. That was encouraging. He's steady. I shared some of the changes about *Heart* with him and he seemed to like that direction. We talked about the look. I asked if he'd help me buy the right pair of boots.

MAY 28, 2019

John Miller called me and we're meeting tomorrow. Damn, it's been too long since we have seen each other. He sounded excited about the Westerns and filming on his ranch, even mentioned helping with funding and that he's writing one. I am excited for our reunion.

An actor turned down a part in *Texas Red* because he is worried about saying the n word. I understand but I feel we must include it in this film, it's a harsh story about harsh times.

The story of Pearl Hart is getting me excited again as I get back to research. I really wonder if KK Starrs could play her.

MAY 29, 2019

That last idea from yesterday doesn't look like it will pan out. For now at least, the passion for acting is gone or dormant in her but perhaps things will change. It's a shame.

Every second away from working on the Westerns feels like cheating.

JUNE 2, 2019

If any time away from the Westerns is cheating then I had a long affair the last three days filming this Mad Max movie.

But it was desert living and I think the more of that I do between now and the Westerns, the better. Jared handles it well. So does Rich. We'll see how tough our cast and crew is. I'd like to find out before I choose them.

JUNE 4, 2019

It's fascinating to see how the female roles in the Westerns are shaping. I told a woman friend about this last night, that with no intention there are many strong female roles in these films. And that's exactly how it should be ideally:

unintentional, natural. I credit this to how much I watch old movies, where women were stronger, not new ones.

JUNE 6, 2019

Getting back to the Pearl Hart story has been interesting. The more articles I read the more interesting little tidbits I find.

I'm torn between giving it a frame story and not. My idea to have her as an older woman telling the story is a good one I think but this tale might be better served to just do it straight. It's almost twice the work but I think I'm going to complete both versions and see what the reaction to them is.

JUNE 11, 2019

I have returned to Mississippi. Driving always makes me feel behind. I seriously need to consider having someone to drive me across the country during the Westerns so I can work or rest on the road. I'm hitting the ground running today.

JUNE 12, 2019

Tomorrow I'm driving four hours to meet Cedric. I hope it's worth it. I hope we have the discussion that confirms for both of us that this is the right move.

Nothing from the Georgia guys... who knows at this point. I need to get back into the mindset that I'll need to raise every dollar to make the 12.

JUNE 14, 2019

The meeting with Cedric went well enough. I'm nervous about talking to his manager and that the business side of it might screw everything up. It's also a big role. No one has shown this level of interest or commitment to it but making that final choice is still nerve wracking.

He said he'd watched *Blood Country* three times and his daughter had detailed thoughts about it. That made me feel most confident.

JUNE 15, 2019

I've reached out to Ritchie Montgomery for the last time. If he's not going to respond or take the time to read a script for a lead role then so be it. I'm not going to chase him or anyone else for these Westerns.

Non-responsiveness is bullshit. If you're too busy to respond to people who hit you up repeatedly then you need to fix that or hire an assistant. It's unprofessional.

JUNE 19, 2019

Today I went with Lynn Wentworth and Bill Perkins to scout in Franklin county. In many ways it was more beneficial as a conversation than a scout, getting to know Lynn, hearing the history of some of the characters in *Texas Red* and some that aren't who lived in that area. It all added background. We did see a really good swamp. And we saw a bridge that might be the one for the finale.

No word from Cedric's manager. I feel like that's a bad sign, that they don't care enough to make it a priority.

Apparently the Georgia deal is still possible. It would be the biggest relief to see it come through.

A couple days ago I argued via email with someone I can't mention about a contract we have related to the Westerns. They stated they wanted a certain right, the ability to approve something that wasn't provided in our agreement. I reminded this person of the terms we agreed on. They argued again. I again reminded them. At this point they informed me that in the South it is rude to bring up the letter of the contract like this. I politely found a way to respond. But that's the whole point of an agreement and if that's the way of the South, I don't agree with it.

JUNE 20, 2019

I've adjusted my method of working because it's been impossible to get my daily tasks done on days when I travel or scout. So now I set a timer for 15 mins per task on those travel days. Any days that I stay home, I go back to the half hour method.

JUNE 23, 2019

Not one but two people in Natchez remarked with surprise at how "calm" I am considering what I'm doing... I found this to be quite a compliment.

The scout in Freewoods went well. I couldn't get the best read on the owner of the cabin and how he felt about me but at least verbally, he is willing to let us film there. These locations will require a lot of work to clean up and design. I hope that people will volunteer...

Tonight I am forcing myself not to keep working but to take a break and watch a western, which of course is a form of work but it's one that refreshes me.

I'd like to know what people making supposedly progressive movies with strong female roles in today's society, "changing" the portrayal of women in movies, would make of Jean Arthur in *Arizona*. Check out this dialog:

William Holden: "Where I'm from women are supposed to need protection."

Jean Arthur: "I don't ask nor get favors for being what I was born."

JUNE 24, 2019

Something interesting and unexpected has happened. A filmmaker I met not long ago, who makes westerns, has parted ways with his main partner, the person who directs the movies they make. He hit me up yesterday about potentially filling that place and making his next western one of my 12. It's an interesting proposition. We spoke today and for the most part that went well. I'm very curious to see how this develops

JUNE 26, 2019

Something that I never thought would be a challenge in this project has become one: the selection of DPs for each project. I've had Nick and Jared read different scripts. It's tough on them I'm sure to have so much reading material sent their way. Sometimes the responses to these are difficult. Today, I spoke with Nick about *Texas Red*. He has good questions and good thoughts about it but I get the feeling that his heart isn't in it much. Not like it is in *Heart of the Gun*. This is the challenge: I need each DP to have a strong passion because this will help significantly with my energy.

JUNE 28, 2019

Last night I heard the news I've been hoping for. Mario and I have been waiting to hear word if an investor liked the script. The word back was "Amazing" and now I hope this means we will have momentum.

JULY 1, 2019

I have once again traveled across the country. Bandit and I made the journey to Colorado yesterday. He is a completely different dog in different places, which is funny and fascinating to observe. He's getting older and I hope he will live through the Westerns with me.

JULY 7, 2019

I'm in Tombstone now. Most of my mind is occupied with thoughts of Bandit. He isn't doing well the past few days and may have an ear infection. But he is tough and with keeping a close eye on it, I think he'll be fine.

The last minute nature of putting this *Ranch Hands* short together proves how valuable the planning I'm doing for the Westerns is. Even having to find a gun or blood the day before is stressful.

JULY 12, 2019

I felt the energy Monday night while making *Ranch Hands*. That extra kick that comes when I go into production. It's great, knowing it's still there, waiting for filming to start.

JULY 13, 2019

Several times now I feel like I've reached out to someone about funding and I'm just two to three months late... another filmmaker, sometimes people I know (some I admire and some I don't), got there before me.

I'm trying to figure out how to incorporate vodka (for product placement) into one of the Westerns. It's first appearance in America and presence in the 1800s is unclear.

JULY 14, 2019

While making the shoot schedule today for *Guide to Gunfighters*, I realized how hard it's going to be, how I need to have a firmer grip on this script than any I've done before both because I won't be able to shoot chronologically and because I must have a good hold on what I want to change and play with on set to remain consistent.

I proposed to Jared Kovacs the other night that we shoot one of the Westerns on an iPhone and I'm serious about this. I also am exploring filming one on 35mm.

JULY 15, 2019

Today I took a shot in the dark and emailed Cinestate, probably my favorite company making movies right now, to see if they might be interested in one of my Westerns. They wrote me back almost immediately saying they're actually on the lookout for a good western to make. I was giddy. So I sent them *Bastard's* and *Deputy's Wife*. Who knows what will happen. It's a long shot. But that was a great feeling and makes me think I should throw more Hail Marys like that one.

JULY 17, 19

I think the Georgia deal is dead. The nail isn't in the coffin but it doesn't seem very positive anymore.

JULY 19, 2019

An opportunity has arisen that is even better than the Georgia deal but equally uncertain. If it happens, it could change the whole landscape of what I'm doing.

I spoke with Jared yesterday for an hour and a half about *Bastard's*, *Texas Red*, and *Slow Death*... he is interested in all three. I'm waiting to close the door with someone else on *Texas Red* who has become unresponsive in the last couple weeks. I'll wait one more week before making that decision. Jared is in on *Bastard's*. For *Slow Death* and *Frontier,* which he was already attached to, I'm thinking of doing them back to back and shooting one on the IPhone and the other on 35mm, respectively.

JULY 20, 2019

My rhythm has been thrown off by actually having a little fun the last couple nights. I feel like, especially next year, I'll have to be like a filmmonk. My life will be the Westerns and nothing else.

JULY 22, 2019

The casting call was well attended and the best part was seeing some new talent that I'd never met before. That's encouraging that there are still good actors left to discover here and also some mentioned they'd recently moved to Mississippi. I left feeling content but without having seen someone who really blew me away, someone who absolutely had to be cast.

JULY 24, 2019

I threw a couple Hail Marys today for *Bastard's Crossing* casting. The rep for Brad Dourif replied asking for a pay or play offer. I figured as much. I hate agents.

JULY 27, 2019

Last night I finally got a date range from Cedric's people which allows me to start planning the schedule for *Red*, or at least seeing how it might go. Breakthrough!

JULY 29, 2019

Once again, traveling really throws off my routine. I go to Jackson for a great lunch with Dorsey Carson then Vicksburg then home to work but I get back and need a power nap and just don't have the momentum to do as much as I'd like. I have to force myself to work a little and then rest to hit the reset button tomorrow.

I came up with this idea the last couple days about casting Richard Anderson in *Bastard's Crossing* after telling Jared that this is the final part in our unofficial trilogy with *Bride of Violence* and *Deadbeats*. I really feel this way and find it ironic considering that I didn't write two of those three scripts. But they have shared DNA. I'm thinking of calling it the "Good Men Gone Bad" trilogy. So I contacted Richard today about pulling double duty as cast and our gaffer. We'll see what happens.

JULY 30, 2019

For the first time, but certainly not the last, two actors have turned down offers to be in my 12 Westerns. One was because of not having enough time off work and another is just too busy to work indie movies, even ones with SAG ULB pay...

AUGUST 1, 2019

Bastard's Crossing is harder to schedule than I thought it would be... these are going to be long challenging days for sure and just because it's one location doesn't mean it won't be as hard or harder at times than *Texas Red* which is more than 15 locations.

AUGUST 4, 2019

I finished the *Bastard's Crossing* schedule, at least the first one. I sent it to Jared. It's rough. It's going to be a hell of a hard one to make. I have to rehearse the hell out of these actors. They can't be unprepared and unguided on my sets like they were before. Nope. They have to be ready.

AUGUST 7, 2019

I'm in Oxford today, taking time away from the Westerns except in my mind. The cinematographer I was interested in for *Texas Red* finally gave me a no yesterday, after many delayed responses. He said he really regretted not being able to do it, that he really wanted to. Apparently not enough to answer me for a week or two...

So I returned to Jared who expressed a lot of passion for the project. Passion always wins.

AUGUST 8, 2019

I finally finished the rewrite of *Heart of the Gun* last night and this morning, powering through over 30 pages. It feels good to be done but also just means there's more to come.

I'm thinking of sending this to my top two picks for the lead female role and see how they each react.

AUGUST 10, 2019

Today I woke up with urgency: perhaps I need to choose what all 12 Westerns are more quickly, perhaps I need to be more aggressive about funding, perhaps I'm more behind than I realize.

AUGUST 11, 2019

We had an emotional freak out from a collaborator who decided he doesn't want to act any more. This effects both my current projects and one of the Westerns I'd chosen him for, both for cast and crew. So we are back to square one. I cannot afford these kinds of stressful people on my team, people who are dramatic. They hurt the work.

AUGUST 12, 2019

This morning I started making day pages for a film that won't shoot till March but I learned something very valuable: this is the kind of task that energizes me, that gets me buzzing more than coffee. I need to do more of this, breaking the script down into days and props and costumes. This is not only what helps me see the production better but it gets me in production mode.

AUGUST 13, 2019

Casting for **Bastard's** is tough. My instincts don't line up with Joe's nor some others I've shown the tapes too. I trust them but I have to follow my instincts at the end of the day.

AUGUST 14, 2019

On the drive back from Natchez yesterday, I argued with my friends as I suggested an unconventional idea for keeping costs low on a stagecoach rental. They immediately jumped on it with the kind of doubt I've seen time and time again on set. I was mad. I explained to them that half the movies I've made wouldn't have been made if I listened to such immediate skepticism.

AUGUST 16, 2019

Well we lost another location for *Texas Red*. First, the warehouse for the Rhythm Club, though we never really had that one, and now the cabin in Freewoods. They got dollar signs in their eyes and when they realized I wouldn't have many, the answer turned to no. The main disappointment here is we might not film in Freewoods, at least at a structure of any kind.

I still haven't heard definitely from Cedric's people. It's driving me nuts. If only I could lock that in, I'd have some security for what to do next.

AUGUST 19, 2019

Well this has been a crazy day. I got yelled at by the widow of an actor who cried on the phone for a half hour and then threatened me with legal action because we're playing a film her late husband was in... I chose to play the damn film to honor him! And we've gone through the legal process to license it. People are amazing.

This morning Bill Perkins and I went down to measure the inside of the trading post. It's smaller than I thought but workable I'm sure. Of course Bill couldn't resist and had to break out the chainsaw. Suddenly he was cutting everything I could, with the presumption that I could haul off the branches to fire piles which of course I did. But after a while I yelled out that we'll have volunteers in September for this kind of work. Nevertheless he kept cutting and I kept piling. Finally the owner of the house next door came with his bush hog and ran over everything. I basically had to drag Bill out of there to keep him from cutting more.

AUGUST 24, 2019

I was pleased to finally cast Cam the other day. Ward Emling and I went to the location. It's interesting to see different peoples' reactions. They all have opposite concerns about the place. What I see, and I think what Bill sees, is nothing but possibility.

AUGUST 25, 2019

The last two days have ended with mental exhaustion but I just wrote two good scenes for the Pearl story, I spoke to Anabella about being in *Turn and Burn*, I mixed *Deadbeats* and went live and did other little things all damn day. That's good enough till tomorrow.

AUGUST 26, 2019

One of my collaborators and I keep butting heads. He wants to do things immediately, spur of the moment, and I want to plan. I want to cross the Ts and dot the Is before we attack. I also want to take full advantage of my time and energy before charging the battlefield without a plan.

AUGUST 27, 2019

Today I drove from Vicksburg to Jackson and back home. I did a radio interview about the festival and opened a bank account. I made a personal appointment and completed most of my tasks. It was a good day.

This character I'm writing, Joe Boot, is one of my favorites. I could feel that before I even started writing, when I first read the story of Pearl Hart, but now he is living right in front of me.

AUGUST 28, 2019

My head aches today, filled with so many things: locations, people, schedules, funding, how to shoot on film, when to make this film and that.

AUGUST 30, 2019

I'm slowly losing all desire to have a personal life during this project. I mean a personal life with other people, be it male or female friends. Week after week, it feels like a waste of mental energy with little fulfillment, a distraction not because of the time it takes away from the project but because of the effect it has on my mind. I may need to abandon these desires completely and find satisfaction in simply spending time with Bandit and watching movies when I need to decompress.

AUGUST 31, 2019

Like *Texas Red*, Nick doesn't seem jazzed about the *Natchez Trace* project. He's right. It needs work. It isn't there yet but he does sound passionate about the barrel racing film without having read a single page... that's good. So it's not for sure but I think I might be looking to find another DP for the Trace project. Jared's already shooting 4 of the Westerns. He's a beast and brave so I'm sure he could take this on too but the move he's planning may hinder that. It might be possible to reteam with Mario.

I'm still fighting the nature of that project and whether I want to go with the direction it's headed or return to my original desire for a *Devil's Rejects*-like disturbing western. The latter is what excites me most.

SEPTEMBER 2, 2019

A friend and ex-lover stopped by for a quick chat and asked me if I was "ready" for all 12 Westerns. I told her that was a stupid question. She then asked if I was excited. I told her that was too. It's funny how you can be close to someone and they really don't know a damn thing about you.

SEPTEMBER 3, 2019

I made a horse list for *Bastard's* today and holy shit, it's a little intimidating. What once looked like a simple movie really isn't.

SEPTEMBER 4, 2019

My head runs wild today with thoughts from five or six projects. As I do props list for one, I email about camera and lighting for another, funding for another, casting for another. I am not a filmmaker. I'm a professional juggler.

SEPTEMBER 5, 2019

The Georgia deal is officially dead. So any funding for the Westerns I'll have to scrounge up myself or with the help of my connections. This is good for only one reason: complete creative control of the 12 Westerns.

I came home mid-afternoon today exhausted, both because of some tense interactions and hearing the kind of nonchalant racist talk that is common in these parts. I was on edge and tried to sleep it off. I couldn't sleep

SEPTEMBER 6, 2019

Yesterday closed with another tense altercation. I informed someone I'm working with that they either needed to commit more time and energy to this specific western or I would have to remove them from this paid position until they could. I thought it was a fair approach; I'd been honest up front that being paid on one of these films means doing a hell of a lot more than volunteer work requires. But I must have pushed some buttons and the person got mad. I insisted we discuss on the phone in a calm manner and a half hour later we did. It was uncomfortable but better. I'm not sure if we truly ended the conversation with understanding. I explained that I have to make constant progress on these films and if someone is too busy to help me, that's fine, but I must forge ahead regardless. It is interesting how connections and relationships dry up. Sometimes there's a pattern to it. This specific one is from a certain region in Mississippi and all my connections in that area, including someone who promised me a good deal of investment seems to have dried up. Can a mood sweep over humans geographically? It seems so. But perhaps it is just a phase and this will return. It reminds me of here in Brookhaven where I was once cheered on and now taken for granted or ignored. Yes, there are supporters here and good ones, but it's fascinating to see the fall off when you become old news.

I can't imagine not doing my own props list. I can't see going back to having someone else to do it, not just because they'd probably do it wrong but because the process of going through these details raises so many questions and ideas for the film. It seems essential for the director to do this.

SEPTEMBER 9, 2019

I called the *Texas Red* actor's manager today ready to deliver the ultimatum that I need to have a signed contract by the end of September. He said we actually should be able to finalize this week. Of course I've heard that before but this time we went over the contract in detail together. I'm hoping I can get this off my plate. The project is so stalled without knowing if he is playing the lead or not.

SEPTEMBER 11, 2019

Completed the first round of SAG paperwork for *Bastard's Crossing* today. It's amazing how many forms they ask the exact same information for. Over and over.

I had a meeting scheduled this afternoon in Jackson but some sneaking suspicion told me to call ahead and make sure it was still on. Turns out the person I was going to meet isn't even there today because it's his birthday! His daughter who set up the meeting acted nonchalant about the fact that she'd scheduled me to come today, seemingly unaware that I would have showed up for no reason... I asked her to please make 100 percent sure that our rescheduled meeting next week was in their calendar and confirmed. She said yes but as the conversation ended, I was positive she had not written anything down. Is that the kind of world we live in where you have to double check every confirmation you get? I don't want to live in it if that's the case.

SEPTEMBER 12, 2019

I am so worn out of people. It's a piss poor culture we're living in. Howard Hawks professionals... Where are they? Do they even exist?

SEPTEMBER 13, 2019

It felt good to get back in the saddle today. I love that Beau challenged me to ride his most difficult horse. I want to get better and better.

Our meeting also went well. Every interaction I have brings up more things that need to be figured out but hey, at least these things are being brought up now and not weeks before production.

SEPTEMBER 15, 2019

I had a major breakthrough with wagons today. Finally met with Randy in Wesson and it looks like we may get at least two wagons for *Bastard's* out of the connection. He's a good guy, I can tell.

I started call sheets too. Absurdly early but that word doesn't really factor into this project.

SEPTEMBER 18, 2019

I have been working on a deal to confirm the *Texas Red* lead role since June. I just looked and it was June 21 when I first texted the talent's agent. Last night I received a signed deal memo. It took almost four months, the longest time it has ever taken for me to secure an actor. I'm happy that this process ended with confirmation and not denial.

SEPTEMBER 22, 2019

I am finally home from the film festival and ready to fall in bed. In some ways, this was a vacation from work and in other ways it was three solid days of work. I feel that it is a success. The greatest highlight is that the 12 Westerns fans made up the majority of the audience, most traveling from hours away and putting themselves up in hotels to attend. This touched me deeply. I almost cried at one point talking about it but kept it together and I don't think anyone noticed. I love this sign of dedication, passion, and interest in the projects.

Also I feel Mitch Ryan was appreciated. That's what I wanted. I hope he leaves with a good feeling.

SEPTEMBER 24, 2019

I made a decision about casting Mabel. After the internal tug of war, conversations I had this weekend solidified my feelings on who should play her. Perhaps the other woman and I will find a different project to work on.

SEPTEMBER 25, 2019

In a little while I'm going to pick up Jared in New Orleans. He's flying in for the *Bastard's* set prep. I admit to not being as ready as I'd like for this because of many factors, the number one being humans and totally out of my control. However I hope we can make great use of these next three days.

SEPTEMBER 26, 2019

I am astounded that people continue to drive hours to help with these movies while most of the people who could drive ten minutes don't care. Isn't that the irony of life? But I am grateful for these film warriors who spend their time and energy to help me make the movies.

SEPTEMBER 29, 2019

I have been too worn out to write. The three days of set construction and design were more exhausting than most days of film production. It was fun, frustrating, and physically taxing. Beyond productive, it was a study in personalities and ego. Some people can't stay focused. Some people work so fast that they don't get the job done well, leaving more jobs to be done in the end. There were long and short arguments, conflicting perspectives, but in the end, I suppose we were victorious in overcoming these personal conflicts to make it happen. Still, it gives me pause. It makes me ponder on how to better work with some personalities and to avoid working with others.

OCTOBER 2, 2019

Yesterday Jared and I drove from Brookhaven to Austin, not a bad trip. Most of it was filled with discussions of movies, *Bastard's Crossing*, and life events. I am trying to laugh first at things that frustrate me, as an initial reaction, sort of a shield. Then process them. Then decide if action needs to take place.

OCTOBER 3, 2019

The remaining journey to Arizona seemed to go on and on but we finally arrived, dropping Jared off in Tucson to be taken home by his girlfriend and picking up Mary Beth to double back to Tombstone.

OCTOBER 4, 2019

The last two days with Mario and Mary Beth have been good, also enlightening about personalities and realistic expectations. We tried to go through every scene of the script but couldn't, getting stuck on the details on so many of them, which led to good work but prevented us from doing as much as we can.

Deputy's Wife is going to be such a hard film to make. But they all will be.

.

OCTOBER 6, 2019

I hit the *Texas Red* schedule hard this morning, rethinking almost everything I'd done before. It's brutal but necessary to go over these scenes over and over again to determine the best order to shoot them.

I'm worried about horses. I'm worried about lodging. Those are my two main concerns.

OCTOBER 8, 2019

Today, I feel like I have serious momentum. I've figured out, after toiling away at it for a few hours, how we might shoot *Texas Red* in 20 days. I feel exhausted just looking at the schedule but it seems like the best possible plan.

Also for the first time since its conception, I know who will play Travers and Sarah. I spoke with Amber Rose Mason on the phone today, finally confirming with her. She's been in limbo waiting to hear if I want to move forward or not. Attaching Miles Doleac as Travers feels more solid with every passing day. Now I have my leads. It's moving.

OCTOBER 9, 2019

No one can remember a damn thing anymore. Literally no one remembers anything anyone says. Our brains are totally screwed as a culture.

I enjoyed lunch with Gus tremendously. I was happy to hear he feels good about my attempt at diverse casting and the way I'm going about it. We practiced our lines for *Two Drifters*. I have to get comfortable with the French to the point where I can really feel the emotions through the language. Right now I'm just trying to sound right.

Spent the day jumping from various projects. It's not tough to keep the stories straight but sometimes it is tough when say I go back into *Bastard's* call sheets after not looking at them for a few days. Then I'm not clear where exactly I left off or what my thought process was when I did. But this work now will make the work later easier.

OCTOBER 10, 2019

An actor on one of the Westerns is testing the hell out of my patience. It's defying my instincts to not immediately replace him as he is the only person giving me any issues. He is constantly missing the most simple communications and directions, and also somehow manages to be stepping outside of his role to do things I never asked him to do... he's an inch away from being dropped from the cast.

OCTOBER 11, 2019

The reading for *Guide to Gunfighters* last night went far better than I imagined it would. I left thinking of all the different ways I need to direct each personality but one thing was evident: the cast will make this script stronger than what it is on the page which is actually proof that the script itself is stronger than it seems.

OCTOBER 13, 2019

I think today's trip to see the actors work with the horses they'll be paired with in the film was just as important for getting to know the humans as it was for their connection to the horses. I don't want to get too close to any of these actors but seeing them interact, hearing more about them does give me insight into how we'll work together.

OCTOBER 14, 2019

Arizona life: black coffee, canned food, no pillow, dust, whiskey from the bottle.

Mississippi life: light brown coffee, steak, a king sized bed, sweat, red wine.

OCTOBER 17, 2019

I feel a momentum today like I haven't felt in weeks. Finally I have a good schedule for *Bastard's*. By the end of these 12 Westerns, I should be able to schedule any damn movie that comes my way.

OCTOBER 19, 2019

Last night I had quite a little adventure. I met Jasper, Gigi, Big Boy, Soggy Bottom, Number 1 and Number 2 (all dogs, cats, and pigs). I also met Zoe, three years old, and her mother Lucy who live on the Lonesome Coconut Ranch, a place that feels like a hippie haven in the middle of the desert. We walked over to Pete and Delight's place, two more kind hippies, and the entire entourage of dogs and cats followed us, even the tiny Soggy Bottom who must not be much more than two months old. These neighbors cooked burgers for dinner and they burned the first round to black charcoal patties because they talked so much. But they tell good stories and have an earthy warmth that made me believe in humans again.

The ranch is close to the western town and might be a place where I can board people during our shoot. I fear that some of them might be too picky to stay there. For me, it is the kind of ideal place to stay while making a western, comfortable enough without separating you too much from the reality of the land.

Merina Khan arrived last night from LA. We spoke briefly before both passing out. She confessed to me that her film job in Mississippi had fallen through. That was the reason she was driving out this way and also the reason we had scheduled her scout of Gammons today. Now she is just coming here for this sole purpose and driving back to California. She asked for nothing. I told her that I must pay her gas to get here and back. I told her about some of the wilder plans of the 12 Westerns. She listened with a skeptical look, reminding me much of Nick whose traditional instincts are often challenged by my crazy ideas.

OCTOBER 20, 2019

Yesterday's scout at Gammons was productive if rushed at the end. Seven hours sounds like a long time but it goes by very quickly when thinking out scenes. I was impressed with Merina's ability to stay grounded in our conversation, present in the discussion of the scenes and story. In my experience, cinematographers have a tendency to get dreamy in these discussions. Their minds drift to exposure, the placements of light and camera, living in the future set moment instead of the present one. Merina didn't do this which helped our conversation flow and left me with a positive feeling from the day.

OCTOBER 21, 2019

An unexpected visit replaced several hours of work yesterday. I found myself divided between the pleasures of companionship, conversation and my duties. Does one replenish the other? When I go to bed after working hard all day, I feel satisfied. When I go to bed after such an interaction, I feel restless, wondering if this personal connection was worth the work I gave up or if it will mean nothing in the days to come.

OCTOBER 22, 2019

Megan Rippey arrived at 4am last night after a long drive from LA. She must be exhausted but I am glad to put the time in to do this. Today we will rehearse at Gammons together and also develop a report as director and lead actress.

OCTOBER 23, 2019

My time with Megan was valuable. We went through just about every scene from the script... and some of our discussions led to realizations for me, things I hadn't thought of before in terms of these characters and their motivations. We spoke at length. She's sharp. She also starts good, starts real. That means she can only get better and better.

OCTOBER 24, 2019

Yesterday I was in the car close to eight hours. However, because of the great landscape on 288, it felt better than many of my recent two hour trips. I drove from Tombstone to Young, Arizona. Nearby, there is the Tilting H Ranch which Nick and I scouted for *Heart of the Gun*. It's a diverse and striking property. Pete, the owner, was different than I thought he'd be but we had a good connection, especially when we started talking Westerns films. I could tell his surprise when I mentioned Joel McCrea and Randolph Scott. We bonded over the dislike for modern Westerns like *Hateful Eight* and *Hostiles*, having the same issues with the latter. I encouraged him to watch *Bone Tomahawk* and said I'd be curious if he'd like *Yellowstone* or not, suspecting he would find it as phony as I do.

Seeing Nick was refreshing, our collaboration has this feeling of age and understanding now. There's an ease that kicks in inside me the minute I see him, like being joined on the street by a friendly gunfighter, a pro, and he knows what we've got to do.

OCTOBER 25, 2019

Our first time working on 16mm film yesterday for *Two Drifters* was super challenging, in ways a normal shoot would not be. Though we did far less takes than normal, the method slowed us down considerably. We had to do far more rehearsal. Our second magazine screwed up and we lost four takes. This was the biggest disappointment of the day since they were good takes and we then had to redo them in different light. This showed how easily on a film things can go bad quickly, especially without experience, though Jared did everything he could to make it work. I enjoyed playing the Frenchman but felt that there wasn't as much time to play with this way of working. Still, when I woke up this morning, sore and worn out, I was not discouraged at all to shoot one of our 12 Westerns on film.

OCTOBER 26, 2019

Mario and I are back to zero on locking in our camera package for *Deputy's Wife*. His top prospect, one that seemed moments away from being confirmed, has become an almost non-option. Everything changed when I spoke to this person on the phone, a terrible conversation that I can't remember if I wrote about in this diary or not. Regardless it can be summed up by saying that this person and I did not see eye to eye at all: he was hoping to work eight hour days and sounded very hesitant at the sound of our usual 12, he approached me with incredible skepticism though he supposedly trusted Mario's word on our previous experience, and he wanted "more" but not more compensation. It was odd and one of the worst interactions I've had recently. Then for the next week or so we've been trying to see if he can get his head right leading to him not wanting to commit. I told Mario that the only reason we want this person is his gear at this point, that the person himself is not bringing value to the team and therefore we need to find someone else. Attitude is the absolute most important thing on films like this and films like this also require a special kind of attitude.

OCTOBER 28, 2019

I'm running ragged in these last couple days in Arizona. I could fill another three months here, full of prep and planning. It's hard to leave. It's hard to think of what I haven't done that needs to be done. With almost two months left, this is where the pressure really begins.

OCTOBER 29, 2019

This is my last day in Arizona. The next time I'll be back in AZ will be for filming in March, by then I will have already made 2 of the 12 Westerns. This month has gone by too quickly... I leave with a feeling of sadness that I was not able to see my friends here more, a feeling of anxiety that I could have used at least two more months of prep on the ground here, and finally a feeling of anticipation for my eventual return to this place I love.

OCTOBER 31, 2019

I'm now in Colorado, spending a few days with my family. The realization is setting in for myself and those around me that things will look different next year than they have before: I won't be able to make trips like this, I may not be at Christmas, etc. My mom joked about when I might get married and I told her next year I'm married to the 12 Westerns.

NOVEMBER 5, 2019

Once again I feel an immense pressure with *Bastard's Crossing* and *Texas Red* around the corner. Somehow now I feel like I'm chasing a hat that has blown off my head and is tumbling down a hill, trying to catch it before it goes off the cliff or is swept away by the river below.

Another image that keeps coming to mind that I would draw if I could animate comic strips: in 2019 I am a man dragging a wagon up a steep slope. The wagon says 12 Westerns on it and inside there are all the actors and crew and props for the film. It's heavy and I can barely lift it to the peak. In 2020, we are going down the mountain and the wagon is out of control. I am pasted to the front of it as it speeds down the mountain, unstoppable.

I have dreamt more vividly the past four nights than I have in years, both good and bad dreams.

NOVEMBER 6, 2019

On the road today from Colorado to Mississippi I had a good call with Kelly, head of costumes at one of the universities in MS. It sounds like she's willing to strike the same deal I had with New Stage Theater, a bargain for costume rental. This could be a major coup for the project.

NOVEMBER 8, 2018

Today is a victorious day for the 12 Westerns. I left the lunch meeting with a five thousand dollar check for *Bastard's Crossing* and a ten thousand dollar check for *Texas Red*. This is what I needed. I move forward regardless but now I can do so with more strength and less stress.

NOVEMBER 9, 2019

It's time to push myself to another level. To stay up later. To work more intensely. Less distractions. Gung ho.

NOVEMBER 13, 2019

My scouts today led to potential breakthroughs for *Texas Red*. I feel very good about filming the Newman Scott drugstore scenes at Serio's, which has changed a lot but thankfully not too much since we filmed there for Porches 1. Jim Bonner was very helpful.

Then I went to Franklin County to meet Howard at his property but he forgot about our appointment. This mistake led to great things as I entered an extended conversation with his son Brett, who I didn't know was his son till halfway through the discussion. He was very engaged and interested in my film work and though he had much to do, took me for a little tour of the property which revealed more possibilities than I was aware of. Howard called before our tour was finished and I went to have lunch with him, which was also positive. It seems the doors are open to us filming there.

A meeting with Jennifer about makeup for *Bastard's* was brief but also good. Other than my computer still acting up from the cold, this is a good day.

NOVEMBER 14, 2019

Great rehearsal today with JD. It's such a high to see novice actors make significant progress. He also told me about his days as a livestock officer and the wheels have been turning since. I don't know how I could fit it in the 12 but I sure as hell want to.

NOVEMBER 16, 2019

My mom called me this morning and told me of what is the most tragic thing that has ever happened to our Mississippi family. You never know what's going on inside someone, what they're truly feeling and thinking, what's going to happen tomorrow or even by the end of today. Nothing is guaranteed. I despise the saying "it's all going to be okay" or "it's all going to work out". I want to hit people in the mouth who say that. It's the dumbest statement anyone could ever say. The truth is that it might be okay and it might not. It might work out and it might not. It might be good and it might be bad. This applies to everything. Work. Romance. Life and death. Happiness.

As I continue to work on the 12 Westerns, this tragic event and it's meaning consume my mind and my heart.

NOVEMBER 18, 2019

Forty four days till 2020. The countdown has truly begun. I feel momentum. I feel extra energy. I also feel enormous pressure.

Today, I'm driving to McComb to sign the agreement for the train location, then to Hammond to rehearse with Ashleigh for the first time. I hope to make some progress with her. Then she's accompanying me to see the *Irishman* in New Orleans with Miles and Lindsay. Hopefully Miles and I will be able to talk about *Heart of the Gun*. I sent him a list of name actors I'd like to shoot for in small roles for that film.

It will be a long day and one mostly away from Bandit but at least I'll return to him at the end of the night.

NOVEMBER 19, 2019

I felt progress with Ashleigh. I tried to explain to Joe that it has nothing to do with her getting the voice right. It's her feeling it. Her being in the situation. Truly in character. Then the voice comes... she doesn't quite feel it yet.

One thing that's starting to occur more and more and become somewhat frustrating: lots of people telling me to do things different ways. This person will say do this with a horse while another person says they're full of shit and says do that instead. Same with wardrobe. Same with just about everything. So how do you manage that? How do you handle conflicting information from people who know better than you do when they contradict each other? I guess I just need to listen to those who are most consistent with me. Even if they're wrong, we'll learn together. Whereas people with fly by opinions can confuse you...

NOVEMBER 20, 2019

I went on my first "Billventure" since returning to Mississippi. Though he's been back for a few days, this was the first I saw of Bill, as he's been too busy to make an appearance back at the homestead. But it was a healthy dose. He exercised my ability to be flexible and patient. I must use my friend as a patience bench press.

In all seriousness, he's a big help too. We ventured off to look at a source for old cars for *Texas Red*, finding a huge collection near Bogue Chitto. The owner wasn't there but Bill called him up, worked his charm, and we may see him next week.

My meeting with Brad Turner, the owner of two wagons for *Bastard's*, also went well. The more strategizing about this the better. Planning is starting to become less theory and more practice. That's when I feel good inside.

NOVEMBER 22, 2019

The best thing that happened yesterday was hearing that two graduate students from USM are going to help me with wardrobe for *Texas Red*, selection and measuring in mid-December. I desperately need the help, not just because their wardrobe collection is massive but because it's tough to look at these things without an extra pair of eyes to suggest things.

I'm off to Jackson this morning to wire transfer our SAG deposit for *Bastard's*. I don't want to go but 40 days out... can't wait for anything anymore.

NOVEMBER 23, 2019

Technical issues and human interactions are slowing me down. Wish I could make 12 Westerns with only dogs.

But sometimes humans do amazing things... we got our first official investment for *Heart of the Gun* today.

NOVEMBER 26, 2019

Distractions abound. Some good, healthy. Others, obstacles.

Rehearsal with Ward and Ashleigh was the highlight of today. I love feeling it come together. Come alive. Ward is going to make this character something so much more than the page, like a true actor does.

NOVEMBER 28, 2019

I drove today with Bandit to Meridian where I'll be for the next few days. We had a good Thanksgiving with Joe Pevey's family. It was nice to exchange ideas with Joe in a non-rushed environment where the thoughts could just flow as they came. I'm grateful for his interest in this project and his dedication to it. He may be one of the most surprising collaborators I've had.

NOVEMBER 29, 2019

Other than a few bumps in communication, my first full day in Meridian was successful. We saw a handful of potential locations for *Turn and Burn*. Considering the movie doesn't have a ton of locations, seeing just a few that very well may work felt like putting a good dent into pre-production.

NOVEMBER 30, 2019

It's raining now on the RV as I am falling asleep. What a day... of course like most casting calls, we were crazy busy at first and then it slowed down. I had my favorites and Joe had his. But we meet in the middle on some of them. It will be a tough choice.

DECEMBER 1, 2019

I've entered the final month of dedicated pre-production.

DECEMBER 2, 2019

Today was a long but good one full of meeting and scouting with Clark Richey and Amye Gousset. Clark and I got to know each other better. He showed me his resources in Baldwyn and the things we might be able to accomplish here for the Natchez Trace. It holds much possibility. At the end of the night, it seems quite positive that we may team up.

Joe and I picked our top two contenders for the role of Jessica in *Turn and Burn*. I sent them both the script and asked them to read it carefully. As we feared, one of them won't do the kissing scene and I refuse to compromise on that kind of stuff. The other has rumors floating around about her past. Because I've suffered from the damage lies can take, I am investigating... I am now private detective/filmmaker.

DECEMBER 5, 2019

Crazy day. Lots of things coming my way. Got a great deal on our desired location for *Heart of the Gun* which suddenly puts me in a spot where I need to decide on our shoot days ASAP. That project just went from poking along to very real and moving in a heartbeat.

Also, heard back from Clark and Amye about teaming up on the *Natchez Trace* films. They're in. This is big news. I need their help and I'm happy to have it.

My head is pounding from the afternoon cups of coffee and these developments. I have about twenty tasks left on my to-do list today... trips to Fayette to see the old school house and Meadville to see Dixie's barn and a visit to Wayne's place to talk further about the use of his vehicles all set me back but hopefully this adrenaline will keep me productive for a few more hours.

DECEMBER 8, 2019

Life is getting crazier and crazier the closer I get to filming. We start in just 24 days. This weekend we did our "horse boot camp", training actors to both ride horses and drive wagons. It was quite an experience. As you know from that scene in Ranch Hands, if a horse knows you're intimidated, it doesn't want to cooperate. The biggest struggle I'm having with these westerns, and specifically with the horse situation, is conflicting methods/opinions from my horse people. One guy wants to teach the actors this way, another wants to show them something else. As a non-expert when it comes to horses, I have to try to find a balance and do what's best.

I had two conflicting personalities this weekend. One of them says, "It's always the rider that's the problem, not the horse" and the other just complains about the horses almost the whole time. I agree with the former person for the most part. Though these horses were challenging, it proved true every time my wrangler could get on a horse the actor was having trouble with and do what was required immediately. I've learned from my own horse experience that sometimes I am tense, scared, frustrated and the horse picks up on that faster than I can even realize it. This other gentlemen complained a lot and I had to explain to him that on a low budget film, we have to work with what we have and to think in terms of solutions instead of focusing on problems. It's hard to describe this dynamic in writing but it's a struggle and one that I hope we will overcome as filming begins.

The actors did an amazing job for the most part. My lead for *Texas Red*, the Grammy-nominated blues singer admitted that he is afraid of horses but challenging himself and was riding fast by the end of the weekend!

My only regret at the end of the weekend as I packed up after everyone was gone is that I didn't have a woman to share the beautiful ranch with. The last time I'd been there, I had a girl with me and I remembered with fondness the places we'd spent time. Alas, Bandit and I enjoyed the pond where he swam as much as possible before driving back to Brookhaven.

DECEMBER 22, 2019

The start date is quickly approaching. I spent this weekend with my small crew making the finishing touches on the *Bastard's* set but of course it's not really finished. There are still so many odds and ends to figure out. The hardest part of this will be continuing to do pre-production on the others while I shoot the first ones.

DECEMBER 30, 2019

I'm now just a couple days from the beginning of this crazy endeavor. What can be said other than it's finally here... I wanted it... I asked for it... and now I got it.

Jared has arrived in Mississippi. Him being here gives me an extra boost of energy. I think we'll have a good crew on this film. I am also excited about what the lead actor will bring to the role. He is very passionate and clearly is giving it everything he has.

BASTARD'S CROSSING

Photograph by Carys Glynne

The first of the 12 was supposed to be easy… yeah, right! What writer Joe Pevey and I originally hoped would be a simple Western to start with ended up being as challenging as the rest. It was set in one location with a handful of characters and long dialog scenes like a play. However, it also included several wagons and plenty of horses. These would have been challenging enough to include but there was another unforeseen factor for this first production:

weather. It was one of the wettest Januarys in recent Mississippi history. Of course it was... because we were filming!

Before you read about our time making Bastard's Crossing, here is a brief synopsis of the story: Cam Talcutt won a remote trading post in a card game. He now lives there, isolated and lonely, unable to make a connection with the passersby. If that isn't bad enough, he learns that the freight company that supplies his store won't be coming his way anymore. Desperate, Cam soon takes advantage of a tragic situation to replenish his supplies but this spawns an evil idea that soon grows in his mind.

January 7th, 2020

The first week of *Bastard's Crossing* went better than I could have imagined. Part of me feels like this can only mean that some really hard times are yet to come. Who knows because going into week one, things seemed poised for disaster. Our first day was expected to be a shit show... I mean, actors and crew were asking me to postpone the shoot. "Start Friday instead of Thursday", they said. I told them what I usually do, "We're working. Even if we get one scene out of six, it's worth it." Sure enough, we got all our scenes and wrapped early. It was like rubbing a cat's head in shit to make it remember not to do that again but they won't learn. When you face disaster, you look it right in the face and proceed, not because you're stupid and fearless, but because you know that any progress is progress. In the end, the elements of rain and mud looked damn cool in our footage as we watched the dailies from day one on *Bastard's* and if I'd chickened out upon their advice, I would have started the 12 Westerns a day behind. Instead, I started it with confidence.

...

Speaking of dailies, Jared and I have made it a habit to watch them after every shoot day. That's something we've never done and it's valuable as hell. We've stuck to it and I like that. Going into production, I told him we needed to be rigorous with our progress. He said the word "meticulous" and that's a good one too. We are working well together with the assurance of familiar partnership. What interrupts that flow is moments when I feel like he should know better the way I make movies. He called "cut" one day when he should know that's on me to call and that burning media time doesn't mean shit to me. This happens in almost every movie, along with his inability to remember how important it is to me that he throws up frame and test blocking first. There's an obstacle there in our relationship on certain things... stubbornness perhaps that he wants to hang onto a certain process and is unwilling to bend or it may just be that he can't remember things that aren't important to him. Memory is so key on set. Some people have it. Others don't at all. He's somewhere in between, unable to remember or retain a lot of our conversations but definitely able to stay focused which is what matters most. Others like my set decorator can't remember a damn thing. It's in one ear and out the next for 9 out of 10 things we talk about. She is, however, doing a good job of decorating. You put up with these faults because you don't have options as an indie filmmaker. This is who you have to work with and you work with them until the job is done, till the movie is finished. Then you try to keep looking for the people who you really like, Jared and others who you can develop with. Chris feels like one of those. He's our gaffer on this show and we almost immediately bonded. Tonight, I asked him to stay on for *Texas Red*. "What do I have to do to keep you in Mississippi?" He makes more in three days in Chicago than working with me for fifteen but he has the heart, the passion for what we're doing. I joked the other day that if he, Jared, and I were in the movie *Jaws*, he'd be Quint, Jared would be Brody, and I'd be Richard Dreyfuss's character. It's super true. He has Quint's smile. I like him a lot. He can be mad on set, frustrated with my answers, and then shake it off and be back to work within a minute.

...

Filming in the mud was tough. I went through a couple pairs of shoes, caked in wet dirt, until I finally invested in some rubber boots. But I loved being covered in it for my scene, even if it seeped through my clothes and got really damn cold. My teeth were chattering as I gave direction for the scene I was in. Unexpectedly, my first take falling off the mule was the best one. Each one that came after could not compare. From then on, we struggled to find the moments to piece it together. As I fell off the mule into frame and staggered my way to the other horse I was supposed to mount for the last take, the horse led me out of frame... I pulled the reins, felt in control, turned around, and then the horse wanted to take me back. That felt right so I followed its lead but as soon as we reached the hitching post, it wouldn't stop. It took off towards the building, the trading post structure. What the hell? I was moving fast towards the overhang, what just hours earlier our horse wrangler Beau said would "decapitate" an actor if we tried to have him ride under it (something I was hoping to do for the next movie, *Texas Red*). Suddenly, I knew I was unintentionally about to test that stunt, not a confident enough horseman to pull the horse to a stop before we both went under. Thankfully, I could think fast enough to duck and not lose my head. We rode through the breezeway and the horse stopped before the other side. I gave everyone a heart attack that's for sure but I have to say that getting off the horse, heart beating fast, I was having fun the whole time. Though I failed to stop the animal, I was conscious of what was happening, aware of both the danger and even the value of this crazy act. Still, it was clear how quickly things can turn wild.

The same was true throughout week one as our animals did sometimes unpredictable things, even with experienced riders on their backs, even with their owners riding them. The truth is that you just have to do your due diligence to be careful. It's like driving on the freeway, you do your best and hope those around you don't screw up and end your life.

...

We wrapped early five days in a row. I've never done that. I've never heard of that. Not even two or three days in a row. It's crazy. What is it? Good crew, good scheduling. Who knows. Really who knows. At some point, it's not going to be that way and the same answer will remain, who knows. There's no science to any of this. But there is experience, confidence, knowing what you want and don't want. That goes a long way.

...

Working with one actor is not quite what I imagined. He's good. A true actor. He can play. He's all in. He does have these little diva moments. They're tolerable. They don't ruin how I feel about him but I still wish he'd shake that bullshit off. I expect it's a symptom from years of witnessing big budget productions roll in and out of Mississippi, taking notes from the bad example of pompous hollywood jerks. Still, he's a soldier for the most part and he's doing good work, he's carrying the picture. That's what matters in the end.

...

I cooked two meals today when I should have been doing pre-production work but it was just a cooking frenzy that took hold, a nice break from the other kind of work. I'm having fun taking care of the crew with great food, wine and liquor when appropriate. It goes a long way it seems.

...

Probably one of the things I feared most on this first movie happened: the owner of the stagecoach we're featuring flaked. See, back a month or so back, I was scheduled to go see the coach in North Mississippi and just days before, Aaron (the owner) said, "My company flew me to Mexico but you can still drop by and see it". I did and pleased, wrote an agreement between the two of us for him to deliver the vehicle to set on Jan. 12th. Well, even when discussing the agreement with him, I explicitly said "Look, you're not going to suddenly have to fly to Mexico again and I won't have a stagecoach, right?". He assured me that would not happen. "A set date is a set date," he said. Well, that's exactly what happened.

Today, I followed up with him, just as a courtesy, nothing else. "My company flew me to Mexico again. You can come get the stagecoach but I won't be able to bring it." Come get it? It's four hours away! Thankfully, after some strategizing, I was able to rely on the incredible support of Brad Turner, a man who has already provided wagons and so much help for this project, to go fetch the stagecoach. I have to pay him but the willingness to do that is amazing. He's a good guy, through and through. When I confirmed with Aaron that we could still get the wagon, I wanted to tell him off but I bit my tongue...

January 15th, 2020

Today was go go go. Even more than days on set. I tried to meet up with a girl. No time for that. Tried to eat dinner. No time for that either. Now I'm home with leftovers in my belly, drinking my second gin and tonic, thinking about why a day off of pre production is more exhausting than a day of production. Is it the lack of creative fulfillment ?

...

I couldn't have picked a worse night and place to have our wardrobe test this evening. The same building as Dorsey's office happened to be the site of a big inauguration thing. Parking was shut down. A bunch of fancy dressed men and women all over the place, all going to the 19th floor and I was headed for the 13th. I had to check with security just to use the damn elevator. Then I have to make several trips to get the wardrobe up there. On one trip down, the elevator door opened and another man in a suit stood in my way. I said, "Excuse me" without hiding my frustration and turned back to see it was our new governor, Tate Reeves himself. Well, now we're acquainted.

...

Yesterday, our seventh day of production on *Bastard's* was a struggle. I arrived in the morning with some pep in my step but it was quickly deflated by one of the actors whose morning grumpiness has been on a steady incline. He immediately hit me with a level of aggressiveness about a bathroom use issue and randomly seemed concerned about when he was getting paid. When I explained the SAG schedule, he pushed for more details. This kind of thing pisses me off. Why hit me with that question in the AM halfway through production? People can't think ahead. If it was a concern, he should have asked long before. After the interaction, I tried to shake it off but the grumpiness hung over the day. Others mentioned it. I was so tempted to confront the issue but decided to wait till the completion of scenes for the day. We had a conversation in the dark of the carport next to the hearse wagon. It seemed like there was an understanding but the next morning would reveal there truly wasn't. However, before getting into that, this wasn't the only carport heart to heart I had that night.

On her first day of filming for another actor, we conflicted in a way I didn't see coming. After giving me the impression the actor was truly tough, things fell apart during a simple scene where the person is supposed to be gagged. The actor complained about the handkerchief cloth being in their mouth. "I'm a mouth breather," the actor said. "But you can still breathe through your nose, right?" I asked. No answer. The actor wasn't having it. Truth be told, this person had been complaining gradually more and more, showing impatience with doing more than two takes. So when they kept doing it here, I did not give it much weight. By about the third take, the actor said it was "uncomfortable". I asked the person harshly, "Have you read the script? We'll do as many takes as I want." The truth is, this burst all spawned from my disappointment with this person and my surprise at their lack of toughness. When the words had left my mouth, I could tell they'd hurt. We continued with a couple takes and at the end of the last one, she was crying, not in character but really crying.

So less than an hour later, we sat in the same carport discussing what happened, though I wouldn't call it much of a discussion because I was barely heard. The actor was upset and not hearing anything but her upset-ness. Yes, I can see some of the person's point... I had probably over-reacted but her statements of "You should never talk that way to anyone on set, ever" and "I thought you were a nice person" showed that this actor and I live in different worlds. They are fully embedded in the sensitive, politically correct world of the modern film industry and I cannot reconcile that with everything I know, want, and have studied. The actor reiterated that doing more than a couple takes was strange. I asked if the person could please use more words than "uncomfortable" in the future to let me know if something was truly a problem, to say something like "Travis, we need to talk", but they would not concede, they would not bend even a little. I left the conversation knowing that I would have to handle this person like a fragile doll from now on, being clever with my manipulations rather than direct.

The next morning, an argument erupted before we even got off the first shot. While walking through a fight scene, one actor demanded that we remove a certain set piece because it was dangerous. I explained that we should discuss it but he insisted, becoming almost belligerent about it. Suddenly, our voices were raised, shouting at each other as I told him that he could raise a concern however much he wanted but he could not tell me what to do or not do. This is a problem with people in general... they don't know how to just talk about something. It immediately becomes an emergency before it has even been diagnosed as a problem. He cooled off in the breezeway as I took a deep breath. One of my crew later said they were amazed at how fast I shook off the argument and returned to work in a normal tone. We got back into planning the fight scene and sure enough, the "dangerous" item did not have to move one inch as we moved the fight scene four feet over. Later in the day, the actor apologized but I don't know if he really learned the lesson that situation should have really taught him. Regardless, his grumpy mood finally lightened over the course of the next couple days.

...

On our last day of week two, we worked towards a sluggish finish. I could feel the team losing steam, needing some days off. I, on the other hand, needed the days off for a whole different reason, feeling the future projects running away from me in a hurry. And now at the end of those two days off, I can say that I have caught up. A little. But a little is better than nothing. James, my good old friend, told me all I needed to do was to make these films and survive. He might be right.

January 21st, 2020

"The end of production is the end of a life."
- Sam Peckinpah's quote on my final call sheet for *Bastard's Crossing*.

I've reached the end of production on the first of 12 Westerns and it's not those fifteen days of filming that have me exhausted but the prospect of having only one week before production starts on the 2nd, a very minimal amount of time to figure out a whole lot. I spent all day doing as much work as I could, my mind working twice as hard as my body, like wheels spinning in mud and not getting far as they could on hard ground.

The last day of filming was a mixed bag. There were good moments and also some incredibly frustrating ones. I hoped there would be a lack of distraction, that the crew, especially Jared would give me one final focused day but alas, this proved to be impossible when I needed him/them most. In the final two hours of filming, I knew we were going to be rushing for every second of sunlight. I pushed and pushed, saying over and over again "We need to be sharp. We need to move fast and be on our game." In the process of blocking and shooting the final scene, when I caught Jared making silly videos on his phone, I barked, "Don't fucking do that agaiin. No fucking around from now till we've got the last shot." It really angered me, that in these final dire moments he would lose focus, especially since he already struggles with keeping the shots and the memory of what we've talked about aligned in his mind. I have to have a talk with him but I'm waiting for the right moment.

Again during one of our final takes, Creek Wilson (our actor) started cracking up. Understandable, the scene involves him getting kicked in the nuts. Fine. One outtake. Then the crew started laughing. Then Creek laughed more and couldn't get straight for another take. I turned to the crew and said, "If anyone laughs during this scene, I promise I'll never work with you again." They all thought I was an asshole but I don't care... their silly joke died that day and the takes we're getting last forever. People still don't get that. They place their little moments over these huge moments that are imprinted on the movie for the remainder of our existence.

Going back in time, it was interesting saying farewell to some of the actors. One had been so ornery through a good deal of the process, certainly always delivering an interesting performance but struggling at times to maintain a good attitude. As the end of the shoot approached, I could feel him lightening up, possibly because he could see the light at the end of the tunnel or because he was starting to put it all in perspective. I see this a lot: people bitch and complain all the way through and then come out grateful as can be at the last second. However, I did take his thankfulness for the role and experience as genuine. I just think the goal as a mature person should be to see through the current moment to what the big picture is before you get there.

...

It's easier to write about the bad things and harder to remember the good. One positive was the way we shot and covered the climax with Cam getting killed. This is how I'd like to shoot a lot of scenes, with plenty of time for takes and lots of angles. Sure, I love getting it in one shot and making that work but sometimes it's nice to get as much as you could possibly want. To give yourself time to play and time for ideas to emerge as the scene marinates take after take.

I'm grateful for all the people who came along to help with this... Brad saving my ass with the wagons, Damon picking up the slack on the back end of production, Martha doing her best with the food. It's up and down but those folks really brought this one home.

Discussing a scene with Ashleigh Lewis, playing Sadie.

Bandit watches a scene, wet from the rain.

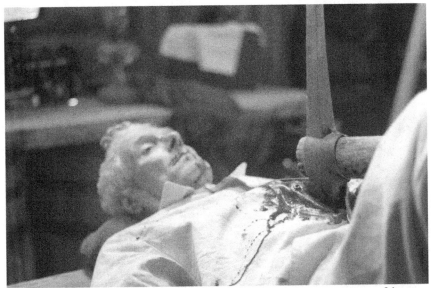

Actor Jeff Buchwald with his pickaxe gag, courtesy of Lee Cannon.

Lead actor Ward Emling stands in the mud we trudged through every day of filming.

All photographs in this section were taken by Carys Glynne.

TEXAS RED

Many will say that Texas Red is not a Western. Well, with people calling No Country for Old Men a Western these days, it's pretty hard to define what fits into the genre and what doesn't. For me, the Western must include the following: 1. A struggle for justice, usually between outlaws and some kind of law enforcement. 2. A variation on Western wear including cowboy hats, holsters, and boots. 3. The action of riding horses. 4. Shootouts and showdowns. If a film has these elements combined, it does not matter as much to me where or when it is set. That's how I saw Texas Red.

I've always been drawn to true stories and though the degree of truth in this one will always be questionable, what happens in the story rings true in the most disturbing way and will always resonate. Here is a brief synopsis of the story:

Texas Red is a successful juke joint owner in the segregated South. He is rumored to have gained some of his wealth through thievery with his partner in crime, the much wilder Oklahoma Kid. When a Constable decides to take the law into his own hands, a midnight raid on Red's cabin turns tragic as a young deputy is killed. With the blood of a white boy on their hands, Red and the Kid are now on the run and a manhunt begins to track them down. From a posse of angry citizens to several sheriffs, the FBI, and even the National Guard, these men are chased through the cold winter of 1940 in Mississippi and must do everything they can to survive.

Photograph by Damon Burks

January 27th, 2020

Well here I am, on the eve of the second production start. This past week has gone by in the blink of an eye.

I've spent the last six days working my ass off to catch up for *Texas Red* and always feeling more behind by the day's end. Today is the only one where I end it feeling a little more up to speed. In many respects, this film is ten times harder than *Bastard's* just because of all the moving pieces.

Also, I must admit that I've dropped the ball in the past couple weeks. I thought I was on top of prep but I was letting things slip through the cracks. It seems thus far like none of that was detrimental but it certainly could have been and could be in the future if I let it happen again. I have to find more time to prep during production...

The crew seems good so far. I like Baretta and Brian, our new additions a lot so far. This will be a crew of men with only one female, something I'm looking forward to as a change of pace.

Cedric continues to prove himself a man of passion and humility. His quiet strength will show through in every scene I think. Today, Herman (Oklahoma kid) and I conflicted about music. I thought a sax player would work fine in the scene and he was strongly against it. I said we'd discuss it. We did and as usual the discussion led to solutions and understanding. I tried to explain to him that's how I work. He admitted that my initial defiance of his opinion made him feel like I wasn't listening to the black perspective. That wasn't it at all. I'm listening to all the perspectives. I am curious to see if this comes up again.

January 28th, 2020

The first day went better than I thought. Almost too smooth like calm skies before a storm. Cedric brought it all. Gung ho. I just wonder if there will be days when it gets too much. I'm sure there will and we will get through them.

I have several stresses on my plate tonight... I heard from Beau that he can't make it tomorrow. His dad had a heart attack. That puts us down two horses, one that Nick was riding today so we now have a continuity problem. Also, I still can't cast the fucking Ben Chester White character. Mississippi is full of black people. How is it so tough to find one to play a damn good role?

I'm behind on extras. Locations. Logistics. Fuck. I need to just keep working hard and find my way to the other side.

January 30th, 2020

When I arrived on set yesterday to see nearly all of the riders who'd signed up had actually arrived, I was moved to the point of almost crying. It floors me how lucky I am that these people help me out and since flaking on commitments is so much a part of our culture, I am always impressed when people pull through, regardless of weather, etc.

We moved real fast, more documentary style which is something I'm enjoying a lot more compared to the long lighting setups. Every project is different but this may be my preferred way of filming. Cedric continues to be a trooper, bringing so much passion and physical energy to the role. The riders were all impressive but this young man Rhett particularly stood out. He definitely understands film and how to be in it the right way. I think he has incredible potential.

I'm a little worried about something. SAG contacted me yesterday asking to have a conversation about some of my scenes... I don't even know what project they want to talk about. Could be *Bastard's*, or *Texas Red*, or even *Deputy*. They did call Ashleigh from *Bastard's* the other day, as she reported to me, asking her if anything went wrong on set. She said all went well but who knows what kind of shit they may be throwing at me. I really hate the restrictions of the damn Guild and on top of that, they're incredibly disorganized. Hopefully it blows over.

I still haven't cast the Ben Chester White role. This may be the toughest casting fiasco I've ever had.

Feb. 2nd

The last few days have been rough. Our second posse day, I fought to stay on schedule from call to wrap and we were behind the whole time. At our creek location, two near disasters happened. The camera, hit by water in a take with Cedric moving down a tunnel, was shut down when Jared discovered condensation INSIDE the lens. There was no easy way to clean it or take it apart. We only have the one lens on this film so it totally put us out of commission. They started guessing at methods to solve it, putting heat on the lens, etc. Nothing worked. For a good forty five minutes we just sat there, waiting, hoping. Finally they figured out that a neutral temperature of air could make it go away. Suddenly, we were back in business.

The scenes went well and then we decided to capture some shots of riders going across the creek. This was tested out for safety; I walked the creek back and forth with my waders several times as the riders watched to see what route had the hardest bottom. The men, who'd more than encouraged us to get this shot, felt confident enough to give it a try. The way over, they did fine. On the way back, though, not far from the bank, a horse suddenly sank in the sand... and then another... and finally, a third one. All three riders went down. One guy got up and rode out on his horse. Another horse had its legs stuck about a foot in the bottom of the creek. I ran out to help them, along with Chris (our gaffer). We pulled its hooves out and suddenly it was free too. The last horse, Jeremiah Gasaway's, had fallen to its side, its head sticking up out of the water to breathe. Thankfully the water wasn't too deep or this would have been a tragic accident. Chris and I went to help him next, taking the saddle off, which was now wet and adding a significant amount of weight that might keep the horse from getting up. Once we removed the tack, the horse flailed again but couldn't rise. Cedric, unable to help himself, rushed into the water to help us, ruining the 15-20 minutes of makeup work Jennifer had done to make his feet look right for the upcoming shot. Suddenly, someone cried out, "His saddle blanket is going down stream!" I looked up to see this part of Jeremiah's kit getting further and further away from us. I took off after it, running through knee deep water. Maybe 10 to 12 feet away, I decided it was necessary to dive for the blanket. Apparently, the crew thought it looked great, like a Brett Favre touchdown someone said. Who knows. But I caught the blanket, soaked to the bone. Finally Jeremiah's horse rose out of the water and made it to land. It was an intense moment and thankfully one that led to no injuries for any of us. It shows how fast things can change when working with horses, even when making precautions.

The next night we moved into our overnight schedule. It would have been nice to sleep in to get ready to shoot till 4am but as I explained to Jared, who expressed, "Well, dude, we can't have you getting tired in the middle of the shoot," that luxury wasn't available for me. I woke up at 6-something as usual and worked, creating the store location (almost from scratch with Damon) till our call time at 3:30pm. From there, we shot all night until 4:30am. There was no dragging. Regardless of sleep, I'm the only one on set who doesn't drag, who doesn't get tired. Once we wrap, I collapse. That's just how it is. The movie carries me.

The actors were damn good that night. Good from take one even. It made my job easy. I was relieved, after two months of visiting Wayne Wallace once a week, that we got his old truck in the scenes. Unfortunately, we killed the battery and were unable to get it back to him without a tow. I hope it doesn't ruin my relationship with him. The truck looked fantastic but what a long, tedious process to get these car people to make any kind of commitment. Oh and Damon ran over my generator with his truck. Miraculously the thing still runs. It's like me, beat up a little but working well.

The juke joint scene was the following evening, Saturday, and I felt a lot of tension, wondering if my extras would show up or not...

February 13th, 2020

I have done a disservice to myself, especially my future self, by not being diligent about writing this diary every day or at least every few days. But this is certainly the hardest film I've ever had to make and my energy has been stretched to its limits, especially during our second week of production. I will do my best to now backtrack and fill in the blanks before I forget.

When I stopped writing last, I'd mentioned the juke joint. This was an incredible experience. The fears of not enough people showing up were immediately relieved as I waited out by the street, during which my crew lit and prepped our location, for people to show up. While directing parking, I was moved that we had barely any dropouts and that these folks did a good job finding their own 1940 wardrobe.

When approaching this scene, I felt more and more like handling it in a traditional way was a mistake. I explained this to the extras as I gathered them all around: "Normally, when we shoot a scene like this, there's set blocking... you move right to left on action, you over there move left to right five seconds after action and so on. But we're not doing that this time. I want this to be real, I want the feeling of a real juke joint party. So when you go in there, just grab one of our prop drinks and do your thing. I'm not going to tell you where to stand, look, what to do or say... just respond to the music, respond to each other." It was perhaps the best direction I've ever given: no direction at all. And what I hoped for came true.

Within a few minutes of setting these people free in the space, the juke joint was alive. It was nothing I ever could have blocked or directed. It was like using a time machine into the past as these people totally embodied the space and let themselves go. Singing. Dancing. Rowdy. Sensual. Real.

Occasionally I would give a line of direction to one of our main talent, asking them to repeat an action so Jared, who just roamed around the room with the camera reacting to whatever was happening, could capture something he'd missed while being focused on something else. At one point, I snuck up to our guitar player Ontario and whispered into his ear to call "Texas Red" out to play a song. I wasn't sure how Cedric would react to this improvised moment but it worked out beautifully. He played one of his tunes and it fit the scene to perfection.

It's amazing how quickly things can go from good to bad on set. Here we were, getting chills and almost tearing up at how beautiful the scene was, all marveling at this great creation and not thirty minutes later, Chris the gaffer is in a fowl mood, stomping around saying it's not okay that we have so many scenes left to complete that evening, not okay that we have a location move... it was like watching a child go from this high of playing to a little hissy fit. It's too bad I don't have the luxury of putting these children down for a nap. However much I like the people I'm working with, nearly all of them are children. Perhaps with the exception of Baretta. He has yet to show me that side if he has one. Though it pissed me off incredibly to deal with that attitude, I did what I do with women... wait it out and sure enough, not too much later, Chris was back to normal. I was not though. When people put me through that shit, it zaps the energy right out of me.

...

The next shoot date was our most challenging yet, starting at 9pm and filming till 9am. A true all nighter. The material was tough too, the raid on Texas Red's cabin, action (aka not my strong suit). But somehow, it went pretty well, all except for running out of time right as the sun was coming out. We just weren't quite done with our final night scene as light started to appear in the sky. That last shot we got might not match... but I sure hope to hell that it does.

As the sun did rise, I was renewed with energy. I felt as if I could film another 12 hours no problem. The rest of the crew did not. They were strung out but our morning scene was strong too and we finished the day mostly victorious, our equipment and props spread out all over the place. I should have insisted we clean up but I didn't and we walked away, leaving a complete mess with loose ends that are still being tied up to this day. Arriving back at my house, I found Jennifer, our makeup artist, and Chris drinking in the kitchen. They asked if I wanted one. I ordered a gin and tonic. A couple hours later, at eleven AM in the morning, we were all drunk. It wasn't the best decision for productivity but it was probably good for my mental health.

Those two days off were barely a break with one clouded by that drunkenness and the other filled with errands, a trip to Jackson, and as many tasks as I could pack into the available hours. I entered week two unprepared and a little scared.

...

As I write this, I just now remembered how crazy that second day off was... I worked as hard as I could in the morning, took off for Jackson to send the payroll deposit, meet our executive producer, exchange the hard drive with our assistant editor and then I headed for Carlisle (an hour away) to scout that for week three, then to got back in the car to hit Natchez... no wonder I was worn out.

Our first day back was an away game in Natchez. As mentioned, I was not ready for week two. That was evident leading up to that first day, the seventh of production, in which I still had not figured out who would play this Military man who has his jacket stolen by Red while he's distracted by a girl in this car. Originally I'd planned this to be my cameo, hoping to find a lady who would be comfortable making out with me in the scene. But as the days went on, I realized there were no real contenders and this is of course not the easiest part to cast... "Hey, this is my director's cameo and I want to cast you as the one who just kisses me in the car and that's all." In our culture, that's the last thing I need to mess around with. So I went on the hunt in the final 24 hours for cast members, something I hate doing. I'd already pushed casting Ben Chester White during week one till the very last moment and here I was again, in the same situation. I contacted Sarah Hanson, a costumer I'd met twice, hoping she'd know a young man and woman to fill the roles, even hoping she might fill it. It turns out that Sarah did save my ass, finding a couple she's friends with to comfortably make out in the scene. She even provided the outfit for the girl.That crisis was averted.

...

But going back to week two, that pattern of being behind continued as the days went on. Each day of production, there were a ton of things I hadn't figured out yet. I was scrambling to bring it all together. Each time I did but what a stressful journey to get there. That's the part of it I don't like, feeling like I'm chasing the production, like chasing *Texas Red* and he's getting away from me. It's an interesting metaphor because making this film about being on the run definitely feels more like being on the run, trying to survive than any other film I've made. Amazingly enough, with all that in consideration, the scenes we're getting still feel incredible. It's the raw nature of this, Cedric's sincerity, and our confidence to tell the story the way we're telling it. That's how it feels now at least. Only time will tell what it comes to be.

February 15th, 2020

Yesterday, we set out to capture the climactic scenes of the film, and also some of the most challenging of the whole production. We filmed on an old bridge, now closed to traffic but safe to cross on foot. With the recent rains and flooding all over Mississippi, Jared and I were astounded as the Homochitto river looked one way when we first scouted and then just two days later, all of what we'd planned was changed by a water line that had risen several feet. Thankfully, on our return Friday to film, the river had gone back down and our plan was possible.

We arrived and started to map out our shots. Cedric showed frustration more than ever as we had him walking barefoot across the cold sand bank. After days and days of showing nothing but patience, it was wearing thin and rightfully so, especially as he dealt with our indecision at times and even little things like moments when I failed to say "cut" loud enough, letting him run on without knowing the shot was ended. It's amazing he hasn't been more grumpy with us but that morning was definitely tough for him.

As the sun came out, things improved and we continued to move through the day's shots but there was more conflict as the actor John Maxwell showed up and we started work on his scenes as the sharpshooter who shoots Texas Red. The tension between a Crew Member and I has been building through production. I like him and he's definitely a hard worker but he lacks some serious professional attributes, often revealing how immature he is for an "industry" pro.

I have been increasingly troubled by the way he moves around and even speaks during takes. He's unable to stay still, either pacing, fidgeting, messing with gear, or whispering comments during takes. It's been a problem since *Bastard's* but it just gets to me more and more. Also, it has ruined a few takes at the very least, maybe more. I've expressed this to him but it didn't get any better. So... back to Day 14, as the sun had come out and we were working on the sharpshooter set up, this Crew Member started talking in the middle of the shot, in which I was holding the sniper rifle, doing the movement for a rifle insert so the actor wouldn't have to. Whatever he said after action, I exploded: "Will you shut the fuck up? I'm tired of you talking during the fucking take and making noise when we're trying to work." He bounced back with, "Oh, so tell me how you really feel." It went on like this, almost humorously as I continued to move the rifle through the shot and Jared continued to operate while we argued. I pulled the trigger on the rifle (no bullet inside it of course) and called "cut". Tension was high but we continued to work. You'd think a blow up with the director like that would lay this to rest... no.

Flash forward to the next day of filming. We're setting up for the scenes with the most extras we've had all production: up to 100 people outside the courthouse, lining up to see Texas Red's dead body. I'm trying to talk to Jared about the shots and blocking. All the while, this Crew Member is interjecting random comments that have nothing to do with the subject. I snapped again. "I'm trying to talk here, dude. And by the way, Baretta (sound person) confirmed you've ruined several takes with your noise. If you do it again, I'll have you leave set immediately." Not two hours later, he tested my patience again, saying I should make all these extras wait for the "right light". I responded, "This is the schedule." Crew Member: "Just think about it, huh? Think about it! Maybe there's something wrong with the schedule, huh?" I told him, "You want to go home? Do you? Go home." He shut up and we kept shooting. Amazingly, we get along well most of the time, especially off set.

...

Going back to day fourteen, it was a wild one, full of great shots and little misadventures. Jared almost sank in quicksand. That's a bit of an exaggeration but while walking along the bank of the Homochitto river, he did sink close to his waist while holding the camera. It showed how unpredictable this landscape can be. Not long after, Brian (our assistant camera person) dropped the slate through cracks in the bridge. This was right after our final take. I was seconds away from leaping off the bridge to get it when actors convinced me that it was too far a drop. Instead, I ran off the bridge, through the nearby camp and down onto the bank. I entered the Homochitto river, wading chest deep to intercept the slate as it floated downstream, encouraged by cheers and directions as to its path. Upon grabbing the fallen item, I clapped it like we do at the beginning of a take and this produced even more applause. It was a fun way to end the day.

Wrangling the extras Saturday was a challenge. Somehow, no matter the number of times I asked them to move "slower" by Red's body, they always sped up. It's this odd magnetic pull a human being feels while following another human, unable to set their own pace or resist the urge to catch up. It was an amazing visual sample of how people truly follow each other.

...

The next day was Cedric's last playing Texas Red. In the couple days leading up to this, I could feel his frustration, his decreasing patience. He is however still probably the leading man with the best attitude I've ever worked with. It's a testament to his character that after 16 days of having him in and out of cold water, running through all kinds of brush, often barefoot on all kinds of surfaces, he never lost his cool. That final day with him was not an easy one, going from some pick-up scenes I decided to add to the script where Red sees visions of his common law wife Dolly in the woods (ones that I hope will fill in some gaps in the character's journey) to a challenging green screen shot at the train station to a big scene we'd pushed back earlier in production: Red and the Oklahoma Kid saying goodbye at the Mississippi River.

Since writing it, this scene has been a big question mark on my mind... how could I pull it off? I'd already had issues with a river in *Blood Country*, sinking an old boat and having actors rescued from the water. That could not happen again... I planned, however, to film in the exact same area, Cooper's Ferry in Monticello. As luck would have it, the Pearl River (standing in for the Mississippi) has been in flood stage for at least a couple weeks and keeps getting worse. I was warned by several sources not to mess with it at all. On top of that, the actor playing the Oklahoma Kid couldn't swim, not even in a pool. Could I double for the Kid, a black character? The idea started to turn in my mind. It seemed to be the only way to limit risk. Getting Herman, the talent, anymore that waist deep in the water was impossible but perhaps I could do a stunt. Somehow.

We planned our shots as if we'd cheat around the Kid never actually getting in the water. I told Jared that the stunt would be a bonus if we had time. Turns out we did, barely. Suddenly, I was disrobing and waiting for the Kid to change so I could put on his outfit. I'd pick out a "safe" distance to swim to. Before the current really kicked up, there were a few trees sticking out of the water and a pile of brush that would be my mark. I stepped into the muddy river, not too cold at first, and waited for Jared to set the camera. I confirmed a few things once he was rolling, worried we'd only have one take at this. Seconds later, I was moving out towards the river. It wasn't long before my feet couldn't touch the ground and I had to swim. It also didn't take long for the temperature to drop dramatically, feeling the cold of the true current. I could feel my breath stolen away from my lungs as my arms pumped and pulled me to that piece of brush, hoping all along that the shot was working, that all this was worth it. I made my mark, a little nervous when the brush moved considerably as I grasped it. Worried that it might come loose and pull me downstream, I started back immediately and could already feel the resistance of the current, not at a dangerous level and certainly one that reminded me how dangerous it might have been if I'd gone another ten feet. I came back to the shore breathing heavy from the cold but I was not so chilly as soon as I saw the shot and could tell that it worked, everyone felt that I totally doubled for the Oklahoma Kid. "Hell yeah", I repeated several times and got those wet clothes off as soon as I could.

Cedric's farewell was an emotional one. Jennifer cried, no surprise there. My voice choked up as I thanked him and he reiterated his gratitude for the opportunity and experience. I would love to know the whole range of thoughts and emotions he has for what's happened, good and bad. Maybe one day he will share them with me. Humorously, he left before filling out his final SAG form.

...

Damn SAG... it makes producing films harder, that's for sure. I've learned so many lessons the hard way with this process: 1. When this all began, I didn't even realize SAG works off an eight hour day so I was immediately going overtime on my actors, paying out the ass on *Bastard's* for working them 10 to 11 hour days (all the time thinking I was doing great by keeping it under 12). It's nearly impossible to schedule an eight hour day with an actor, at least the way we shoot. My goal with *Deputy's Wife* is to find a way because with six SAG actors on set, I'm going to be screwed if I don't. 2. I learned how much it hurts to push a lunch past six hours. The day our horses went down in the creek, we had a "working lunch". Cedric, going by the books, didn't count this as an actual lunch and I got penalized thirty dollars every thirty minutes until he actually got one. That was brutal.

...

Finishing out week three of production with filming on Monday and Tuesday felt a little odd now that our lead actor wasn't involved. These were big travel days, with hour drives to begin and end each of them. Monday we were in the "town" of Carlisle, now only four to five buildings. I was attracted to this place because you can shoot nearly every direction and it passes for 1940.

Near the end of the day, Jennifer alerted me that she saw Andy Shelley (one of the people harassing us on Facebook about making *Texas Red*) drive by in his white truck three times. I told her to immediately call the cops, alarmed that she hadn't told me the first time he went by. There's no screwing around with stuff like that these days. You can't take it lightly with all the shootings. How do I know some redneck asshole might not decide it's a good idea to blast one of my crew out his truck window with a shotgun? People are stupid and that can't be underestimated. They will ruin their lives and others' lives in a heartbeat over the most ridiculous thing. The sheriff's department showed up and took down the info. Damon even managed to get a picture of the truck's license plate. I hope we get through the rest of production with no issues.

February 23rd, 2020

I have now officially completed filming on the second of the 12. *Texas Red* is done. It feels like we shot for two months, not one. This has definitely been the hardest film I've ever made in many respects: the volume of extras in many scenes, the multiple locations, the ensemble cast, the limited (and sometimes problematic crew)... All of it combined has been an exhausting and yet rewarding process. Though I don't believe in "best", I do feel this movie is some of my strongest work. Only time will tell as we piece it together.

I must say I am relieved to say goodbye to some of these people. I am also excited to say goodbye to the mud, to the consistent rain, to the Southern fried food, and to the racism that pervades this area and becomes more and more apparent with every movie I make here.

Saturday, Feb. 22nd, our final day. We filmed at this historic African American school, a fitting place for the scene and to end this movie. The six black children who showed up were quite good and super well-behaved, unlike most kids I've worked with. Herman, an actor I'm very happy to have hired, delivered once again, especially with his last line about Red being a "true rebel". This required no direction. He said it exactly how I wanted him to. I feel this scene has some real nice subtle subversiveness... playing off the idea of a "rebel" in Southern culture, comparing someone like Red to George Washington, contrasting school room history to a "real story". Should be interesting to see if anyone picks up on that stuff.

All I wanted to do after wrapping was relax. After our celebratory dinner, I was able to resist the temptation to follow some of the crew to the bar. Instead Morgan (my assistant) and I came back here and had a couple of glasses of wine with some nice conversation. She encouraged me that I would make a good Joe Boot in the Pearl Hart movie and now I keep seeing her and I in it together, quite a duo. Time will tell, on both fronts.

I have two days to pack as much of my life as possible in a Toyota Corolla and move to Arizona for six months.

Lead Actor and Emmy-nominated blues singer Cedric
Burnside during filming.
Photograph by Travis Mills.

Retrieving the slate that fell off a bridge into the Homochitto river. Photograph by Damon Burks.

Actor Nick Murphy riding with the posse on a cold February morning. Photograph by Travis Mills.

Legendary theatre actor John Maxwell plays the
sharpshooter Coochie.
Photograph by Travis Mills.

Directing Cedric Burnside (Texas Red) in the climactic scene.

Photograph by Damon Burks.

SHE WAS THE DEPUTY'S WIFE

She was the Deputy's Wife is one of the first Western scripts I wrote. Its long period of development, from 2014 till production in March of last year, allowed the story to develop and the characters to deepen. I feel we went into filming with a solid script but unforeseen circumstances derailed this one

more than any other. The COVID pandemic, which was nothing more than a blip on our radar at the beginning of the month turned into a crazy crisis that would change all of our lives.

If it weren't enough that we faced this unexpected disaster and had to navigate through it to finish the film, we also experienced the greatest tragedy of the year. The loss of Mack Mumford, our assistant camera person, was devastating. He was a charming young man with a bright future but clearly he was also a person who struggled with depression and a bipolar disorder. You will read below the account of making this film, still probably the hardest of my career.

The story: a horse thief is about to hang when a telegram delays his death for a few hours until the Marshal arrives to question him. Meanwhile, the sheriff's deputy is unaware that his wife has fallen in love with this outlaw. She takes the biggest chance of his life, attempting to break him out of jail which leads to a tense standoff. As the story progresses, this love triangle grows more complex and everyone's loyalty is tested against the evil Marshal.

Photograph by Gerald Marrion.

March 10th, 2020

As usual it has been too long since I recorded my thoughts and the events of the passing days. After arriving in Arizona, I immediately went to work on preparing for this third film. Part of that preparation was getting the place where we're staying ready for the crew's arrival a few days later.

I'd booked the "Lonesome Coconut Ranch" as the lodging for most of our crew, a hippie farm house I'd visited months before. It is rough around the edges but a serene place in many ways. I prepared my main collaborators and crew members for this unconventional home base. In those couple days, I saw Lucy (the owner, a single mom with a little girl named Zoey) turn the place from a semi-cluttered home for her and her many animals (cats, dogs, ducks, and a pig) into a good living situation, by my standards at least. Upon arrival of the small crew, I could tell that not everyone would feel the same way about the ranch as I do. I communicated with the whole team to let me know their concerns and that we would address each one to the best of our ability to make it the most comfortable environment possible. You'd think that would be enough for a group of adults... more on that in a bit.

We did two days of prep on site at Gammons Gulch: camera tests, lighting tests, working out the logistics of production. I never could have guessed what the biggest obstacle to overcome would be: shit, literally. After experiencing some immediate issues at the Lonesome Coconut ranch with a toilet that was getting overwhelmed by the bowel movements of many people, we suddenly faced another crappy situation on our movie set. Joanne, the lady who runs the place, had given us special permission to use the bathrooms on set that are normally closed off to cast/crew because they can also be easily overwhelmed also with a large number. On top of this, we knew port-o-potties would be coming in the next couple days but those would be used for extras. No later than halfway through the first day, I had Joanne up my ass about the bathrooms. "Someone had diarrhea in the men's bathroom and got crap on the inner lid! If you all are going to use it, then you need to make sure it stays clean throughout the day!" This immediately triggered the practical side of my brain and produced only one answer: it would not be possible for us to use the special bathroom. Why? She was setting us up for failure, whether she knew it or not. I mean, you're telling me that in the middle of a shoot day, when my gaffer has to shit his brains out, that he needs to worry about cleaning the INSIDE of the toilet before he hurries back to keep us on schedule? Hell no. Clean it all at the end of the day? I proposed that but it was not enough; it had to be consistently cleaned. I battled over and over to talk sense with her. She claimed we'd brought more people than I'd originally said. I countered this by asking her to look at the list I'd sent. She claimed that I had actors there who weren't on the list. I asked her to point them out. She said that perhaps it would work out if only a certain amount of people used the bathroom and others used the port-o-potties. I said sure, how many? She wouldn't give me a number. I said, just give me a number and I'll put that into practice. Nope. It was nonsensical. The final consensus, which I disagreed with, was for her to leave a spray bottle in the bathroom for each person to use after using it.

Sure enough, the next day, Anouschka (my production designer and now a close friend of Joanne's from her long hours of pre-production at the set) comes storming into the saloon where I was, angry. "I just cleaned up the men's bathroom and there was shit on the inside of the toilet again. I mean there was shit on the upper inside. How does someone do that? This is ridiculous." I should have taken a deep breath but I didn't. "First of all, Anouschka," I began, "No one asked you to clean the bathroom. If you discovered it was such a mess, why didn't you ask me to come see it and clean it before doing so resentfully? Second, this is just not realistic.

Men take big shits sometime. They have diarrhea sometimes. It's not something we can all control and we definitely can't control it in the middle of an intense shoot day." After some banter back and forth, she exclaimed, "Men are pigs". I lost it. "Fuck you," I said, in the most sincere way I could say it. She shut up. Things got quiet. Our main investor was in the room. Later I apologized to her (the investor, not Anouschka) for losing my cool but she did not seem to mind. Perhaps she understood my frustration. That night, I planned to tell the crew that no one could use the men's bathroom to avoid more issues.

Ironically, the next morning I received a text from Anouschka telling me that a leak was found in the men's restroom and that it would be out of commission anyway. She was adamant about adding that this had nothing to do with the issues of the past couple days. Who knows. I was happy to be done dealing with this shit and weary of the way both Joanne and Anouschka had acted throughout the experience, completely driven by emotion and lacking any logic.

...

Thankfully, the busyness of production has given some of our people too many tasks to bother themselves with drama. The first five days have been increasingly intense and mostly good. The cast truly is one of the best I've worked with. Megan, our lead actress, makes my job easy, coming in to deliver solid stakes which require only little adjustments. Robert, as her husband Jonathan, is also solid. I feel I may have to push him later in the production to surprise us but he has it in him and that was clear on the first day. John Marrs has exceeded everyone's expectations, even mine. I knew he'd be reliable but he's more than that, an actor who truly comes to life in the wardrobe and location of the picture. Vincent is fun, if a little too worried at times about what I think, what is being communicated instead of just trusting it.

Shayn is in another class... dangerous, unpredictable, like a taste of working with Brando or Dean.

Struggles on set for the first week of production have included the slowness of our camera crew (getting too caught up in details). A good example of this came the other day while setting up for a shot on the gallows. This was one of our biggest days and I returned from a task to find Mario at a standstill. "I'm trying to get the app to work on my phone so I can see what lens to use for this shot," he explained. "That's why you've got a camera". The expensive piece of film machinery sat aside, unused. "Well, that's tough. Takes times. If this app would only work..." He kept staring at his screen. "What lens do you think you want to shoot this on?" I asked. "A 35," he answered. "And what lens is on the camera?" "A 35", he admitted. "Pick up the camera and put your phone down. See how it looks." This is the kind of odd obstacles people create for themselves instead of just making progress, moving forward.

...

According to my friend Blaize, the 30ish background extras have been very pleased at our efficiency and organization, something I'm proud of because it may lead to more support on future westerns. But yesterday, we nearly ruined that. The extras were called at 10am and by 11:30am, I still hadn't done a damn thing with them, struggling to finish a complicated scene (for reasons that I will explain in a bit). I felt our pristine record slipping away when suddenly I came up with an idea to shift things in the schedule, capture the extras in only two shots and clear them in no more than an hour and a half. To my relief, it worked and everyone left surprised at how quickly we'd gotten them done.

The thing that set us behind was one of our supporting actors. He was good on some days, definitely a great look on screen, but as soon as he was given a few lines and some not-so-complicated blocking, things fell apart quickly. He could not listen to the most simple direction, "stand on this line, move on that one". Nope. He screwed up take after take. I fought hard to retain my patience, trying to find little ways to encourage him while making it clear he wasn't doing his damn job. He prided himself the day before with never missing a mark and this time was missing everything, including the marks! It was a draining day because of this and I wasn't the only one who felt it. At the end, we collectively knew what we'd overcome and were happy to also know that it was over, the majority of his scenes on the picture were complete...

...

Well, back to the Lonesome Coconut Ranch, some of my crew started getting hotel rooms on their own dime without even telling me. Suddenly they were just not here and I was wondering what happened. Trying to pin down a reason through second hand knowledge produced multiple confused answers... was it the cold? was it sharing a single bathroom? Noise? Spiders? I couldn't find out but it frustrated the hell out of me that I'd told them to tell me if there's a problem and that I'd do my best to solve it. Throwing up my hands in the air, I sent one more email stating this and saying that if they really wanted to waste their money on hotels, that was their choice. Oh well. I tried. People just don't know how to communicate. To me, this is a great place, the perfect kind of place to stay while making a Western, comfortable enough but not so comfortable that it removes you from the elements, from the very things you're trying to capture on screen.

March 11th, 2020

Today has been one of the roughest days so far in this journey. It is the first time I wanted to scream, the first time I wanted to cry. And nothing crazy happened. It's just the culmination of human drama and the stress of production.

From an altercation with the teller and manager at the bank (where they wouldn't do what every other Wells Fargo branch has done for me to send the payroll money), to one of my crew bitching about having sloppy joe's for lunch tomorrow, to finding out that three of our crew won't be staying at the ranch I've paid for to house them at anymore (not to mention that sweet Lucy has worked hard to make it comfortable), to knowing I'm over budget and figuring out how to fix it... On top of that, everyone's talking about this coronavirus.

I just want to focus on these films. That's all I want. Make the movies and shut the rest out.

March 18th, 2020

It's amazing how much can change in a week. Just seven days ago the threat of the virus did not seem like it could slow me down. Today, I am certain that it will slow me down in certain ways. However, I am determined that it will not stop me even if I end up making these movies completely by myself. The actors on this film have grown afraid that they will not be able to get back to California. They are concerned about a potential ban on travel between states and this might mean that they would have to go home in a hurry and halt production on this film. I can only hope that that will not happen as it would be detrimental.

Cat Roberts had to drop out of her role on Deputy's wife. She has quarantined herself with her family in the mountains. As a doctor, she is very concerned about the state of things and does not even think she will be able to play the other role I had for her in April. I understand where she's coming from but I must keep pushing on. It seems inevitable to me that this will spread. Are we delaying the inevitable or are these restrictions really helping?

...

It has become clear that I do not think John Miller's script is going to fit in the 12. What he sent me last, an outline of sorts, does not show much change from what he sent before. There just isn't enough time to make the script right especially with the pace that he works at. I would have to get in there and start rewriting it, which is something that I have no desire to do nor the time. So instead I am now thinking about moving the Pearl Hart movie back to August when it was first scheduled and creating a whole new Western for May, the fifth Western. This movie would be very simple, something that incorporates what we have at our disposal and something that we could make regardless of what happens with the virus. I am actually thinking of doing something that incorporates a virus into the story, perhaps some men that discover a ghost town stricken by a disease. It would be interesting to do something with a little bit of a Twilight Zone type feeling.

...

The virus is not the only thing that has changed in the past seven days. Last Friday I think it was, my producing partners for the Natchez trace movies decided to quit. This was not a complete surprise as I could tell their increasing frustration that I did not want to do exactly what they wanted to do. This began when they wanted to cast a somewhat recognizable actor in probably our best character role of the movie. I tried to explain to them that this person would cost us money but have no distribution appeal. Furthermore, I tried to explain my previous experience casting people like this and how easily money could be wasted if you do not choose the right person. No one would look at this guy and know his name. I could tell this frustrated both of my partners. Not long after, they decided to send me a comprehensive document outlining all of the cuts they wanted to make from the existing script. Some of these cuts I agreed with, others I did not and some I felt were absolutely absurd.

One thing that bothered me most was how easily they were willing to give up on finding certain locations months out from production. I tried to explain to them that if I had that perspective, I would not have accomplished most of what I've done in my short career. Furthermore, they wanted to split the first movie into two films and drop the second movie completely. The math on this just did not add up. For the first script, we're working with 107 pages. If that was split in two, we wouldn't even have two 60 minute movies. Not to mention the fact that they already want to make cuts from it. I didn't say it but while reading their email I couldn't help but think that their lack of experience in never making a feature film made this experience overwhelming to grasp. Instead of trusting me or turning to me to try to find solutions, they decided to have a strong and unbendable position. My response must have pissed them off because when I asked one if we could talk on the phone, I got a simple answer "I quit. No need".

It sucked. But what are you going to do? I would rather know now than later. So now I'm back to where I started, and perhaps better to be there. I have no idea what I will be able to accomplish on my own but I'm certainly determined to not only make the movie that I wanted to make but to also prove them wrong.

...

The cast continues to be a pleasure to work with. The first day with Les, the actor playing Marshal Graham, was a little challenging. He came in with a certain idea of the character, one who had very little humor. His first scene scheduled was a six page dialogue scene, his heaviest load of lines in the whole film. In many ways this was a blessing in disguise. It forced us to find the right voice and attitude for Marshal Graham. We would not have needed to do so if it was a simple three line scene. However this was not easy as I worked take after take to inject more humor into his performance, inevitably setting the schedule behind and forcing us to push two scenes to later in the production. However, eventually he did find the right tone and from then on has been able to touch on it in every scene. Once an actor finds the right button, they know where it is and can push it whenever they want to. I feel so good about this movie but I know that how you feel on set does not always translate to the finished product. What I feel now is that we are making an interesting hybrid between classic westerns by directors like Delmer Dave's and even Howard Hawks' *Rio Bravo*, but with more modern acting and filmmaking styles. The combination seems to be working and excites me with every passing day. I love the humor that we are playing with, very much like those classic films, and how it is contrasted with the violence that they lacked. I also love how distinct the characters are and that it is a true ensemble. Only time will tell how all this comes together.

March 20th, 2020

We have moved into a split shooting schedule, starting in the afternoon and filming late into the night. Yesterday was our first day of this and a challenging one to start for many reasons. We had a sluggish beginning, struggling to get the right angles in a tight saloon space. In these instances, I always want to drop the wide shots completely and focus only on the performances in the closeups but Mario really wants to get the wides, and he's right, many of our wide shots have been some of our best this whole production. But it's tough when we're working on a shot and I don't feel like I've even begun to dig in with the actor. I told Mario, an hour into filming, "I don't even feel like I'm working yet. The scene hasn't even begun." More and more, I want to focus on performance, maybe because I'm working with some serious talent who are fun to play with.

During our first night shoot, the crew got cold and kept going inside to warm up whenever they could. I felt the temperature at times but most of the while I was too busy working to notice. At times it frustrated me that most of our people were inside while we were still picking off shots. Mario echoed this in a light way when he said something like, "No, Travis, it's just you and me out here in the cold." For all his bathroom breaks, coffee breaks, and moments of focusing too much on little details that don't matter, he's a trooper and a really good collaborator.

Also last night, the paranoia of the California actors was at its highest so far. Just looking at them arrive on set, I could tell something was wrong. Their minds are preoccupied with worries about getting home, how it's going at home, etc. I don't blame them and at the same time I hope they will keep level heads and finish their work here. I am already prepared to fight for them to stay through week three if they push for leaving. That would mean we'd only be missing the extended flashback, scheduled to shoot week four, which could be picked up later in the year. I don't want that to even happen but it's a plan in the back of my mind if they start to freak out. Thankfully, once we get into filming, they sink back into their characters and do excellent work.

March 26th, 2020

The last week has been the hardest of the 12 Westerns, the last day one of the darkest of my life... I will take us back to

Friday, March 20th and eventually make my way to this current moment.

What started as an ordinary day of filming, the 12th of our originally scheduled 20 dates on *She was the Deputy's Wife*, quickly turned into a giant mess. When I arrived on set, our makeup artist Candice complained of feeling a little sick, stomach ache. It did not sound like coronavirus but any kind of sickness was worrisome. The reason I did not react is that nearly everyone on the crew had suffered from a short term stomach bug at some point during production. But it was a mistake. I should have notified everyone immediately, considering the state of paranoia that had already overtaken our team. An hour and a half later, when she told me that she was getting worse and feeling a tightness in her chest, I realized my mistake and hopped into action but still that wasn't enough. I told Mary Beth, our AD/Associate Producer that Candice needed to be dealt with and that she shouldn't be touching actors without gloves and a mask. Somehow, this didn't get filtered down the line soon enough and before long, I had actors showing up, finding out after the fact or seeing their makeup artist dressed that way and started freaking out. Vincent and Robert, the first two actors to be made up, did not lose their cool but Shayn, the actor playing our 2nd lead male role, lost it completely. I was told that he was not happy and needed to be talked to but still had no idea just how dramatic it would be.

Meeting him on the street of the western town, Shayn immediately told me, "I think I'm done after tonight." "What does that mean?" I asked. He explained that the next day he would be driving home to California and not completing his work on the movie. Now for more than a week, Shayn had been the actor most troubled by the virus, already confessing his desire to go home to be with his wife, worried that the borders of California would be shut down and he wouldn't be able to return. This situation with Candice was just enough to push him over the edge.

Considering the nature of our conversation, it's surprising that we both remained calm, though we could hardly see eye to eye. As I tried to plead with him and use reason, he would not budge. Not completing the movie was a side concern compared to getting home. He was practically convinced at that point that he'd been infected. I tried every way I could to help him see that stopping the production then would most likely lead to it never being completed. So many small indie movies that halt production never do return to finish the work... Somewhere in the talk, Shayn said, "Just kill my character off or something." Now this got my head turning. What if I could kill him off and save the movie?

I needed to talk to Megan, our lead actress. I knew she was frazzled by the situation too but for this to work, she'd have to hang in there. More calm than Shayn, Megan and I discussed this too. She'd felt betrayed that I hadn't immediately let them know Candice was sick. I explained the order of events. I apologized for any mistake I made. She seemed willing to stick around.

Next, I started to discuss the possibility of killing the Paul character off with different members of the crew, the ones who I trust and who knew the story well. John Marrs thought it could work. Mario, my DP, did too. Thankfully, Mario was up for finding a way to continue. The significance of making this change was huge. The original script ends in a *Casablanca*-like decision for Megan/Mabel as she chooses between her lover, Paul/Shayn, and her husband, Jonathan/Paul. So killing Paul is the equivalent of having Bogart shot three quarters of the way through *Casablanca*, leaving Ingrid Bergman with only her husband to choose from... well, maybe not quite like that but you get the idea. Could it possibly work? By the time I'd explored these options in my mind, Shayn was singing a slightly different tune but not one that made me any more at ease. Now he said, "I'll stay till I get sick." Well, that wasn't much to count on. Considering how easily he'd freaked out, I suddenly felt the fragility of the whole project. To finish the movie, it seemed I needed to make some major course corrections and get done as soon as possible.

Oh, and one more thing before I proceed. During my first conversation with Shayn, we had this exchange:

Travis: "A couple months from now, I promise you, you're going to regret what you're doing right now."

Shayn: "Is that a threat? It sounds like one."

Travis: "No. It's the truth."

And it soon would be…

...

So the rest of the night, we shot Paul's death. I suggested he die with the same sudden surprise as DiCaprio in the *Departed* and Petersen in *To Live and Die in LA*. Here is the sexy outlaw that Mabel and all the female audience members have fallen in love with (at least that's my guess from how our females have already responded on set), he's a badass, clearly the "hero", and then out of nowhere the bullet that was originally scripted to fire from Lemmy's bullet into his thigh now enters his skull. He drops dead. Mabel is devastated and the audience is (hopefully) in shock, not sure what to expect next. That's what my instincts told me to do and as of now, it still feels right. It was a hard night shoot, lasting all the way till 5am because of our delay in filming from all the drama and long negotiations.

As we returned to the homestead, nearly dawn, I still did not know what would happen next. Would Shayn stick around long enough to film the flashback scenes (something key to show how Mabel fell in love with him) or would he get sick and go home? How would I structure the rest of the story after Paul's death?

...

With two hours of sleep, I made coffee and went straight back to the script, scrapping everything that originally happened and starting fresh from Paul's death. That felt like the only way to do it. Yes, I saved some situations and lines but my perspective was new direction, new path. After a couple hours, I had something I was pleased with and even excited about. Could it do justice to the script and what we'd filmed so far? Could it be equal to the original ending? In some ways, I liked it more. But no one had seen it yet. I printed the pages and gave them to Mario. It was his opinion that mattered most to me. I waited in anticipation as he read the 10-12 page ending. Finally, he reported that he liked it, a lot. "Last night, I laid in bed thinking of all the obstacles there were in having a non-Paul ending and you've solved every one of them." That felt damn good. I was renewed. Next I sent it to our main investor, I was hoping she'd embrace this as Mario had done. She did not respond enthusiastically but did not say no either. Then I sent it to John Marrs, whose opinion holds more and more weight with every day of working together. He liked it but had one suggestion: at that point, I still had Smithey, the barber, killing off our main villain. John said, "Let Jonathan, the husband, do it. He needs a victory." This was a fantastic suggestion and I immediately incorporated it. Now the ending really did feel stronger than the original, giving our "deputy" of the title a heroic moment he did not have to start with.

This was all the more reason why I was shocked when Robert, the actor playing Jonathan, called me back after reading the revision to confess that he did not like it, that we'd screwed up, and that he did not feel we were doing justice to the film. I respectfully disagreed but did confirm I would listen to his ideas on how to improve it. He did not seem interested in improving what I'd written, feeling as if it was too far off the mark to make small tweaks. He wasn't the only one who didn't care for the revision. A small group of the actors got together and came up with their own ending. I was curious what they'd thought about but as I read it aloud to John Marrs a couple hours before call time, we both started to laugh. Not only did it betray the nature of the characters and the spirit of the movie, but it would take at least three extra days to film it. I knew they'd be pissed that I did not want to go with their concept but I had to bite that bullet.

...

The reason I was on set early is a whole other dramatic issue. So Candice, the one whose sickness had triggered this mess, had woken up Saturday morning feeling completely well and, of course, also feeling like she should naturally go straight back to work. When I told her this was still up in the air and that I needed to discuss her return with the actors before making a decision, she got upset. I was trying to take an hour nap before starting another long night of filming and ten minutes in got a call from Anouschka: "Candice is on her way to the set to get her things and leave. I think you need to come down here." So I crawled out of bed, packed up my own things, coaxed Bandit into the car and headed out, knowing a nap was now a fantasy.

Candice arrived on set, huffy. She was rightfully emotional about the potential of not being allowed back but also, like the actors, unable to listen to logic. I kept telling her, "I get where you're coming from but I just can't bring you back without making sure they're comfortable." She went back and forth between crying, getting mad, saying she'd take her name off the project, etc. Finally she left us enough makeup supplies to get through the night and agreed to return to her hotel room until I could talk to the cast that night and hopefully bring her back. Mary Beth was against it completely, perhaps living more in a state of fear than the thespians, but she reluctantly agreed that if I got a unanimous decision from the ensemble, she'd accept it. The balance with her was hard, trying to make her feel as if her opinion mattered while also making sure it was clear that the final decisions on set belonged to me and me alone.

So that evening, at call time, exhausted, I called the actors together in the saloon. Their faces were grim, not even the hint of a smile in the room. I poured my heart out, explaining that their safety was important to me but so was finishing the film. John had advised me to make this ultra clear and I found it to be a wise suggestion. I explained that I was not compromising in any way with the new ending and truly felt this was a great new direction. They did not seem convinced. Finally, I asked if anyone was unwilling to continue work on the film and do the best with what I'd written. Everyone agreed, solemnly, they would continue to do their jobs as professional actors. And the Candice situation came up. I explained that she was well, that she didn't have coronavirus symptoms, that she'd wear gloves/mask from now on. I asked for a unanimous vote and to my surprise, it passed. She was back.

Oh and Shayn was there. He wanted to say something and admitted that he'd acted rashly and apologized to everyone if the story had been ruined by him. I'd told the team that night too that my new plan was to wrap the movie up in 17 days total instead of 20, filming through our upcoming days off to get it done in less time but as soon as possible. Shayn asked him to tell him in all honesty if he was the main reason the movie was being cut short, condensed. I told the truth. By then, he wasn't the main reason. Though he'd angered me, he'd also opened my eyes to how shaky the ground was that we stood on. The cast or even the crew might fall apart at any moment. It was imperative to get it "in the can" and at a fast pace. Those regrets I'd promised Shayn he'd have didn't take two months... they didn't even take two days. I hope this is a lesson to him not to act rashly, that such actions and behavior can completely change a film forever as it has this one. But humans rarely learn lessons.

That night was another long one. We shot till 3am this time. But something cool started to happen. As we worked the scenes, I could feel some of the cast started to feel the strength of the rewrite. Vincent, who plays an Iago-like character, came to life as I let him play with some of the dialog, reminding him that I'm always up for exploration. Les Best, our main villain, loved the rewrite from the start and in many ways, led the cast through this. Only Robert seemed to remain unchanged, but to his credit, he delivered a strong performance without faith in the material.

...

I slept for a few hours again and woke up early, knowing I now needed to rewrite the flashback scenes. Keep in mind, this section of the movie was originally going to be shot over the course of five days, our final week on the film. Now I was hoping to film it in 2 and a half days. I dug in, writing, trying this and that. I took 17 or 18 pages and made it 12, still a lot to film in that short a time with a demoralized and exhausted crew. Most of the team seemed different now, not just drained but their hearts weren't quite in it. Mario, who was still very passionate about our story, could feel this with me and we struggled hard over the past few days on the film to carry the crew with us. Some stayed strong, others faded off. Some of this fading came close to disastrous: example, our makeup artist not being ready for some blood effects, though she'd been told to do so, as we shot the lead villain's death in the last minutes of daylight. It nearly screwed the whole movie, just one person not being on point, not being present.

Anyway, somehow we got through and not only survived but seemed to preserve quality. Both Mario, myself, and a small group of loyal crew felt till the very end that our efforts were way worth it and had made a good, solid film. Others did not even care enough to stick around for that final wrap moment, antsy to leave the set as soon as their own work was done. This pissed me off. They showed no sense of being on the team in these final hours. Even Mary Beth left hours early and after all that? In the end, we finished the movie in the early afternoon of day seventeen with a tiny but loyal group. Ironically, this last pack included Shayn, who wanted to finish the film with us even after his scenes were complete. I regained a little respect as he offered to help us carry gear and stuck around till I announced it was all over.

We drank a cold beer and hot wine (left accidentally in a car trunk) in the saloon, smiling at each other, worn down and accomplished. Mario and I both felt stunned that we'd pulled it off, wrapped the scenes and done something with them we were proud of. I went to sleep, ready for a day of rest to follow before getting to work on the next film. I could not have imagined what I would wake up to.

...

Before I went to bed last night, Mack, our assistant camera, seemed like a completely different person than his upset self that afternoon. As we wrapped, he'd told Mario like our main investor that it was a mistake to finish the film, an opinion that we all found baffling as we safely reached the end of production. But now, he was full of positive vibes and smiles, talking about how great it felt to finish. We'd seen this up and down before and Mario had told me he suffered from bipolar disorder, on medicine to keep him balanced. He'd also been dealing with some intense, traumatic life issues: only a few days after his arrival in Arizona to make the movie, his wife told him she wanted a divorce and moved out. So he was dealing with that all production. Still, he was chipper day in, day out.

This morning, I woke up ready for a new day and wandered across the ranch to make the morning coffee. Mario had already gotten up and beat me to the punch. He was standing at Mack's tent, calling inside that it was time for them to hit the road back to Texas. There was no answer. Soon we discovered he wasn't in his tent. Both of us felt this was weird. "Maybe he took a long walk," we figured and went back to our respective morning routines. But as time went on and a long walk seemed to be less likely, an eerie feeling came over me. I looked around the property. I checked the pool. I thought for a moment he might have even gone to bed with our host Lucy. I now realize that I did not venture much further for fear that I might discover something I was fighting to not believe. I returned to the RV and within minutes, a visitor came. From the windows, I saw her talk to Lucy and then Lucy's sense of panic. The single mother, our sweet host, ran to the gate and back. I could see her go to the house and then back to the RV. Now I could feel it, what I didn't want to be true was true. Mario was rushing out of the house as Lucy walked my way. "Travis, Mack is hanging from a tree outside the gate." Morgan was there too and fell apart immediately. I ran to catch up with Mario, my heart hurting for him already.

On the other side of the gate, Mack hung under a small three, his jacket and hat on, a half finished beer bottle and pills on the ground. He'd taken his own life while we were all asleep. An older couple who lives in the area had found him before we did on their morning walk. The woman, who had been a nurse for years, immediately told Mario and I not to blame ourselves, that she saw this many times. "Humans make irrational decisions and sometimes they make permanent ones." Mario and I stared on at his lifeless body, in shock. My friend/cousin/collaborator was stoic as usual but clearly shaken too. He told of how he and Mack had laughed and laughed the night before, drinking and smoking, talking about how great of an experience it had been. He reported that Mack said it was one of the best times of his life. There was no sign that he was about to do this.

We found the note that we hadn't seen in his tent that morning. It was simple. It told us where to find him and a simple explanation, "I just couldn't go home". With the pain of his divorce, returning to that life, to an empty house was just too much for him. As we all do in these situations, we wished he'd turned to his friends instead of suicide. We wished he hadn't given up. But he did. He made a decision and there was nothing we could do about it. His note also asked us to wait till April 20th to tell the rest of the crew, or to wait at least a week. But that didn't seem possible. What he'd done and how he'd done it was a mystery and always will be.

Seeing him there is something I'll never forget. He didn't look like a human anymore. He looked like one of our mannequins on set, the ones we used to pass for dead characters instead of having actors lay down in the street for hours. It's the first time I've seen someone dead like that.

I tried as much as I could the next few hours to help Mario, to help the Sheriff's department with information, to comfort Morgan, to comfort Lucy and her little girl Zoey. Mack had played a lot with Zoey. It only hit me later, the anger that he'd done this there at her home instead of waiting to get back to Texas.

I suppose there is not much more to say about it and maybe I have already said too much but I must record this now as I feel it, as I process it. What happened today feels like one of the darkest days of my life as I stand in it but I know I must move on, continue not only with my life but this project. Mario left for Texas ready to move forward too. We can get through anything, he reminded me. Yes, we can. And as one of my favorite movie endings goes, "Hemingway once said, 'The world is a fine place, worth fighting for.' I agree with the second part."

March 27th, 2020

Today I tried for the first time this year to have a day to myself. I hung out with Bandit and cut his hair. It felt good to be closer to him and less preoccupied in our time together. I watched two westerns and now I'm working on a third. The first was Quigley Down Under which I liked a lot more than I thought I would. The second was Conagher which I haven't seen since I was a kid and have wanted badly to see again. It was great at first and then got a little messy towards the end. Now I'm rewatching Jeremiah Johnson.

This morning I made calls to all the cast and crew about Mack, one after another. Around noon, Lucy and Zoey (the single mother and little girl who run this farm where we're staying) and I went out to the road where he hung himself and placed items in that spot. Along with Annie, the neighbor who found him, we'd all thought of doing this separately around the same time. We will pass the spot every day and it feels good to have some things there. I took half of the marks Mack made for actors and placed them on the ground.

I am glad I stayed here and did not try to leave this place for a couple days. It feels good to work through it here and Lucy confessed it has helped her for me to be around after the shocking event. That makes it worth being here no matter what.

March 28th, 2020

Earlier today, I met John and Anouschka at the movie set to help clean up. There wasn't much I could do but grab a couple trash bags.

John told me today that he thinks I should delay the next production by two weeks. I heard him out but don't quite understand his logic. He thinks this is a smart move, mainly to save face I think, because we're starting to get criticism (I'd call it persecution) for continuing to work. He thinks a two week quarantine would solve this and keep us more safe but I don't see how. In two weeks, the virus may be worse, Tucson and Phoenix will most probably have more infections by then. Also, there is no stay at home policy right now but there may be in two weeks, which would cause an even further delay. When he said we might get shut down during production, I agreed, but at least we would have gotten some days shot while we could. Better to start and stop than to hold off from ever starting for no reason other than a guess that it might work. We disagreed that people would be more likely to drop out of something that has already started versus something that hasn't. From his point of view, people would be more likely to stay on if I delayed and also more likely to drop out if we stopped in the middle. I see it differently. If we don't start, I may lose some of my crew and the crew are the ones I really need. Actors can be replaced. I mean, I'm replacing 2-3 right now. In the last couple days, three actresses dropped out of their roles. I don't hold it against them. It's a choice they were given.

If someone gets infected with coronavirus on our cast/crew, I'll stop production for two weeks. If the government announces a lockdown/stay at home policy, I won't break it.

But I'll be damned if I stop in this very moment. It just doesn't make any sense to me...

March 29th, 2020

I asked Morgan to try to make it back from Santa Fe by 9 or 10pm last night. By 5pm she still hadn't left so she didn't get back till 2 or 3am. I'd asked her to wake me up but by the time she did, I just told her to get some sleep, we'd talk in the morning. Fat chance... she was charged up with fears of the coronavirus and could not suspend the conversation, regardless of my desire to sleep. So she went on, explaining just as John had why I should delay production and I responded with the same points I'd made before, in a grumpy worn out tone I'm sure. By the time she'd satisfied her end of the conversation, my head was spinning and I could not get back to sleep. "This is why I said we should talk in the morning. Now I'll be awake all night." "Travis, a fifty year old person died in Tucson." "Morgan, people die of the flu all the time." Eventually I was able to sleep.

In the morning she seemed more pacified. The whole time she lobbied the night before, she wasn't even aware that Arizona is under no lockdown or stay-at-home orders. She just assumed we were. More fake news. I told her that the 8pm curfew our last crew had talked about over and over was complete bullshit, debunked by the cops themselves... The coronavirus is real and it kills people but nothing does more damage than ill-informed, irrational humans.

...

This afternoon, after the failed nap, I went to Gammons to help put out another "fire". Over the last couple weeks, I've heard bitching about not having enough outfits for Diana, the lead actress in this fourth film. Between the two women supplying the wardrobe, who should be helping each other but are doing everything except that, there has been so much drama and mixed messages about these damn costumes. Finally, I just said screw it, let me handle it. We met today at the movie set. The actress brought what she has. Our wardrobe person opened up her stock and within less than two hours I'd picked close to thirteen different outfits for the actress. Problem solved with little effort.

I feel like I'm putting out a fire every five minutes these days. Just an hour ago, my cinematographer for this next film (*A Guide to Gunfighters of the Wild West*) Merina hits me up and says her sister might be infected. She's getting tested and who knows but waiting for the test might take five days... we'll be filming in less than five days. Merina might either be delayed or may not be able to come at all if she's infected. I proposed to Forrest, the gaffer, that either he or I DP. Our current plan is to tag team it. It was tough enough already with how spread thin our crew is... now this. I don't know what to say other than every blow like this makes me want to succeed even more.

John Marrs (Sheriff Bob) stands in for a shot.

Texas actor Les Best as Marshal Graham.

Actor John Schile, playing newspaper man Wilson, watches between takes.

Assistant Camera Mack Mumford on set. He tragically committed suicide the day after we wrapped.

All photographs by Gerald Marrion.

THE ADVENTURES OF BANDIT AND WILD WES

In the back of my mind, I always had a card up my sleeve for the 12 Westerns project: if I ran out of money, if I was totally abandoned by my cast and crew, if everything just went to hell… I'd make a Western with just my dog Bandit. As COVID

changed all our plans for the 12 Westerns and I faced suggestions that I should postpone the project completely, I knew it was time to make this truly simple Western, giving us a chance to regroup and move forward through this challenging time. We did so in secret, as some of my team members had already been persecuted for continuing to work by various industry people during the making of Deputy's Wife. The entire project was funded out of my own pocket: the budget was $1,200... my stimulus check.

Feeling him near the end of his life, this film was also a way to preserve my friendship with Bandit on screen. I am so happy we made this film together and that I will always be able to look back at the connection we had. In short, this film tells the story of a not-so-smart outlaw named Wild Wes (me) who is betrayed by his partner, then saved by a dog (Bandit) who he teams up with to find the one who did him wrong. It was inspired by Buster Keaton and Charlie Chaplin.

April 1st, 2020

On Monday, I had a full day of travel planned. It began with a drive to Tucson where I met with one of the investors on *Deputy's Wife*. He was also one of the cast and the most difficult to work with, not because of attitude but because he doesn't know how to listen. I'd give him exact blocking but he couldn't follow the most simple direction. However, his positivity about the production and working with me overwhelmed my frustration.

From there, I drove to Phoenix to rendezvous with Nick for the camera package. Like with *Bastard's* and *Texas Red*, we rented his equipment for *Guide to Gunfighters,* the fourth Western we were scheduled to make in just a few days. It was good to see my old friend Nick and also humorous as he showed me some basics on the camera package while trying to remain six feet apart, practically impossible. We said our goodbyes and headed opposite directions. Less than an hour later, I received notice that the governor announced a stay at home order. I knew it was coming and I knew when it did that I would finally have to delay production... it just came sooner than I hoped and expected. So there I was driving back to Tucson, on the phone with everyone explaining that we would in fact have to postpone filming *Guide to Gunfighters* BUT that it would get done and that I would still make 12 Westerns this year. Somehow, I will.

My last meeting of the day, after picking up 600 feet of rope that I ordered from Home Depot for *Deputy's Wife* (an expense for nothing since we didn't even film long enough to use it), was with John Marrs, a story conference about *Counting Bullets*. It's fun to craft this new Western together. We get along really well, especially when it's just the two of us.

April 4th, 2020

Working on pre-production the last few days has been productive but I can feel a growing restlessness, wanting to film. I've decided to proceed with making a secret fourth Western during this quarantine month. It's the idea I've had in my back pocket this whole time, the one I was saving in case 1. I ran out of funding. 2. All my crew quit and I had to make a movie by myself... well, almost by myself. Anyway, it's a silent comedy picture in the style of Buster Keaton and Chaplin starring Bandit and I. Of course, I'm no Keaton or Chaplin but I've always played that style of comedy with a degree of success and I think this will be a fun project to explore. We begin filming tomorrow and have a total of seven filming days set. The only consistent people working on this film will be myself, my assistant Morgan, John Marrs, Anouschka, and of course Bandit. We'll have to act in it, help plan it, and shoot the damn thing. The camera I got from Nick just an hour before the stay at home policy was put in effect will be our filming tool. For a small fee, which will come out of my almost broke account, I'm able to hang onto the expensive camera package for a couple weeks. It will be worth it in the end, at least that's what I keep telling myself. But making this movie, however simple, will keep me on track so that if the virus persists in the coming months, I won't be so far behind that I can't catch up.

I am also determined to make *Counting Bullets*, the new Cavalry picture I'm writing with John, in May regardless of whether stay at home restrictions have been lifted or not. We went scouting in the Dragoon mountains yesterday and there are plenty of people out there camping. That's basically what we'll be doing for 10 days. We just need to find the right cast and crew who are up for it. It was fun to show John this terrain as he continued to say "This is fucking cool." When he was sure we'd discovered the best spot for the action to take place, I kept saying, "Just wait. There's more to see." Sure enough we kept going and finding even better places. Finally, we found a spot that fits nearly all our needs and there wasn't a single person camping there. We are moving forward with this area as we finish writing the script and begin planning the production.

April 6th, 2020

Yesterday, we shot the first scenes from my "secret" silent film. It was just John, Anouschka, Morgan, and I. Of the four of us, I know the most about camera, but not much, and was not only in front of it for most of the time as the lead character but tied to the tree for half the day, unable to assist with setup and settings. All things considered, I think they did a pretty good job. We had an issue with one lens that still hasn't been resolved. For some odd reason, the longer lens would not allow us to change the aperture at all. With no manual way to change the iris, all computerized, this prohibited us from using it, stuck with the 18 to 35, not a disaster but an interesting challenge for sure. While troubleshooting the lens issue, it was fascinating to see how both women reacted in contrast to John, who mostly stayed out of it, knowing how much he doesn't know. Morgan was all up in my business, head literally getting in my way, saying "maybe it's this,maybe it's that" to every button on the damn camera. Anouschka claimed she could probably fix it if I just got out of the way, then she sat there and did the same exact thing that I did. Neither was helpful.

All this said, it was a fun day because we were creating again. I love the inventions of the moment that come with making a movie, the things that are not scripted. Most of what my silent comedy character does around the campfire was not on my mind until sitting there in the space. Other ideas get suggested by the collaborators and the best incorporated. Sometimes it's a combination of the two. When tied to the tree by Slippery Slim (played by Corey Busboom), John suggested he leave me a canteen before deserting his old partner. I revised this suggestion with potential hilarity: he puts the canteen in my hand but because I'm tied up, I can't reach it and start to swing the canteen to try to reach it with my mouth only to swing it too hard and knock myself out cold. The first two takes of this went just fine, hitting myself in the head with the metal object, which hurt a little but reasonable pain, and then faking a knock out. The third take, knowing it would probably be the last, I went all out, firing all cylinders from the action to cut... well, we didn't quite make it to "cut". This time I swung the canteen, not much harder than before but apparently at the perfect angle and busted my head open. It didn't hurt or feel much different than the previous takes but as I slumped into my fake passed out pose, I felt blood dripping down my forehead onto my cheek. I waited a couple seconds, probably should have waited more but I was slightly concerned at just how much damage I'd caused, and announced "I'm bleeding" in a calm tone. There was a gash at the top of my head, just under my hairline. Anouschka and Morgan helped stop the flow and we continued filming not long after, sure that we'd gotten the hit enough times. Sadly, the blood didn't really show in the take. Oh well, another scar and another good story.

April 9th, 2020

A little about my daily routine since it may interest me at some point to look back at it:

Wake up around 6.

Hot coffee. Cold water. A cough drop.

The first thing I do is my daily post tracking how many days I've worked on the Westerns. Then I load footage into Premiere and start syncing the audio for DEPUTY'S WIFE.

My deal with Morgan is that we work from 8am to 8pm. I get started early. For the most part she's been able to keep the schedule, minus distractions, smoke breaks, etc.

Now, around midday, we do about 30 minutes of labor for Lucy who owns this place. This is trade for our breakfast. It might be moving heavy things or tearing drywall down from one of her many shacks. This is followed by pond time, where Bandit loves to swim. I got in the cold water yesterday too. Zoey the little girl is enthusiastic to say the least about swimming and have others join her. I drink a beer during this time, cooling down and then back to work.

Lucy rings the bell for brunch and dinner. It's interesting that when I want Morgan to focus on something, she often struggles, but when dinner time is called she is (or likes to play that she is) so focused that she can't even break away.

Yesterday she said she'd join us at the pond and 20 minutes later I found her in the RV staring into space... humans.

April 10th, 2020

Last night I set out three traps to catch the rat or mouse that's been in this rv for a couple weeks. We'd already caught one before but this fella was too good, working around the regular mouse traps. About a week ago, I thought I caught him in this new device, woke up to see this little critter trapped in a box kind of contraption. I didn't feel like drowning him in the middle of the night, so I just set the trap outside. In the morning, I woke to find it empty, curious if he'd escaped or if some bigger critter had gotten to him.

Well the noises continued and I put up with them, a little lazy at night to set the traps but last night I did again. I woke to major rattling, figured I'd caught him, got up to check and swear that I found the cage empty... the noises continued throughout the night waking me up here and there. I guessed it was the mouse in the walls, screwing with me. But this morning, I just got up to find the son of a bitch in the cage. How I had not seen him last night boggles my mind? Perhaps I was too sleepy or perhaps I only dreamed of getting up.

I made some coffee and followed Lucy's instructions, dumping the trap in one of the small ponds here. It happened quick of course. I don't like killing things unless there's a purpose. I suppose the purpose here is to give me better sleep.

April 11th, 2020

I woke up down today. The situation with Morgan just keeps getting worse. I am now certain that I must either tell her it isn't working out or give her a definitive amount of time to get her shit together.

It's the most simple things now that aren't working... yesterday morning (after asking her specifically the night before to wake up in plenty of time to help pack and get ready to film), the minutes passed and passed with no sign of her. Finally, as our 8am call time approached, I decided to pack the car myself. She suddenly showed up in a hurry, ten minutes before 8 (when we should have been pulling into the location), rushing and asking where the stuff was to pack. I told her I already packed it.

By the time we arrived at the movie set and started to set up, she was sitting smoking a cigarette and saying that she had a migraine coming. I told her she needed to go back to the ranch, lay down, knowing she'd be useless the rest of the day.

Surprisingly we worked better this day than we did our first time shooting the silent western and part of that was her absence. Her manic energy was missing and therefore things worked more smoothly. But it wasn't just her not being there, the three of us genuinely worked well together yesterday and I hope it continues that way. Anouschka, John, and I had a great rhythm of setting the camera up and blocking the shots. "We were focused on the craft," as John said at the end of the day. Our buddy Larry Judkins was there too to play a cameo and lend a hand. He's always super helpful.

The material wasn't as funny as our first shoot (or maybe we're just used to it now) but we seemed to make a lot of progress and capture some solid scenes. I enjoy playing the character, though I feel that silent movie acting is more difficult than regular acting. There are so many things to do, to communicate, especially in a comedy. With the Morgan thing at the back of my mind, it was hard to concentrate but I pulled it off, if maybe as spontaneous as the first scenes had been.

April 14th, 2020

On Saturday, we finished our scenes at Gammons Gulch, getting the rest of the "Ghost Town" episode, followed by the Doc Holliday (John) part and a horse scene with the Lady Bandit (Morgan). John had some good fun with the Doc part and it was a great time playing off of his drunken antics. The time he's put into his craft really shows. He's an actor who worked for it, not someone who was just naturally "talented" and doesn't understand that this is in fact work.

Caron brought her two horses, Chance and Dreamer. The gag we decided on involved me stealing Dreamer, the paint horse, from the corral. I would climb the fence to mount him bareback and while climbing, get turned around, stepping onto the horse backwards. I notice there's no horse head in front of me but before I can correct this mistake, the true owner of the animal points his gun out a window and I fall off the horse... well the plan was to kick my leg to the side and slide off but in one take I felt it get caught and truly fell to the ground. It looked good, totally worth it. Ironically, it was in one of the takes where I did land on my own two feet that I got hurt: an old left knee injury comes back now and then, even when I'm walking, and I must have landed just right to activate it again. Just means a limp for a few days, nothing serious. After falling off the horse, I try to leave the corral in a hurry, bouncing off the fence boards back into the dust again. Doing these "stunts" gives me such pleasure, the ultimate pleasure of filmmaking when they are successful. Maybe there's something to the connection of physical action/comedy and film with Buster Keaton/Tom Cruise and why I like doing my small, untrained versions of these: it's when motion picture telling is all about motion.

...

Morgan and I had a conversation that night, one that was hard to remind myself to have after a positive day. I confessed to her that I was not happy with how things were going, that I felt more like her assistant than the way it should be. She didn't say much. She just stared in her non-communicative way and agreed that the end of April was a good time to assess moving forward. She was more concerned about taking a week off then to go home to Santa Fe. "Do you think I could take a week off and go home?" "Sure but Morgan, don't you hear what I'm saying? I'm telling you if things don't change, then it will be more than a week off, it will be over. Your work on the 12 Westerns will be done." I told her to take some time to really consider this but it's hard to tell if she did or has since. Her work habits did improve the next couple days but it's consistency I'm looking for.

...

On Sunday we filmed in Tombstone and the Dragoon Mountains, where we plan to make this new Western *Counting Bullets*. Anouschka played the Lady Bandit's strict aunt, who the young female outlaw brings her "new husband" to. We did a shot on the couch that was my little ode to Buster Keaton, with me stiff and stuck between the two women, though I'm not really like Keaton at all... not doing the stone faced thing with this character. It's hard to tell how the humor will play for these when they're all strung together or if it will play at all. The only thing we can do is to follow our instincts and make what we feel is good.

We ventured out into the desert hills to complete the Lady Bandit scenes and I was happy to do another stunt, trying to retrieve a honeycomb out of a tree (one of the many tasks this western woman asks me to complete) and fall out after getting stung by a bee. Anouschka remarked, "Why are you so good at falling?" I grinned.

...

On Monday, I spent most of the day sneezing from bad allergies and finishing the hard drive of *Deputy's Wife* for Tony (Editor). I had a few more days of footage and audio to organize/sync. This is a tedious task but one that should help post-production move along once it gets into Tony's hands. In the end, I'm glad I did this for all the mess that I've discovered. Over the weekend, I found out that we are missing audio on an entire night of footage: the night we changed the movie's script and killed off one of the main characters. It's just not there at all, a huge mistake. And yesterday I found more missing sound on our second to last day of filming, five random scenes where there is no trace of recorded audio. I double checked with Mario, who also has a copy of all the files and he confirmed that these are also missing on his end. What a discouraging discovery this was... I also asked Baretta, our sound guy, who was certainly at fault for the misnaming and mismanagement of his files but he confirmed that he recorded audio those times and I believe him. In the end, the fault is most likely on the shoulders of the one person we can't talk to about it, the young man who killed himself. It was his job to transfer all the media and make sure it was done so correctly. There's no changing the past. This will guarantee the necessity for ADR, something I was trying to avoid diligently. It also guarantees that I will never trust sound or the media transfer that much again and will have to keep an eye on it from now on.

April 15th, 2020

Yesterday's scout to Globe was productive and not quite what I expected. Within the first ten minutes of meeting Molly, our contact to show us around and a member of the board for many of these historic spots, she named dropped another Arizona filmmaker Robert Conway and how much she loves working with him. I immediately told her, "Conway is not a fan of Travis Mills, though he's never met me." Conway is in fact one of my biggest non-fans. A few years ago when I broke up with his friend Carrie, I even had a voicemail on my phone of him threatening to beat me with a baseball bat. The guy has consistently tried to convince people that I am sexual and physical abuser, blah blah blah. So this made me immediately nervous, mainly because the whole scout and any planning put into it could be a waste of time if Molly was the type to listen to gossip and decide not to work with me because of it (something that has happened many a time before). This was at the back of my mind as we looked at the various impressive locations she had to show me. Later on, as we waited for our burgers to be delivered from a local joint, I straight up asked her, "If Conway tells you not to work with me, is that going to effect this? Because I don't want to put the time and energy into planning to film here if gossip will be trusted over experience." She confidently said that there would be no issues unless they happened directly between us. I hope she means it.

The jail, train depot, and even the courthouse had possibilities. I continue to debate about how exactly to make this movie: 1. as a straight western with big production value. 2. as a straight western but made with an iphone and a kind of on the street/New Wave realism. 3. an anachronistic punk rock western, mixing modern and old elements together. 4. something even more experimental with a different person playing Pearl in each section of the film, from a black woman, to a child, etc. All versions of this film circle my mind.

April 17th, 2020

Today we get back to filming and that's a relief. I could film all day, every day but be less tired than I get working on pre-production. It's also during pre-production that people have too much time on their hands and start causing trouble.

...

Yesterday, I drove into Tucson to open the bank account for *Counting Bullets*. The bank took hours, waiting outside because of the virus and waiting for the banker to figure out over 45 minutes or more what it usually takes the folks in Mississippi 15 minutes to do. I returned to the ranch, played with Bandit in the pond, and got straight to work on the *Wilderness Road* script. I don't think I've gone through more drafts of a project before. The first iteration was one big movie with the Harpes, Samuel Mason, and all the little side tales blended together and split in two (Kill Bill style). This had many different forms in itself, moving chapters around in the order of telling, before the idea came to split up the movie into only the tale of the Harpes/Mason (*The Wilderness Road*) and all the side stories (*Tales of the Natchez Trace*). Then of course was the proposed concept my old partners had before quitting to ditch the Tales completely, cut twenty or so pages from the *Wilderness Road*, and split it into two feature films, which by my estimation would have been 45 minutes in length each. I rejected this. Now, I am once again re-envisioning this project. They were right that it is ambitious and looks even more so in the light of our current conditions and everyone's hesitation to provide funding but I remain unwilling to give up on the vision. While compiling the chapters this time and touching up parts of them, I decided to ditch the non-chronological Pulp Fiction style format. I asked myself why it was there? Was it serving any purpose other than my own amusement? With all the stories together in a gigantic epic film, it made more sense. Furthermore, perhaps it is better to see the stories lined up in a chronological way before moving forward. They can always be moved around, if not in the script than even in the edit. But to see the story, I now want to look at it straight through.

April 18th, 2020

I was back in the pink long johns yesterday, walking, stumbling, and sometimes even crawling through the desert landscape. But first the day began with yard work at Gammons Gulch to pay Joanne back for our recent days of filming there. Thad, Morgan's "significant other", has arrived from New Mexico to participate in helping/filming and ultimately return back with her. He's an alright guy but talks too much and too quickly when he does, like he's consumed five too many energy drinks. We cut weeds and the difference on the movie set was significant, enough so that we're excited to go back and continue cleaning up.

When we started filming, I told Morgan that she and Thad could just relax, the simplicity of the shots only required Anouschka, John, and I. The truth is that the three of us have a good rhythm and I did not want it interrupted. As we worked together, hauling camera, sticks, lenses, setting up each shot and blocking at a time, I felt more and more that this is the way I may want to make movies. Frederick Wiseman has spent most, if not all, of his career making films with a 3-4 member crew. Camera, sound, him and maybe one other person have produced countless notable works. Yes, they're all documentaries but why can't features be done the same way? It may slow me down some but the process is much more enjoyable. The more crew added, the more spread out people become from each other, the less intimate the experience is and it inevitably becomes much harder to communicate. In addition, there is the wrangling of personalities (the ultimate struggle of making movies). 2-3 is manageable whereas even 10-15 is not. On a crew of 2-3, there's no real place to go off and gossip, to spread negativity about the director. You either do it straight to my face or you suck it up. I am strongly considering this method of filming when I complete the 12 westerns, making small movies or even big ones over extended periods of time with a good team of no more than five people.

...

Over beers, when finished with our shots for the day, we got into an argument (though not a heated one) about camping for *Counting Bullets.* I mentioned that a prospective actor asked about possibly bringing his RV if he were cast and communicated to John my concerns about this, those being that suddenly with one, two or maybe even more RVs, we'd have this big footprint out in the wilderness instead of a small one. This would make it harder to shoot around our camp. To my surprise, John and Anouschka announced that they'd been considering renting an RV for the experience too. "Aren't you going to bring yours?" John asked, referencing the one I'm staying in here at the ranch. "No," I responded, "I'm going to camp like we said we would."

Then it became a discussion of comfort, saying that I was "insane" for wanting to actually camp. This started to get my blood boiling, calling back memories of other bad sport situations like the one with people suddenly not wanting to stay here at the ranch during *Deputy's Wife.* I brought this up: "As soon as one person expects and requires special treatment, it ruins the whole thing. When Baretta decided to leave the ranch, suddenly more and more people wanted to and I had a problem on my hands." Anouschka retaliated: "No, he wasn't comfortable." Me: "He didn't give us a chance to help him be comfortable. He didn't communicate at all!" This idea of communication seems to still be a loss for people, the understanding that talking about something is the first step to simple problem solving. A little heated, I told them that if they wanted their damn RV then they could do it but that the whole plan of making the movie out in the Dragoons and camping out as we agreed was much less appealing to me. Suddenly there would be an imbalance: some people sleeping in a climate controlled space on a mattress and others on a cot or sleeping bag on the ground in a tent! This is not good for camaraderie and it's my definition of being a bad sport. How can two able-bodied people like John and Anouschka not camp for two weeks? Fucking pussies... that's what I honestly felt. They're not willing to toughen up or live the experience at all. I thought about bringing up the fact that Christian Bale slept on the ground with nothing at all for weeks on Rescue Dawn with Herzog but this would have fallen on deaf ears. They would have without a doubt said, "But he gets paid millions of dollars" and nothing I could have said would have helped them understand that it has nothing to do with that. At least John admitted he could see some reason in my logic about creating an imbalance of conditions on set. He started to think about buying a cot instead of renting an RV.

This reminds me of one of my main concerns in the years leading up to the 12 Westerns, wondering how the hell I'd find a crew tough enough to really do this with me. I guess I was right. People just have no grit anymore.

April 19th, 2020

Yesterday we gathered together our biggest group so far for this "secret" quarantine movie, our last day of filming at Gammons Gulch for this project at least. Abe drove from Phoenix. Thad, Morgan's significant other, was there. Kim Williams, came to play Crazy Kim, the film's main baddie. Larry returned as Wyatt Earp. The other Larry returned as Lazy Larry. And Caron brought Dreamer, the horse.
Our rhythm of filming continued well for the most part. In our first set up, I asked about my missing pants (which one of our team members had taken to sew up). "You need the pants today?" "Yes, they're in the script and the list of props we need." Nope. She left them in Tucson. Why leave part of the main character's wardrobe? Yet another mistake that

changes the story. I love changing the story but out of choice, not because I have none! The problem is that she and many others I've worked with don't read the script, at least in detail. They don't read the emails, the call sheets, etc. You put all this work into describing things, it doesn't get read.

...

Morgan announced to me at the end of our shoot, "I had the best day on set that I've had all year." In some ways I was happy for her, that she had a positive experience especially as her work on the 12 westerns nears its end. On the other hand, I thought to myself, "This is probably the day you worked the least of all those days. All you did was sit around and then get to jump on a horse and ride away." The child side of her showed straight through. She is still a kid in a woman's body, not an adult yet, or at least one who truly understands work. I'm glad she got to jump on the horse and ride away. For now, I am ready for her to keep riding.

...

Halfway through our shoot, I was pulling my character hat (an old one I'd bought a year or so ago in Tombstone) down on my head and the brim ripped right off. Shit. Anouschka tried to tape it up but it was clear we wouldn't be able to use it this way for very long or effectively. I can't remember if it was John or her, maybe both, who suggested it get shot off by Wyatt Earp as I rescue the Lady Bandit from hanging. It turned out to be a humorous solution.

In our final shot of the day, we pushed the slapstick to its fullest, abandoning reality completely. During my escape from the baddies, I pass by the ghost (a character in a white sheet straight out of Abbott and Costello that we featured in our ghost town episode). To hide, I steal the ghost's sheet and put it over myself. The ghost, wearing an under-sheet, feels exposed with only one sheet on and covers himself as the heavy (Abe) runs by and sees neither of us. When he's gone, the ghost grabs his sheet back and stomps off. I see Abe coming back the other direction and quickly hide in an upright coffin, pretending to be dead. It was absurd. I told John, "When people see this part of the movie, they'll either be with us and enjoying the hell out of it or they'll say screw these people."

April 20th, 2020

Our weekend shoot concluded yesterday with more scenes filmed at the Lonesome Coconut Ranch. We are running out of backgrounds to shoot in this spot, finding shots between the various buildings and abandoned vehicles. However, we ultimately were able to make one small area work for several scenes, further showing our ability to work with very little.

Lucy, the woman who owns the ranch, and Zoey were surprisingly very easy to work with. I thought Lucy might be stiff to start like most non-actors. On the contrary, she was way into it, with lots of expression and color in your performance. If anything, she has to be slowed down. Zoey, only four years old, was incredibly co-operative. Her "tough face" that her mother taught her this past week worked wonders and I think any weaknesses in this part of the movie will be overwhelmed by her charm. I continued to have fun with the character's antics, from lassoing myself and falling over to eating a giant grub. Well, I did not consume the huge earth worm but inspired by the *Quigley Down Under* scene and taking it a step further than Tom Selleck, I did bite into the squirming creature. I appreciate its sacrifice for the shot.

We only have two more days of filming for the project and that's a relief. It's been fun to make but also reveals how hard the process is even with a "simple" project. Filmmaking is challenging and truly only the few are suited to do it.

April 21st, 2020

I am now leaning towards a decision that did not occur to me until last week: moving *Heart of the Gun* (originally scheduled for June) to December. It was a passing thought that has developed into the most probable plan. Most of those involved, actors and investors, think it's the best way. Nick, though he would prefer to work in June, thinks it is also the smartest move. The only element of production that will not most likely (I only mentioned it as a random idea the last time we talked) is the ranch where we're supposed to film. This may mean the loss of the location but only time will tell. I must spend this week talking to various people involved in the different projects before making the final move. This would mean I'd make *Counting Bullets* in May, *Guide to Gunfighters* in June, *Frontier* in July, *The Woman Who Robbed the Stagecoach* in August, and then back to Mississippi. The one reason I like moving *Heart* to December is that of all the scripts, it is probably the one I care most about and so this would be a fitting end to the massive project we've undertaken.

...

I made some notes of things to write about from this past month before I forget them. The most of these are the accounting issues I've had from the end of *Deputy* onward. I knew that as we changed the schedule, went even further into overtime, and still would be required by SAG to pay for days the actor didn't end up working, I'd be screwed financially. The biggest part of this is the SAG deposit, required prior to production and not returned for weeks, sometimes months after. For Deputy, it was $3900. That's a lot of money on a 50k production to be missing. About halfway through filming, I approached one of our investors about loaning the movie that amount and getting it paid back to her as soon as SAG returned the funds. The person immediately agreed, no problem. This was a huge stress relief as I knew I'd have an extra 3900 to cover expenses and payments. But sure enough, by the time I sent the investor the loan agreement, she had a different response: "Oh, I talked to my mom and things are just too tight financially with the virus and all. Sorry." Now I was super screwed with less time to fix it.

So I did what I really did not want to do. I went into further credit card debt to cover the amounts. There was no other choice. Waiting on the 3900 will take a long time so I did what had to be done, bit that bitter tasting bullet. And if that didn't taste bad enough, then came all of the bullshit SAG expenses chasing me back to the bank. Our SAG rep (the person who handles all paperwork etc) had been a pain in my ass, disorganized/unreliable/non-communicative, for a while. Now suddenly she hit me with things she'd never mentioned before: I had to pay per diem for breakfast for all the LA actors (not the Texas actor or John who lived in another part of California and now lives in Phoenix), I had to pay mileage instead of gas compensation which was in my own deal memos (and always has been), and worst of all, I had to pay their days off (something I'd agreed up front with the talent that the film didn't have a budget for). The funniest part of this horseshit was that SAG did their typical thing, cherry-picking instead of being thorough. So they hounded me about paying mileage for one actor while completely ignoring another one, who also drove from LA... You want to raise your hands and tell them how bad they are at their jobs but you just shut up and take in the ass, glad that there isn't more coming. Thankfully we have a good cast and they want to help me out. Vincent, the one they hounded me most about, straight up emailed them saying he didn't want all this extra stuff. They replied telling him there is no choice. Hell, what a system when they won't even let the actor decide not to take something!

I finally put together a long email with examples of the issues I've had with the SAG rep and sent it to her boss. Though there was no apology, the supervisor did say "I am surprised at this. She has never had a complaint before," and then she moved the rep from our projects and took the responsibility on herself. I believe she was still in doubt about whether I was right about the person's incompetence until she started asking for a bunch of documents that were not in our file and I proceeded to forward her email after email from weeks before when I'd diligently sent them to her assistant. A small battle won with SAG in a big losing war. It's too much for a small production to take on. I'd love to pay the day rates for actors but it's far more than that: over time after 8 hours, taxes, mileage & per diem. Pension & Health payment alone is 19% of all salaries.

Right now I have two more productions that need to be SAG, because of the actors involved. I'm going to avoid doing so for all the other Westerns as best as I can and after that, I'd like to stay away from them for the remainder of my career as a filmmaker. I don't care if I have to make "small" movies with local talent. I'll even pay them the day rate. But I won't put up with the bullshit anymore

April 22nd, 2020

John and I scouted Harkers, another little western movie set, yesterday morning. This was is smack dab in the middle of Tucson with planes from the nearby airport flying overhead. When this was brought up by the owner, Rick Harker, I simply said, "That's okay. We do things Good, Bad, and the Ugly style," referencing my reliance and trust in wild lines. Rick recently lost both of his legs, an old cowboy-rock-n-roll type. He was very friendly and seemed appreciative that our 12 Westerns might include his place, one that like most of these set builders has taken him decades to put together. He said, "Blaize kept telling me to contact you. I told her, I knew you'd be comin' around one of these days. I knew you'd be comin'."

We will most likely film there for the first scenes of *Counting Bullets*.

We retreated from the scout to John's place where we hunkered down for several hours to work on casting, logistics of the production, and the in-progress script. During this, we consumed coffee, ginger ale, beer, whiskey, and eventually a couple cigars sent to us by a potential sponsor. We talked about women, politics (of which we are on different sides but find no reason to argue), cops, death, and of course filmmaking practices. I shared with him the news I'd just received that Bethany, a woman in Mississippi I'd been intimate with for a brief time, had just died in a four-wheeler crash. She is the second "lover" of mine who has died, to be followed by many more unless I go first. Death feels very real to me, now more than ever. I do not feel shocked by it but I do feel saddened at the loss of life.

By the end of the time, it was dark and we had a full outline completed for the movie. I drove home with whiskey on my breath and Bethany on my mind. I could not get the taste of the cigar off my tongue. In fact, it is the flavor of my coffee this morning.

April 23rd, 2020

I am back to my old ways of working now that Morgan is gone. It's amazing how much of my day was taken up by interaction and management. Now it's just me in the RV pounding away at the work. I'm trying to finish as much of the edit for the silent film as I can before we film our final two days this weekend. I am almost certain the film will come in at 40 to 45 minutes tops when I was hoping for sixty. By some standards, 45 is a feature but I will make more efforts to stretch the length to 60 over the next few months even if I have to add scenes. Last night I also dug into the sound work on *Bastard's*, something I can tell is going to be quite challenging at times but not impossible. At least we're doing this now with a projected screen release of January.

Speaking of the big screen, I am not sure what to think about Paul Schrader's recent proclamations that the theaters' fingernails have been chopped off the ledge. I certainly hope not. The idea of releasing these films next year without movie premieres is daunting as that is the first chunk of profits I always get back for the investors. Will the world return to a fairly normal way? I have to believe that it will. We've been in the storm like this before and people cannot see out of it. They always call for the end of things but it seems that one day we will look back on this time and say, "Remember when that coronavirus thing happened. That was crazy." Then again, who knows.

April 24th

Thursday turned out to be an unexpectedly shit day. A bomb dropped out of nowhere. One of our investors suddenly announced that he was reconsidering his investment in *Counting Bullets*. On April 9th, he'd agreed to put 5000 in. "Travis, I will give you the $5000.00 for the May project." In that original offer, I'd made it clear that the script was still being written and shared as much info with him as possible. He made no mention of reservations and we continued with plans. Furthermore, I proceeded as if I had a fully funded film, able to count on the sources that had committed (that 5k is half the budget of this micro-budget Western). So flash forward two weeks exactly and the investor tells me yesterday that his investment is now dependent on the script. He demanded to read it. I told him again, we're still working on it and offered to send him what we have of the script. I also told him that we've been making progress under the assumption that we were fully funded and that a pull-out would deeply hurt the production just weeks before we start filming... He didn't seem to care one bit. Just wants to read the freaking script which I told him wasn't ready in the first goddamn place. "My money, my decision." Yeah, and my ass.

So I was super clear with him about what had been agreed on in writing in our text and email threads, sent him the 30 pages of the script we have completed plus the full outline, and scheduled a call for this morning, an hour from now precisely. Who knows how it will go. I'm trying to enter the conversation as calm as possible but it's real hard when you feel like you're getting screwed. If he does decide to pull out, a few things will happen: 1. I will no longer trust this person that I was developing both a friendship and good working relationship with. 2. I will no longer pitch any projects to him and just complete the ones we've already agreed on. 3. I will make the damn movie if I have to sell my soul to the devil.

April 25th, 2020

The conversation with the investor yesterday was at least calm. Again, the main issue was that he did not do the C word, communicate. In the last week, he'd spent forty thousand out of pocket at the hospital and lost more than three hundred thousand in the stock market. This would have been useful information to know if he'd been more vulnerable about his uneasiness to let go of five thousand. Once we started really getting into it, the finished script is nothing more than a baby's blanket for him, a symbol of comfort. It was clear that he might not even read the whole thing. He just wants it to ease his anxiety. I still wish he had not done it this way. It makes me on edge and there has been a loss of trust but I do think he will come through on this film. We'll know as John delivers the script this next week.

April 26th, 2020

Yesterday was our second to last filming the silent movie. We spent a majority of the day in the Dragoon Mountains, near where we filmed *Ranch Hands* and will also be making *Counting Bullets*. It was our biggest group yet with a return of Corey's character Slippery Slim, the three heavies, our core team, and some extra bodies that didn't really need to be there but oh well. We stayed focused and got some good shots. In my favorite moment of the day, which of course involved falling, Doc Holliday is sitting at the base of the tree with a big boulder rock behind him. He's drunk, taking swigs from a bottle of whiskey. Suddenly, I fall into frame, jumping down from the rock which was about six feet high, not a big drop but definitely a solid impact. After landing in, he casually offers me the bottle without thinking twice about this person who has pretty much fallen out of the sky. I take a swig and see one of the heavies come around the corner. I get up to go and Doc drunkenly thinks about shooting me before deciding to randomly blast the bad guy instead. I hope the physicality of this project gets some recognition.

I was worried about its runtime, realizing there's no way we could reach 60 minutes but the more I read about feature runtime, the better I felt. For one, the Academy rates a feature at 40 minutes or more, so does AFI and BFI. Furthermore, *Sherlock Jr.* was only 44 minutes along with a bunch of other silent, feature film classics. So maybe we're alright.

April 27th, 2020

It was such a relief to finish the film yesterday. As usual, all of the work caught up to me, my body, mind, and spirit feeling worn out as we rolled back into the ranch after accomplishing our last couple shots. It might have also been the nature of those final set ups. You see, we saved the film's biggest stunt for last, just in case I killed myself doing it. I'm only half joking. Down from the Lonesome Coconut Ranch, there's a dry river wash and a sort of cliff face of clay that surrounds it. Lucy showed me this weeks ago and immediately my wheels started spinning about how to do a scene here, specifically how I might fall or climb down the cliff. There were a couple spots that looked safe enough to try. A couple weeks ago, we filmed some preliminary shots where Wes, my character, approached the ledge and sees the drop. The major danger with this spot isn't actually the height, it's the fact that the ledge is gradually crumbling away. You can see the large sections that have broken off and fallen into the wash below. You can also see the cracks forming on top where it's starting to break.

On that preliminary shoot, I stood out on the ledge and we discovered the best spot for my eventual stunt: the corner of the clay cliff where several roots are protruding. In general, it seemed the spots with the most trees near the edge would be the safest, the ground more stable with the deeply embedded vegetation. Instead of climbing down with these roots, risking a fall, I theorized that climbing up might be the best bet, reversing the action when editing, and that final hour of the production, we put theory into action. I approached the cliff face and tugged on the biggest root. Some small chunks of dirt and clay broke loose but my natural rope held firm. I put all my weight on it. No sign of breaking. John and Anouschka set up the camera. I waited for their call, worried about my upper body strength and ability to pull myself two thirds of the way up the cliff at least. "Action". I started to climb. Only a couple feet up, I could feel more of the earth breaking loose, above my head and by my feet as I searched for footing. Big rock like chunks fell by my face and I was reminded that those might not feel so good if I received a direct hit; if a bigger chunk came down and collided with my body, I might not be getting up. Nevertheless I kept climbing. Suddenly I was there, two thirds of the way to the top and resting on a little outcrop which did not feel steady at all so I clung to the top of the root and breathed harder than I have, maybe in my whole life. I'd used all my physical energy to do this. "How did it look?" I asked my team of two below. Anouschka said she was breathless watching it. John said it looked pretty damn good. I was happy, checking to see if I might be able to continue up but with no firm root to grab on from there, I quickly determined it was impossible to do so without major risk. I would not see the shot until thirty minutes or so later but upon viewing, their opinions were confirmed: it did work and looked pretty intense watching me climb with all the dirt coming down.

But we needed something to tie the action together. Since I hadn't been able to make it all the way to the top, we needed something with me climbing down from the ledge and piece the two together. After looking at a few options, we found a possible spot where I would only drop 10-12 feet if I lost control. This stunt felt tame compared but still tested my nerves as I climbed backwards off a ledge and felt with my foot for another root. On take two, I slid completely out of frame, without hurting myself, causing a giant cloud of dust to rise into frame. Dusting myself off from the dirt avalanche, the team once again confirmed that it looked great and sure enough it did. I was very proud of these two shots. With no stunt training, this is the closest I can get to a Buster Keaton moment and I'm glad the film has it in there.

We celebrated with Lucy and Zoey: beers, brisket, cigars, and pond time. Upon returning to the ranch, I quickly stripped off my accessories and got into the pond in my long johns, happy to finally retire them from filming... at least for a little while. We all felt accomplished. There's an incredible feeling that comes from finishing a feature film, no matter how small of a production it is. There's also a deep sense of gratitude I feel for my closest collaborators. "Thank you," I told both

John and Anouschka. "You didn't have to be here. You didn't have to help me. You could have stayed home. It was your choice." When we parted that night, I hugged each of them and hid the tears that were filling my eyes.

After I busted my head open with a canteen for one scene.

Larry Judkins dressed up as a ghost for one scene

John Marrs, who also played a ghost in the film, and I outside the saloon on a short break from filming.

I spent many afternoons with Zoey Jean Blair, playing in the pond at the Lonesome Coconut Ranch.

Bandit, happy and free, filming on location in the Dragoon Mountains.
All photographs by the production crew.

COUNTING BULLETS

This was the first of the 12 Westerns to be born in the process of making them. Its conception came out of necessity, as we were forced to rethink how we could keep

making Westerns safely and without causing a stir on social media. We quietly planned this Cavalry Action picture, a throwback to the Men-on-a-Mission movies I loved as a kid. It would be shot with just a handful of actors, a crew of two or three, the most minimal budget, and out of the middle of nowhere to limit both infection from the virus and public exposure.

It was also the first time John and I collaborated in a significant way and where we learned that we work well together. Here is a brief synopsis of Counting Bullets: a group of misfit soldiers is formed for a routine mission to escort some nuns across the territory. After they find the nuns murdered, this small band of Cavalry find themselves facing an unexpected enemy. A group of Comancheros has surrounded them and it will be a fight to the last man to survive.

Photograph by John Charles Dickson

April 29th, 2020

Yesterday I hit the road to Phoenix to return the camera package to Nick. It was a six hour total road trip, there and back, listening to music and interviews with the windows rolled down, feeling the temperature rise degree after degree as I entered the city.

I made a pit stop on my way home to talk with one of our crew members, a long overdue discussion. John Marrs continued to make me aware that this person was griping behind my back to him and others. We've often talked about the crew member's issues on set from staying focused to the biggest: being too sensitive and letting emotions hinder the work.

I was prepared to have a positive talk, especially coming out of a mostly good experience on this silent film. I gave this person the floor first, allowing her to express any issues. She really had nothing to say that held any weight, painting it all as a great experience. I pressed her a little: "What mistakes do you think you made that you've since learned from or want to learn from for the next production?" She went on to describe her challenges to figure out what is a priority on set, what to do in which order. This is accurate. I was glad she recognized it. However, pressed for ways she might handle it in the future, she simply said, "I think I learned on this one. It won't be an issue." Easier said than done and I've already seen evidence on the set of the silent film that it will still be an issue... I urged the necessity of routine on set, not much different than a morning routine where you wake up, make coffee, take a dump... same thing on set. You show up, read the call sheet again, get your walkie talkie, get your cup of coffee, go through your tasks for the scene, etc.If you get distracted, you handle that distraction and then get back to the routine. She seemed to be listening, maybe. At one point, there was confusion about what she should do first again and

I said, "Do what the director tells you to do. You can't go wrong. If I ask you to do something, that's your priority above all else. This way, if someone asks you to do something else, you just say 'I am doing what the director told me to do' or if even I ask you why you're not doing something else you can tell me 'Travis, I am doing what you told me to do.'" This is the safest way to proceed on set. She laughed. Then the conversation turned to shit...

Upon bringing up the sensitivity issue, she leaned forward in her chair: "Travis, when I first met you, you told me lots of things about you that I didn't believe. Now I see they are true. You know your own faults... Travis, you are a sexist." She went on to explain that I specifically pick on women instead of men. Just as when someone said "men are pigs" on set, my defense system was triggered. I don't know why she doesn't get it but this is like calling someone a racist! I reported back, "I am not a sexist. I get upset at the people who do not do their jobs on set. I don't care if they have a penis or vagina. Look at Paula, she is a woman, and I did not get mad at her even once in 17 days of filming. Why? Because she did her job. There are four people who did not do their jobs on set. I cannot help that these people are women." Seeing that I was upset, she then claimed that she did not call me a sexist. I responded that she did. "You said very clearly, "Travis, you are a sexist'. You meant it and you're wrong. I've explained why you're wrong and you have nothing to say back that can counter it. I am all about equality. I like people who do their jobs and dislike people who don't, regardless of whether they are men or women." I explained to her, now blunt, that if she wants to make this Counting Bullets movie with us that she has to be tough, that we don't need to worry about hurt feelings while we're working hard in the goddamn desert.

The conversation ended soon after and I drove away unsure if she'd truly heard anything. I reported back to John and he confirmed that she'd called me a sexist in the past, a remark that he refuted, "Travis gets mad at people equally." But she doesn't listen. Exasperated, we decided that if she says she can handle the production, we'll give her a try.

...

A bit of humor: after driving five hours I looked down at the floorboard of my car to see I had a passenger. A mouse! He must have jumped in at the ranch. The crazy son of a bitch. Hopefully he's decided to move on and find a vehicle with air conditioning.

April 30th

I watched *Tennessee's Partner*, an Allan Dawn directed Western with a lot of merit. It inspired me to look back at the short story. I'd read it several times in college and made a short film adaptation during the 52 films project. This in turn got me interested in Bret Harte again, possibly making a movie of *Tennessee* or *Poker Flat*. That led me to his play, *Two Men of Sandy Bar*, featuring the gambler character from Poker Flat. I'm curious to now read it. When I first started the 12 Westerns I had two adaptations planned, *Outcasts of Poker Flat* and *The Bride Comes to Yellow Sky*. Now I have none... This might be another last minute addition to the project now that things have been turned upside down, especially if I can come up with a simple script for either *Tennessee, Poker Flat*, or this play (if it's any good).

May 2nd, 2020

After finishing another rewrite of *Frontier* last night, I felt at a crossroads. Though a big part of me wants to make the movie, another part of me feels it is time to put the project back on the shelf and fill its spot with something else. Why? For one, I know that raising funds for an experimental erotic western with lesbian content is going to be nearly impossible right now. I'm sure there are investors out there who would jump at it but I don't know those people and in this economy, getting funds for anything is tough enough. That means a tiny production with a small crew and unpaid cast. On one hand, I love that. On the other, can I find those people who will love it too? With my main makeup artist now out of the picture, I need to find someone else willing to make the Hes/werewolves costume. Also, the trouble of finding a location that really fits this story continues to be a challenge. I told Jared and the two actresses I'm courting for roles that this is the last rewrite I'm going to do, other than changes to match whatever location that may be. At this point, this is either the script I want to start production with or one that needs to wait till another day.

May 3rd, 2020

Yesterday, we returned to do yard work at Gammons Gulch as trade for filming there for free on the silent movie. I went through three weed whackers in two hours, frustrating pieces of equipment but highly effective when they work right. It's amazing the difference we can make in this town by working for just two hours.

John relayed the reaction to my heart to heart with that one crew member and said my advice to "always do what the director says as your first priority" was interpreted by her as "big ego". He tried to explain to her that this is the complete opposite! That it's how a set works. But she just can't see clearly how any of this is supposed to work. I wish I could send her back in time to work just one hour on a John Ford set. She'd either be enlightened or destroyed.

Anyway, other than our camp cook (John's hippie friend from California), it's going to be an all male crew and that's kinda what I wanted. Boy, are we going to be stretched thin... but I think we can do it.

May 5th, 2020

The irony of my last statement a couple days ago is that yesterday morning, when I arrived to scout at Harker's old west town, I learned from John that we also lost our camp cook. With things opening back up from the virus, suddenly she needs to return to work. This is the kind of thing I predicted: there's going to be a scrambling for jobs and money as things return to normal. Anyway, we're truly an all male crew now. But faced with the prospect of cooking and crewing with just three people started to sound pretty nuts. We'd have to adopt a much slower, more casual pace to production which wouldn't match the twelve shooting days we have scheduled.

That night, I spoke to Lucy (owner of the ranch where I stay) and she quickly adopted the idea of taking care of food for the production. She wouldn't be the "camp cook" as in always being there but would be responsible for planning the meals, buying all the groceries, and prepping what we needed. So it might be "Tuesday, lunch. Put bag of this in a pot and heat up for thirty minutes." If this works out, it will be a real relief. She has a talent for that kind of thing for sure.

...

Being with Jared for the scout was a pleasant reunion. We haven't seen each since *Texas Red*, which both feels like a lifetime ago and just yesterday at the same time. I filled him in on all the craziness of the past couple months: the struggles of making *Deputy's Wife* in Covid, the production of the silent movie, and of course the suicide. He was amused by the stories and in shock to hear about the tragedy.

The days are getting hot, even away from the city. I have to develop a new strategy for work, unable to edit or work on sound in the middle of the day, baking in the RV. Of course, all of that will soon change as I jump back into production.

May 7th, 2020

Our trip to Phoenix yesterday was half-a-bust. The costume fitting with Wayne went well and meeting him made me more confident about his ability to play the role.

Our meeting with Larry, the civil war enthusiast, was time well spent if it works out in the long run but not the short term. His outfits etc can't really accommodate our cavalry needs right now. His enthusiasm for the battle of Picacho Pass is interesting but like most people with a movie idea, he doesn't have much to offer other than that.

Finally, we went to see the wagon, owned by Corey's dad, which we hoped to purchase. This would have solved our needs on a few Westerns where we're looking at a high cost for wagon rentals. Sadly our plan did not work out. After inspection and checking with our "wagon people", we determined the wagon isn't worth more than 500 bucks. Corey's dad wants 2500. There's no point in even negotiating. At least we got an answer and now we are back to square one on the damn wagon situation.

I feel stressed today, more than I've felt in a while. The things we need to do between now and filming several days away feel tremendous. Only the history of having done it before makes me feel better.

May 10th, 2020

Tomorrow I leave the ranch for three weeks of living in the Dragoons. I'll be camping mostly alone the first three days, with Lucy & Zoey helping me settle in the first night. In many ways, I'm looking forward to being out there, the solitude, the desert living experience. I also have a nervous feeling, not the bad kind, for doing something like this the first time.

I found out the last couple days that Ashleigh, the lead actress from *Bastard's Crossing*, was in a serious car accident and had surgery. She had a spinal fracture and some of her intestine removed. According to a statement from her family, this may be the end or her career as a stunt woman (that was her focus more than acting) and I assume as a figure skater, equestrian, and aerial acrobat. However odd our parting was, I feel an immense sadness that she has lost her ability to do what she loved. However there have been more surprising recoveries.

I do not feel this will be the last tragedy that strikes us during the 12.

May 11th, 2020

I am laying down in my tent now, a one man tent or you could say a one man, one dog tent. Lucy and Zoey came along for this first night of camping and to help haul all the water and gear. It's nice to have them here but I look forward to being alone tomorrow.

After just being here an hour, we already ran into a snake. Little Zoey almost stepped on him right in our camp. Thankfully he was not startled and did not even use his rattler. We chased him away from camp and I hope he decides to sleep somewhere else.

May 12th, 2020

This morning, while drinking coffee at my campsite, I received the most unexpected message. A person named Graham, who I vaguely remembered speaking with at some point, sent me the following Facebook note: Ummm well, Thad tried to kill me and I shot him and called the cops. Him and Morgan are wanted in NM and on the run.

When I asked why Thad would try to kill him, Graham continued, "Because I was sick of their tweeker shit. I locked my door and put a sign on it that we needed to talk. He attacked me unprovoked, told Morgan to tase me said he was going to rope [and] tie me up and I grabbed my gun. He is a psychopath with violent history."

Now let me explain. The Morgan he mentions is my recently fired assistant. Thad is her "significant other" who visited the ranch and helped some with the silent movie. My immediate reaction to this was to not believe it, just as I don't believe any kind of accusation or gossip I hear but pressed, Graham seemed not to hesitate if I followed up with the Santa Fe cops. He even delivered a half-remembered detective name. That was enough to get me past the police secretary who didn't want to help at all. On the line with Detective Ernest, he confirmed, "Yes. Graham is telling the truth. They are both wanted." Is it possible to be shocked but not surprised?

What I mean is that after observing Morgan's behavior, I have been thinking in the back of my mind that she might return to New Mexico and get herself into some kind of drug problem or other legal issue. At the same time, the wildness of this situation was baffling. The pieces added up to a picture I was still not prepared to see. The detective confirmed they might be coming to Arizona. I assured him that I would let him know if I received any word from Morgan. His description of the crime was a "heated moment gone wrong" and he did not seem to think they were dangerous. He wanted a chance to talk Morgan into giving herself up.... before getting off the phone, he relayed that she already had a warrant out for her on a domestic violence case. "How old is that warrant?" He confessed it was from 2019. So the entire time she worked for me this year, she was wanted by the police... what can be said after learning that information? Should I have known better than to hire her? Should I have sensed something like this? I don't think it's possible that I could have. She's a good liar. A good pretender. A good actress, better off screen than on.

I called all the people she might hit up to warn them: Lucy at the ranch, Corey who she became friends with, Anouschka and John.

Blaize joked that this was like the Pearl Hart story playing out in real time (Morgan was at one time my top choice to play Pearl). I reported that I wasn't in the mood to joke about it.

May 14th, 2020

I woke up and recorded sounds of desert birds before the sun made its way over the mountains.

May 16th, 2020

Now, actors Shannon and John Charles Dickson are here in camp. So is Jared. It was much easier to be out here when it was just me. The more humans, the more hassle, the more supplies, etc. But it's also nice to have their company.

Yesterday, we did camera tests up in the boulders where we'll be filming a majority of the movie. Not more than thirty minutes into this, we ran into a rattlesnake. I was walking towards a specific spot to show Jared where I might want a character to sit. Just a couple feet away from that landing, I noticed the venomous creature curled up. It was not rattling. We moved back and debated if we should kill it or leave it alone. Here's the thing, we're going to be filming in this exact area for the next two weeks. If we don't kill it, then it's going to hang around and there's a damn good chance someone is going to get bit. So... we set ourselves towards murdering the fanged foe. My idea was to smash it with a rock, something I've heard done, but after John tried this with a big stone, the snake just got pissed. He then grabbed a very long stick and drew the snake out, eventually smashing its head with the end of this handy tool. We took the dead creature back to camp, hung it in a tree, and eventually I did my best to skin and gut the thing. Our plan was to cook it for an appetizer but later I learned that's easier said than done.

But our encounters with snakes that day were not over. Just a few hours later, Jared went back up into the rocks to pop off some more test shots at dusk. I stayed back at camp, working at my desk. The generator was roaring, I had music playing on my phone, and Shannon/John Charles continued to converse, nevertheless I was able to hear the sound of the rattler from 50 yards away. I was immediately worried for Jared, wondering if he might have accidentally startled one of them and been bit. I took off in that direction, finding Jared on top of a boulder. He'd heard it too of course but wasn't quite sure where it was. We eventually identified the second rattlesnake, bigger than the first, in a crevice between the rocks we were standing on. John Charles showed up with the "snake beater", the name I'd given to the stick that killed the first one. Once again, logic led me to the decision that we should kill this guy too, a threat to us at any point during filming in this immediate area. He was harder to get than the first one, tougher and more difficult to get a direct hit on but John eventually got him. This one, I tried to start skinning immediately but even with their heads cut off, the snakes keep slithering around. Every time I took the knife to its skin, the deceased creature squirmed around, an unnerving sight. Nearly an hour later, even after I took its skin and guts out, the bare meat of the snake continued to move around on our stove... what a creature.

I cooked each snake differently: 1. with the small one, I tried to pull meat off its many little bones, a tedious and not very fulfilling task. I sauteed a tiny bit of meat and we had our first taste. 2. the bigger one I cooked with the bones, breaking the spine in four to five sections. This was better to eat as Jared and I consumed the pieces like ribs but with very little meat. It's not the kind of thing you want to eat when you're very hungry unless of course it's the only thing you want to eat.

I hope we don't have many more to kill and as a territorial animal, I hope that once we do remove the threat from this area, we won't have to worry about it as much.

May 18th, 2020

Our first day of filming on *Counting Bullets* was rough as hell. I suppose that was inevitable with trying to shoot 15 pages in one day but there was a lot that could have made shooting those 15 pages easier (as always).

The first sign it was going to be a hard day came as Jared and I traveled to Tucson from the Dragoons in the early morning dark with a jam packed Toyota, the camera resting in his lap and Bandit in mine for the two hour drive. Somewhere along the desert highway, a deer popped out at the last second. I was able to dodge it, grazing the front headlight of my car with its legs. Jared was ecstatic about my maneuver, continuing to say "good job dude" as we drove on, knowing that might have put a major stop to our day.

On arrival, we immediately got to work. The call time for crew passed and I wondered where John and Anouschka were. I texted John, "Are you late?" He responded, "No." I then informed him call time was six... I'll never understand how experienced people don't read the damn call sheet. So we got started late but with Jared and I moving fast and efficiently, we got through the first three or four scenes without much issue. We hit lunch a little late however and I felt a struggle coming on for our afternoon scenes. It sure did come. From struggling to get good audio with blaring afternoon boom shadows and traffic noise (Harker's is right in the middle of the city), to actors not quite getting it, to finally a very frustrating scene with bad horse riding, stilted blocking, and a loss of light. The actors got on their horses with plenty of time to practice but no one pushed them. I kept asking, "How much more time do you need to be ready for this routine?" I was told they were ready and they were pretty freaking far from ready. This is the typical problem of people waiting around on set when they should be constantly working.

Thankfully, after driving back two hours and getting in close to midnight, we watched the dailies and some of the shots I had cringed during were not as bad as I thought it would be.

May 20th, 2020

"That's a hard working mother fucker right there," John said to the other guys as I laid on my cot. They thought I was asleep but I'd retreated to have some private time. It was nice to hear, especially coming from him.

The last couple days have been better than the first, progressively improving as we get into a rhythm as a team. I was relieved to wrap our horse scenes yesterday. Though Ron (horse owner) was good to work with, horses add such a complicated element to any shot. Just getting them to stay standing in the right spot wasted numerous takes and time. And we did our best to make the shots as simple as possible. What I think will really help the film is seeing these guys travel through the Dragoon landscape. It does have such a unique look and yesterday I kept thinking of what my friend John Miller has said several times, "Travis, the Dragoons could be your Monument Valley."

I let myself get too burned yesterday and something weird is happening with my toes. I think rocks keep getting in my shoes so now I have blisters on my toes. Hopefully it does not get worse as this is a very physical production. Seeing the men ride all day, I wanted to get in the saddle for a while. The way things worked out, after our last scene, the actors were required to ride back 2 to 3 miles to the horse trailers. Shannon was worn out. He said he'd pay a hundred dollars for someone to ride his horse back for him. He didn't have to pay a single cent. I was damn happy to take that ride.

May 21st, 2020

Yesterday was our most successful day yet. We no longer had horses. It was more about scenes than shots. We could really dig in. Jared complimented my instincts for blocking in frame and it came easily for once. The action did too as we used blanks and paintballs to create some simple fight sequences. I died twice in different outfits, playing two Comancheros but not my main character in the film. In one, I launched myself back from a shotgun blast, a moment which looked damn good in the dailies. The whole cast watches them with us, crowded in the office tent. With this team, it seems like a healthy and positive thing to see what we've all done at the end of each day.

May 22nd, 2020

And just like that, it's a wrap on week one of production for *Counting Bullets*. We're halfway through. This morning, we finished work before 10am, waking up around 4:30am.

How could it be easier to make a film with a crew of two than twenty? How could it be easier to make a film in the middle of nowhere without running water or electricity? How could it be easier to make this Western than the others before it? Simple: we're away from people.

May 25th, 2020

It's nice to have the actors back in camp, though since some have wrapped their scenes, it feels like we're missing some members of the team. Michael, the lead actor, admitted how much it has helped to camp out here, that it has created a "unit". They can relate to their characters, having to work together in the wilderness.

May 27th, 2020

Yesterday may have been our longest day of filming yet. We woke up at 4am to start filming at 5am with the goal to get our first scene before the sun showed itself over the mountain. This was accomplished, followed by a breakfast break, and then back to work on an intricate five to seven page scene that we split up into four parts: my character being tortured, the men huddling about what they learned from me, getting a surprise attack, and the aftermath of that attack leading to the final fight. Filming this stretched out over the rest of the day as we worked on the complicated blocking bit by bit.

My torture scene involved getting stabbed with a burning stick to make me talk. The plan was to put a piece of leather underneath my shirt in one spot where the actor could hit me without burning my skin. We talked it out in detail but of course humans don't listen well and on the first take, though we said we'd would end before the burning stick stab, he went ahead and poked me. I certainly got a good taste of how that really feels. It wasn't a big deal and we all laughed about it. The real pain actually came later with the piece of leather present as hot embers fell off the stick onto my arm during the take. I could feel them singeing my skin but continued on with the scene. It at least made things real. Once complete, I had three burn blisters on my arm and one on my belly. To be honest, it was an incredible time. I love playing bad guys.

When Jared said, "damn you just look mean," after one take, I glowed with accomplishment.

May 28th, 2020

My final day acting on this one went well: the leap off the boulder, the fight with Jefferson, getting shot through the neck with an arrow. The jump, which wasn't as high as originally planned, still looked pretty great upon review and better yet, I didn't hurt myself after several rehearsals and takes of tumbling onto the mattress. Anouschka actually came through with the arrow, delivering what she said she could.

May 31st, 2020

The last couple days of *Counting Bullets* were exhausting. Adding more people to the "crew" made things far more complicated. Turns out that many hands might make light work, but few hands make right work. About a dozen people showed up to be Comancheros. Jon St. Clare drove all the way from Mississippi to be one of these background bad guys and even brought me a bottle of whiskey and cigar as presents. I made sure we killed him twice, in two different outfits. That's what we had to do with several people to make our final action work. I hope this film demonstrates progress in my staging of action sequences.

...

On the eleventh day of filming, we pushed to wrap production which would be ending ahead of schedule by a day, all anxious to return home. For the first time in three weeks, storm clouds gathered around us out in the Dragoons and it seemed quite possible we might get rained out. Somehow, only a few drops landed on us and we completed our day.

In those final hours, Anouschka played one of the Comancheros, disguised by a wig and makeup to be a man. The camera was behind her anyway. She was set to fire a blank with a rifle at John and then get shot by Michael. As I marked the first take with the slate and made my way behind the camera, suddenly gunfire erupted. She'd started the action before my call for "action", scaring me half to death. Regardless of Jared's call outs to "Stop! Stop!" the actors continued to play out the scene, killing each other. I wouldn't have been surprised if Michael, wielding a saber, had just continued to actually kill Jared and I as well. That would have been quite a way to die... out of control actors.

...

Overall I ended the production with a feeling of accomplishment which increased as I felt John's confidence in what we'd made. His opinion of how this was done is important to me and bringing the story to life, capturing some of his vision as the co-writer, was one of my main goals.

I'd love to say that we walked off into the sunset and enjoyed ourselves when it was all done but that's not how a production goes. They're messy. The next morning we woke to pack up camp. About an hour into it, I could tell we didn't have enough space to take everything in one trip, even with John's flat bed trailer. So I suggested that I leave immediately in my Toyota with as much as I could carry, dump it all at the ranch (1.5 hours away), and return for the last things that they couldn't take. To my dismay, after making this three hour round trip, I returned to our camp and realized that a second load wouldn't transport everything... I'd have to make a third trip. My day, planned for relaxation, would be eaten up by driving in and out of the desert. I couldn't blame John, who tried his best to fit all he could, and to his credit even offered to come back when I relayed the bad news but I didn't want to make him do that. He confirmed the others departing had not tried their best to take what they could.

I left with the second load, knowing that it would be 4 and a half hours before I finally settled down at home. I was mad but by the time I returned to the desert for the third time, Bandit along for the long ride, I was feeling pretty damn good. I packed the last of our things and all of our trash, once again filling my small car. Every time I traveled in and out of the Dragoons over the few weeks, I wondered if I'd get a flat tire on the stretch of rocky road and sure enough, it finally happened on this last journey. I changed the tire and noticed my spare looked kinda flat too. I crossed my fingers that it could take me another 45 minutes to the tire shop in Benson. I got a strawberry milkshake and waited my turn, lucky that they could repair my tire. As the day was ending, I returned to the ranch. Bandit had a well deserved swim and I had the longest shower I've taken in months.

Cinematographer Jared Kovacs on a group of rocks waiting for a take.

Lead actor John Marrs (Sergeant Whitlock).

In my Comanchero outfit, ready to be tortured in a scene. I didn't bathe for three weeks.

Actor John Charles Dickson as McAlister. He also took these photographs.

A GUIDE TO GUNFIGHTERS OF THE WILD WEST

This was actually the first of the 12 Westerns to be fully funded. Wendy approached me to do her script and I accepted, anxious to get the 12 Westerns moving and show my followers that we were making significant progress. The

plan to make the film during April was derailed. We moved it to June, not an ideal month to work outside all day in Southern Arizona. There were other events that sometimes made me wonder if this project was cursed but eventually, we got it done.

Wendy's script tells the story of Tate Butler, a man who has accidentally developed a reputation as a gunfighter. He is constantly plagued with contestants who want to challenge his fame and earn their own by defeating him. Tate wants all this to end so he can safely be with his love, Katherine. For me, this humorous tale is a throwback to Western Comedies of the 60s. Wendy's intention was to create a "Western Romantic Comedy."

Photograph by Production Crew featuring Shanda Renee (center) and John Marrs (right)

June 3rd, 2020

The most interesting event of yesterday was a call with Wendy, writer for *A Guide to Gunfighters*. I saw a post she made about her movie not being a "spoof" but a romantic comedy. It was a clear response to a post John Marrs had made saying we'd accept background extras on this with more colorful, less authentic clothing, even Roy Rogers looks etc. because we're making a comedy. Turns out his use of the word "spoof" set Wendy off so I decided to check in and sent a message asking how she's doing. In return, she asked me to call her. "Hey Wendy, what's up?" First, she asked for the shooting schedule, which I promptly sent. Finally, and I was waiting for it, she launched into offense against the "spoof", explaining to me the tone of her work, etc. I explained that we're making a comedy and that comedies should be fun, that's all we're trying to accomplish. Unsatisfied, she attacked John for not liking her script (something she'd been told by people on the set of *Deputy's Wife* apparently) and trying to sabotage it with his "ego". I could not help myself from sounding defensive when the person who works second hardest on these 12 Westerns gets attacked. "You don't know John. You haven't spent any time talking to him or getting to know him. He's a good guy and doesn't have a big ego. You're taking one post and blowing it way out of proportion." To this she responded unconvinced, "Well... I hope. You know, he calls himself some historical Western expert." Me: "He is." Her: "I hate to tell you this, Travis, but I have a degree in history and I wrote this script..." I told her that we are making a comedy and we want to have fun with it. The conversation pretty much ended there. Human beings... why the hell do they freak out so easily?

June 5th, 2020

The trip to Yuma felt like quite the pilgrimage as I left early Thursday morning, windows down, ready for the heat. I saw the temperature rise from the mid 80s to 115 degrees. I consumed more water than I thought possible and regretted not bringing more. At one point, I set my GPS to the next gas station and could not wait to quench my first, at which point I bought two gatorades and refilled my water, all of which was consumed within the next hour. That part of the Arizona desert is no joke; it will kill you.

On top of traveling with no AC (something I need to get fixed as soon as possible), I managed to leave home with no wallet. Thankfully my first stop was dropping a check off to my friend Kim and she loaned me forty dollars. I drove the rest of the day more conscious than usual of cops, knowing that being pulled over would cost extra without a license.

The two sites I visited produced very opposite reactions. Though Yuma's prison is still impressive in many ways, it is more tragic to see how little was preserved. When studying the original photographs, it's amazing to see what once was and could still be if we were better at not letting our historical structures go to waste. It is also shocking to see how different the Colorado river was just a hundred years ago... a hundred times what it is now.

My reaction to the Castle Dome western town was completely different. I was prepared to be underwhelmed. Never could I guess I was about to see the most impressive Western movie "set" so far. Better than Gammons and Old Tucson, Castle Dome is a hidden gem. It has no wide main street, just a big group of buildings that Alan, the eccentric who has been working on this place since 1998, saved from falling apart, restored, and filled with the most impressive interior design. I mean, I cannot describe in words how cool this place is. The inside of buildings are spacious, not cramped as usual. There is not one but three saloons and a gorgeous hotel. Every entrance produced a feeling of wonder. And Alan was fun to talk to. He's dug up a lot of this from the local mines, one of which he now owns. Most of these types bore me as I listen to their stories but not him. The tales of Spanish soldiers fighting and dying in the rocky mountains nearby or his crazier friends scaling more than 300 feet down into these tunnels to find old denim jeans that can be sold for thousands of dollars each... I could have listened for hours. The only thing that pulled me away was knowing those hours needed to be spent on the road headed home. As we said our goodbyes, he asked me what the world was like these days. I confessed not much had changed for me. He said the same about his own life. "I'm out here. This is non-coded land. I'm free to do what I want. That's what I want, to be free."

It was a long road back to the ranch, all the time hoping I could easily locate my wallet upon arrival. Unfortunately, I pulled in at dark and searched everywhere I could think of: no sign of it. Thoughts started to cloud my mind of how fucked I'd be this weekend going to Globe with no cards, no ID, no way to get money other than to borrow it. I figured I'd somehow dropped the wallet in the pond when I swam with Zoey the other day. I drank a glass of whiskey and went to bed, planning the next morning to get in the pond and walk every inch of its floor, feeling for the leather with my toes. After two cups of coffee to wait for the sun to peak over the trees, I did that very thing and found nothing. But right before I was ready to give up all hope, the wallet was discovered, half hidden beneath my printer where it must have fallen. Funny how such a small thing can cause so much stress.

June 6th, 2020

It always happens. Every casting call, the actors all show up at the very beginning, creating a couple hectic hours and then it slows way down to the point where I am sitting here and haven't seen anyone for close to an hour. If only it could be spaced apart.

June 7th, 2020

There was one true surprise in yesterday's auditions. A woman who has a kind of natural, hippie prettiness came to read for Pearl. She said she'd never acted in her life. We started to read and I was blown away. She doesn't know how to act and therefore wasn't acting, she was being Pearl! She was real. She was connecting with me as if the scenes were actually happening. An architectural student from Taliesin, she just thought she'd give it a try and in the process made me reconsider my plan for casting the lead. There's an actress in LA who has played Pearl before and is up for the low budget production. She feels like a solid choice. Safe. This woman here, Lorraine, feels like a dangerous choice. And maybe the right one.

I feel so lost with these upcoming projects, *Pearl* and *Frontier*. For the former, I don't know how to approach the material. Do I make it with anachronistic elements, allowing me to work around location and budget issues with modern elements? This could open up a lot of doors creatively. But I'm not sure it feels quite right. Or do I just make it with new wave feeling, shooting on iPhone with all correct period accuracy? This feels better, almost as if we're really there with iPhones filming Pearl really doing all this stuff. My hope would be that it would have a more grounded and raw feeling, less constructed than the other Westerns. But can it be done with what I have at my disposal?

For *Frontier*, I can't find a cabin that works for us. It seems like it would be easy. It isn't. Without the right cabin, I don't have a shooting location which means I can't set exact dates,

I can't make a schedule, I can't sign contracts with my actors...

These two films feel like the most elusive of the 12. Somehow I hope the next couple weeks lead to answers.

June 9th, 2020

I've spent most of the last two days cutting. Counting Bullets is nearly half edited. So far, it feels like the most direct, tough-minded work I've done. If anyone ends up calling it "tough minded", I'll tip my hat to Aldrich and Walter Hill and feel slightly successful.

June 11th, 2020

It's amazing how much can change in less than a day. Yesterday, someone was telling me they'd be my "fan for life" and also my love for life (not something I put any weight on). Today, that same person has refused to talk to me. Because of something I did? No. Because of more bullshit rumors posted about me on Facebook... This actor Austin who worked on *Deputy's Wife* suddenly messaged me asking that I not use anymore pictures he took for marketing purposes. I followed up to see him posting about "sexual predators" on his page. Who the hell knows what suddenly turned him against me. We live in a weird world, a crazy reactionary place that sometimes feels like it's on the brink of just boiling over. Anyway, I thanked him for messaging me and said I would not use any more of the photos and would delete all the old ones I posted. Apparently in the last twelve hours, he's managed to turn others against me. Good. These things are a nice weeding out of people who are easily swayed by bullshit and those who are steady, solid. So be it. I'm grateful for the recent reminder from the Woody Allen interview where he talks about keeping his nose in his work and not letting it bother him. Of course it bothers him. It bothers me. But there's no choice but to keep working.

June 12th, 2020

Just a few more brief thoughts on the drama of yesterday. The person I mentioned had promised to 1. be my "fan for life". 2. be my lover for life. 3. send me money for one of the upcoming westerns. 4. loan or practically give her truck to me for use on the 12 westerns. Within hours of saying many of those things, poof! Vanished. Disappeared. Not surprising but nevertheless another notch in the "I can't believe some people" bedpost.

I'm 45 minutes into the cut for Counting Bullets.

June 15th, 2020

The last few days have flown by. Tomorrow we start filming the sixth western. Today I have more to do than I can wrap my head around, starting with a four hour drive that wasn't planned until fires broke out, closed roads, and caused us to rethink how to get our camera package from Nick.

That isn't the only adventure in recent times. On Friday, Blaize and I went on a crazy location scout to find the Apache Springs Cabin as a possible contender for *Frontier*. I suggested we venture out to find the cabin in her little suv. It has more ground clearance than mine Toyota and the road didn't sound too bad. Famous last words.

What was supposed to be a two hour drive to the cabin got longer and longer as we turned off pavement onto a "primitive road". Early into the drive, we encountered some rocks on the dirt path and Blaize said, "Do you think we should stop?" I dismissed her concerns and said it was up to her but I think we should keep going. From there we had to drive 11 miles and only 9 of those took us an hour and a half. What she'd first been concerned about paled in comparison to what we encountered, pushing her non-4-wheel-drive vehicle to its limits. I honestly can't believe the areas we went through... finally getting stopped at a spot that was just too crazy to pass. We had 2.5 miles left to go until the cabin and maybe 2 hours of daylight. I suggested we hike it. She was hesitant because of the light but I insisted it was a 45 minute walk and we could get back before night. With Bandit in tow, we took off. It was a long walk that's for sure but we finally found the cabin and if the hardship of the journey hadn't already convinced me that this was no realistic contender for filming, the site of it did. It's a cool little spot but not right for the film and not worth the trouble to haul everyone out there. So we turned back and made it to the car with just a little light left in the sky. The whole way back, I couldn't help but think we wouldn't make it out. It seemed inevitable that pushing the vehicle back through the hell I'd already subjected it to would lead to some kind of breakdown. Somehow though, we bumped our way back to pavement, a rejoicing moment when the tires left the dirt road.

...

On Sunday, I met up with John. Haven't seen him since we wrapped *Bullets*. We helped Caron set up her horse pin here at the ranch where her two will be staying during the shoot and then ventured out to Mescal, another Western movie set near here. I'd heard a lot about it but never seen the place with my own eyes. It's legendary, the location for *Tombstone*, *Quick and the Dead*, *Monte Walsh*, and more. But Old Tucson, who owns it, has let the place go to hell. Nearly all the buildings are in some kind of disrepair. But a full tour was just a bonus (and one that got me thinking about the possibilities of filming there later this year). Our main goal was to scout a cabin at the edge of their property for *The New Frontier*. It's been a pain in the ass finding a cabin but in the last couple days, two solid options have presented themselves. This one and another up north. Each has its pros and cons from the landscape, interior design, temperature, bathroom situation, etc. An important and tough decision lies ahead of me this next week.

...

I've been glued to the computer finishing this cut of *Counting Bullets* and thankfully was able to successfully reach the end of the rough edit before starting production tomorrow. I feel good about it. I don't really believe in "best" anymore but there are some "mosts" I feel this one hits: the most successful action sequence, the most effective use of coverage, the most traditional of the Westerns so far. I look forward to seeing how it continues to improve through the post process.

June 17th, 2020

Well, this production certainly has begun with some bumps. On day one, we started with all our cafe scenes, a series of interactions between the hero Tate and this Walter Brennan-like character Wilson. Tate is played by an opera singer named Andrew. Wilson is played by Glen Gold, a man who looks old enough to have acted opposite Douglas Fairbanks. He's had bit parts in 90s westerns and definitely brings plenty of crust to a scene. There's also a waitress played by Blaize... with all the best intentions, she struggled to incorporate the most simple direction and blocking. "But I was getting so many contradictory directions," she said on lunch. John and I bit our tongues.. After falling behind because of much of this, somehow we made up time with the next few scenes and still managed to wrap a half hour ahead of schedule.

Another hurdle came when the opera singer, who had consumed plenty of prop pie and beef stew, started to feel a stomach ache. He worked through it but after leaving set he continued to send me voice messages about how bad he was feeling, probably with some kind of food poisoning. Even as I write this, I don't know if he's well enough to work this morning.

...

And the final hurdle, other than working in the heat, came in the evening as we settled back in at the ranch. Merina, our cinematographer from LA, asked me to speak alone, never a good thing to hear. Apparently, her sister is having an emergency with Merina's two year old nephew. She has no one to be with her except Merina, though I failed to understand why Dillon (Merina's husband) couldn't help and Merina was unable to answer that either. Regardless, she felt compelled to return to her sister's side for the kid's surgery. How long will she be gone? It's totally unclear. She might be back in a few days or gone for a couple weeks. If it's a couple weeks, then there's no point in her rejoining the production. Therefore, Forrest (our gaffer) and I will be sharing cinematographer duties. That adds to my list of already doing sound, script supervising, assistant directing, directing, slating, producing, fuck you name it. But it will be done.

..

I am now at the end of this day. Andrew was never able to film today. Apparently he had uncontrollable diarrhea. We made the most of it, working with our new system of sharing DP responsibilities and filming some coverage without him. This means tomorrow will be packed with scenes to catch up, almost doubling the amount of pages we were originally going to film. I hope we can get back on track. I don't think any film I've made has had a more rough beginning.

June 19th, 2020

Yesterday was both good and bad. Let's start with the good... Andrew made it to set and we were able to complete all the scenes we'd missed the day before plus capture the ones we already had scheduled. We did this without even going overtime, proving how efficient this small team can be.

The bad. When I first glanced at the footage Merina shot, I asked a technical question, "Is there a lut on this footage?" She said it was not. She was wrong.

The footage gets recorded "raw" and looks very bland/flat, giving the colorist the opportunity to fully control the later process of designing the look of the film. A lut is like a color template that gets placed over the footage to give a general idea of what the color might look like. With Merina back in California dealing with her emergency, Forrest and I are now handling things. The last couple days, we've been a little confused about the difference between what we "see in camera" while capturing a scene and what we're seeing when processing the footage later, especially in terms of things being too bright. He had received the same answer from Merina about the lut but once again, I asked him about it last night. "This footage doesn't look raw. It looks like there's something on it." Soon we discovered the problem. Somehow she'd managed to embed a lut into the footage. So normally, you just put the lut on in editing to see the potential look but this one is BURNED in to the footage. It can't be taken off. And this means that our first three days of footage have very little flexibility, very little range of color. This is why what Forrest and I were seeing in camera is different than what's being recorded. Is anything ruined? I wouldn't go that far. Some shots are on the edge of being too tough to work with. But we have to move on, we have to fix the issue and keep shooting now. At least we caught it three days in instead of six.

It's amazing how one little mistake can really screw a production!

June 20th, 2020

The last couple days we've really fallen into a rhythm, wrapping early both days. Today we finished before we were even scheduled to start filming our final scene. I credit the experience Forrest and I have from working together a couple times before, plus our personalities which are confident and assured in our decisions. We move very quickly, on the same page 9 times out of 10 and able to adapt easily when we're not. I think I would have had a similar relationship with Merina if she'd been able to stay and get into the rhythm with me. But that won't happen and with each passing day, we have such a groove going that I really don't want her to come back.

June 21st, 2020

We wrapped up the first week on GUIDE yesterday. Even with hiccups, like forgetting to change the lead's wardrobe before we drove 45 mins to a new location, we wrapped ahead of schedule. Our last scenes were filmed at an RV park in St. David with a couple ponds to use for a baptism in the story. Sounds silly to go all the way there but water is scarce in this part of Arizona. We successfully framed out the highway, trailers, and cars. This was my cameo, dressed in my Wild Wes wardrobe and being held under too long by the pastor when he sees his brother. As usual I was surprised at how hesitant the other actors were to get their feet wet, literally. I tromped into the middle of the pond and one person remarked, "you look pretty comfortable in there" as the other actors tiptoed their way in.

June 25th, 2020

Yesterday was the roughest so far in terms of heat and dealing with actors. We were confined to the general store, a location where a good portion of the movie takes place, and with the addition of lights, the temperature rose and rose throughout the day. It was certainly the first day that I can say the heat bothered me a couple of times. And that was only accentuated by the frustrations with some of our cast.

One actress, a nice lady who has been very supportive of me, even defending my reputation against recent attacks, was hard to work with. Like others in our cast, she could not implement the most simple blocking without it throwing off her lines and delivery. It's like these people memorize the words, imagining that they'll stay completely still. Typically, giving business to an actor helps them... not these people! They fall apart and require many takes to give a serviceable performance. Direction such as, "Say this line, bend over, say that line" is too complex. What you instead get is, "bend over, say the first line, second line gone completely." They have no good training, only bullshit acting classes that encourage their newfound hobby. Someone needs to break them hard like a drill sergeant and really teach them something about how a set works. My mind continues to be blown, as it was yesterday, when we roll a take of coverage on one actor and the other actor doesn't play the scene. "Oh, you want me to say my lines?" My response: "Yes, I want you to do exactly what the other actor did for you when it was your shot." I lost patience yesterday more than once.

...

Back to the heat, it wasn't just our bodies that were effected but the camera had issues for the first time. When trying to record 120 frames a second for a slow motion effect, it would cut itself, stopping the take automatically 10-12 seconds after recording began. We assumed that taping at this high speed was just too much for the machine in 107 degree heat. So we adapted into a kind of rapid fire method. I would say, "One, two, three, action" and Forrest would hit the record button right on action (no slate, no pre-roll at all) and the actor would immediately perform. Actually, it was fun working in this super fast way to capture our shots and proved effective.

June 26th, 2020

Good actors, even decent actors, make all the difference. Yesterday, same space as the day before, same heat (even a couple degrees hotter), same amount of blocking and scenes: totally different experience. We wrapped two hours early because we were sailing through set up after set up and the sweat didn't bother us near as much. We weren't suffering through performances.

In the final scene of the day, I decided to have the actor slide across the general store counter, the kind of move you might see in an old Cary Grant movie as he enters the scene in a dazzling way. We practiced and Andrew seemed to have it down. He suggested we not tell the actress what we planned, to get a genuine reaction. The actress also happens to be his intimate partner off screen. So take one. Andrew enters frame, hops up on the counter, slides across, and kicks Diana's hand! Thank goodness, she's a good sport. Clearly in pain, she continued through five or six more takes until we (or he) finally got it right.

June 28th, 2020

The last 36 hours were rough. Two nights ago, I planned to be in bed by 8pm for much needed rest but first I needed to meet our wagon team, coming with the wagon and horses all the way from Mississippi. The plan was to rendezvous at the Gammons set and drop the wagon for proceeding to a ranch

I'd rented for them to stay at. I waited in my car just off the road and the time of meeting came and went. Suddenly, Joanne (the set owner) was rolling down the dirt road in her golf cart. "They've had a breakdown right off the freeway." I couldn't know this of course because there's no cell service near the ranch or movie set. So the message had to be relayed through landlines.

Anyway, I headed their way. Thankfully, Caron (the woman providing horses for this film), followed me in her truck. We found the travelers only a short distance from the freeway. They'd successfully traversed the country only to get stopped a few miles from their destination. There was no fixing the truck and no idea what went wrong with it. Now the problem was what to do with the horses, the wagon, and ultimately where to put the people. Taking them to the ranch now seemed silly; I'd rented them a (not cheap) place there so that they could stay with the horses and that just wasn't possible anymore. So we went through a series of troubleshooting: Caron taking the wagon to the movie set, me taking the women to a hotel and then returning to watch the horse trailer alongside the road, Caron coming back and switching the horses to a smaller trailer so they too could be taken to the movie set. By the time it was all over with, four hours had passed and I was in bed after midnight. So much for catching up on that rest.

...

The next day was the most exhausting of our production so far. It did, however, have some great moments. John had thought of the idea to have one of us ride on top of the horses as they pulled the wagon, filming our actors as they drive it. This was the perfect angle and something daring we'd never tried before. Brad didn't bring two sets of lines for the team so there was no way he could hide in the wagon and have the actor "fake drive". Therefore, he had to teach Andrew how to drive a wagon in ten minutes. By the time he was done, the opera singer looked like a professional wagon master. Forrest got on one horse with the camera and I mounted the other with my boom mic. I won't lie, it was a little scary at first as the wagon moved and we rode backwards with no saddle, only a leather strap to hang onto, trying to avoid getting in the way of the driver's lines, aware that if the team spooked we might be down under those wagon wheels.

..

The rest of the wagon scenes went relatively well. Even starting an hour later than I'd originally scheduled, we were able to wrap early. The main struggle on set continues to be our actors. The two leads I have no issue with, both professional and prepared, fun to watch on screen. The others all struggle with everything from getting their lines right, hitting their marks, nailing their eye lines, incorporating my blocking, and ultimately giving us something interesting to spice up the scenes. They also struggle with listening, the ultimate human problem! When trying to block out this handheld tracking shot yesterday in which the main character is stalked down the street by a female gunfighter who wants to be famous from killing him, the actors wouldn't stop trying to complicate the process: "Where are the extras going to be?" "What about the horse?" etc. I just kept saying, "Focus. I'm not worried about that. We don't even have your movement down. Stop getting distracted and listen to me." They're worried about all these other things when I haven't even seen them give a usable rehearsal...

Every time Kim (playing the female gunfighter) returned to her mark, she'd re-enter a conversation with Anouschka (getting her cameo here) and this girl Maribel. Kim said after a few rehearsals, "It's so funny to do a take and then jump back into these little conversations over here." The distracting discussion coming from my own team member was already getting on my nerves and this gave me the opening I needed.

"Yeah, actually you two shouldn't be talking. You're not here to chat and have fun. We're here to work. You're distracting Kim. Focus on the work." Anouschka gave me one of her not-so-happy gazes. I could care less at this point.

...

You'd think the person with whom you share intimate moments with would be the least likely to giving you problems on set. Wrong. Of all the cast, someone I have been dating is the only person who has given me schedule issues, signed up for filming two days ago but suddenly asking, "when's my call time? Can it be earlier in the day? When can I leave?" because of a new gig she got on another film. For me, professionalism is that you stick with the job you signed up to do, not screw that job over when you get a new one. And again, she's supposed to be close to me, yet she's the one being a hassle. In such situations, I just shut down. "Don't come to set. It's fine. I don't need you in the scene." So I cut her out of that scene, frustrated. Then the day of filming, I get this text, "well, ya know, I might try to make it down in time. I'm just not sure." Blah blah blah. I said, "We talked about this. I already told you that you've been cut from the scene. I even removed you from the call sheet." She accused me of being mean. I told her that the truth isn't mean. We talked about it. A decision was made. I made the mistake again of trying to explain myself, sending a long message about professionalism, about how I need support not stress from the people closest to me. All I got in return was replies about her, her fun on this other set, etc. No acknowledgement of my statements. So my final reply was simply this, "Please don't text me again unless it's urgent. We don't understand each other. Thanks."

I feel this Southern Arizona chapter of my life, of my project, finally coming to an end. I must admit that I need to get away from these people, other than John. It's time for a change, a new direction for these Westerns.

June 30th, 2020

Yesterday was the end of week two and also the end of Forrest's work on the film. I believe we grew closer during this production, not in a personal way, but as comrades. Yes, it would have been possible to make the film without his assistance as a co-cinematographer but it would not have been nearly as easy or as fun. I'd sign up for another war with him any day.

Now the third week awaits us, one man down. Thankfully, it is a lighter load of scenes. I watch a piece of Bergman's *Passion of Anna* every night, yearning to see a different kind of cinema than I have recently and also hungry for making a different kind of Western with *The New Frontier*.

July 1st, 2020

John and I went to Tombstone, on a mission to complete the female wardrobe pieces for *Frontier* that we hadn't found from the generous donation by Renee (Gaslight Theatre in Tucson). From store to store, we searched for ladies' pants and more, confused by women's sizes. After being somewhat successful and spending a hundred dollars, we retreated to one of the only bars open because of COVID, had a few beers, and share stories about women.

July 2nd, 2020

Well, it's happened once again... I wasted weeks talking to this couple who assured me they could provide tons of horses and a stagecoach for our Pearl Hart movie. I repeatedly told them, "Let's just focus on the stagecoach," as they continued to talk big about how they could provide all this, costumes, extras, etc.

Yesterday, they informed me that their schedule has suddenly become so busy that they cannot even commit one day to the production. What is wrong with people? So many people I encounter in this journey to make 12 Westerns in 12 Months are neither reliable or honest and ironically that's what Westerns are all about! Also, what is wrong with Arizona? You'd think we'd have an abundance of people eager to help make Westerns with wagons and stagecoaches. For this recent movie, I had to bring a wagon all the way from Mississippi. That was more affordable than getting one right here! Furthermore, the main wagon person in Southern Arizona won't answer his phone the last couple months and has a full voicemail... it's frustrating and comical. Alas, I am looking for a damn stagecoach once again.

...

Yesterday though wasn't a complete bust. John and I drove up to the cabin I've chosen for *NEW FRONTIER*, meeting Jared and his girlfriend Elizabeth along the way. This proved to be a fruitful journey: it eased my fears of how much design would need to be done to make the location work, it gave John and I a good idea about what to do on our three prep days, it also relieved concerns about logistics such as cooking, keeping food cold, lodging, etc.

Molly, whose husband owns the place, is such a big help. She's provided a ton of locations for the Pearl Hart movie and now this. I am grateful for our connection. There's so much to do in the next two weeks but I now feel more steady about what needs to be done.

July 3rd, 2020

I made the budget for *New Frontier* this morning, a project I'm funding out of my own pocket and a few hundred in donation money. It's scary but necessary. I'm having to pay myself ahead of time for doing sound on *Guide*, sound on *Texas Red*, editing, etc. in order to have enough funds to cover the costs to make this little film. Even with only three leading ladies, camera and everything adds up to more than five thousand, maybe seven thousand when it's all done. I'll make it work somehow. My mind keeps returning to what Herzog said, that he never worried about money. Somehow it came.

July 4th, 2020

This is our last day at Gammons. Originally we had a scene to shoot today but we got it in the can a few days ago so it's just clean up. I have no sentimental feelings about leaving the place. It's been enough fun and it's been enough trouble. It has served its place in the 12 Westerns just as certain people have. Time for new places and people. Time for a new chapter in this project to begin.

July 5th

After a terrific steak lunch prepared by Lucy, we departed from Gammons. The load out was not as challenging as I thought. As predicted Joanne had many things for us to move back into place or move to new places but not nearly as much as she made it sound, always making a bigger deal of things than they need to be. That's her nature and it won't change.

July 6th, 2020

I was on edge yesterday, a feeling that may have started as the plumber helping fix Lucy's well at the ranch unintentionally blew several of our takes in the first set up by walking through the frame, talking, slamming doors, etc. He just didn't understand what was going on but it was nevertheless frustrating as we tried to get the shot while life at the ranch continued on, not giving a shit about movie making.

I heard from my makeup artist that the actress playing the young woman in *Frontier* is concerned about her nude scenes. This was frustrating for two reasons: 1. That the actress didn't come to me directly, a trend that I told the makeup artist needs to end immediately. 2. She agreed, as the others did, to my "nudity breakdown". This puts me more on edge and I fear that I may have a last minute replacement just around the corner. The problem is, I have no options for that replacement.

July 7th, 2020

The final day of Western #6. It does not feel like an accomplishment to be halfway, just as I don't think I would feel accomplished halfway up the ascent of Everest. I know where I am. I know what still needs to be done. Tomorrow is another day doing it. Here is something I wrote for facebook this morning reflecting on lessons learned the last six months.

Six Lessons I've Learned So Far While Making 12 Westerns in 12 Months...

I reflected on these this morning and may elaborate on them down the road but here's a brief summary:

1. SMALL CREWS ARE BETTER THAN BIG CREWS

I've always preferred a small crew but on these Westerns, I've learned that even 4-5 people is better than my usual 8-

10, especially if those handful are hard workers. On the films so far where we had a larger crew, we suffered more issues with communication, workflow, and morale, which brings me to the next lesson.

2. NEGATIVITY AND BAD ATTITUDES ARE THE NUMBER #1 PROBLEM ON SET.

I'd seen this before but the last six months have confirmed this is the biggest problem making movies. Whether it's a person who can't avoid creating drama, someone who doesn't understand the damaging effects of complaining/gossiping behind my back, or an individual who just can't put the movie in front of their own emotions, bad attitudes are worse than a virus on set. They're contagious and ultimately destructive. There's only one solution to these kinds of people: don't work with them anymore.

3. I WANT TO RELY LESS AND LESS ON THE SCRIPT

Whether I wrote the screenplay or someone else did, I find myself leaning less and less on the pages. There can be downsides to this, like missing details but it feels like the direction I want to go. For me, the scripted scene is just an idea to bounce off of. From there, the actors move around the space and action/dialog both change to work in that moment. This requires flexible actors who can think on their feet with me. Instead of fighting this direction, I'm going to follow it and see where it leads me.

4. ACTION IS BEST WHEN SHOT IN THE MOST SIMPLE WAY

Certainly with *COUNTING BULLETS*, I was challenged to shoot more action than I have in any other films. With Last of the Mohicans and traditional Westerns as a model, we decided to avoid complicated choreography and shots.

Instead, there's the simple tool of cutting from cause and effect, action and reaction. This proved to be more successful than my previous attempts to stage fight scenes and I want to continue to improve these methods.

5. KEEPING UP WITH POST-PRODUCTION WILL BE THE BIGGEST CHALLENGE GOING FORWARD

I have already felt how difficult it is to make films and move them through post-production at the same time. This phase isn't just editing; it's sound mixing, color, music composition, and more. It's a lot. Trying to sound mix *BASTARD'S CROSSING* has taken far longer than I hoped it would. At the same time, we aren't behind schedule with post. I just know that it's going to be a continuous struggle to stay on schedule!

6. "JUST BECAUSE THE WORLD IS CRAZY DOESN'T MEAN THAT YOU HAVE TO BE."

Wise words from my friend and mentor Gus Edwards. We live in a crazy world right now, no one can deny that. It's made even crazier by our inability to see beyond ourselves and our fear. From the media to our politicians to everyday people, we are surrounded by a culture of in-the-moment hysteria. I have tried to stay steady, to always fight falling for the trends, to not to swept up by the waves. In the past six months, I have tried to stay the course and I think the 12 Westerns in 12 Months has been one of the rare, consistent things we can all count on. The words Gus shared with me continue to be a daily inspiration. The world may be spinning out of control but, if we are strong, we can all remain steadfast and true.

Leading lady Diane Ouradnik.

For a wagon shot, Forrest Sandefer and I mounted the horse team with boom and camera.

Scottish actor John Peacock framed up for a tight close-up.

John Marrs "wrangles" Harry the dog, who has sadly since passed away.
All photographs by Production Crew

THE NEW FRONTIER

Also conceived at the dawn of the 12 Westerns, first scripted in 2014, The New Frontier or Frontier as it was originally called has always been a passion project. I knew it would be difficult if not impossible to find funding for. My investors tend to be more conservative with their choices and a lesbian-themed B&W Western with werewolves seemed a little far fetched to appeal to their sensibilities. I ended up funding this entirely on my own, paying myself for various jobs on the other projects and going broke to get it made.

It also seemed challenging to find the right actresses to pull off these characters, not to mention people open-minded enough to even dare to approach the material. I was very fortunate to find the three leading ladies and I will always be grateful for this experience, so far my best collaboration with actors. I will do my best to describe the bizarre plot:

Morgan and Willa live in an isolated cabin in the Western frontier with no connection to the outside world. One day, a stranger arrives on horseback. This new woman intrigues the young and impressionable Willa while posing a challenge of power with Morgan. As the tension unravels and a supernatural force lurks in the mountains nearby, the truth of this alternative Western world is revealed to both us the audience and the film's characters.

Photograph by Todd South

July 8th, 2020

There's barely any time between productions this time. Today, Corey's coming down to get the RV, all my things packed to leave the ranch, and it will probably take all of the day to get up to Superior.

Tomorrow will be the only day in between as the next I'll be headed to the cabin location to start prep with John for *Frontier*. At least the new environment will be a kind of break.

July 9th, 2020

My prediction about it taking all day was accurate, unfortunately. The Adventures of Travis and Corey continue. He arrived late with Abe, a Phoenix musician who also had a cameo in the silent film. Immediately, problems began as we couldn't get the RV to start. Corey went through a series of troubleshooting: trying different batteries, re-wiring things, etc. Finally, Lucy offered for us to take a battery out of one of her own vehicles, which she then offered to sell to Corey. "You didn't want to sell it to me when I asked," I interjected. "A lady is always allowed to change her mind." "At the expense of men," I grumbled as we continued to work, getting the RV running and backed out of the driveway. We had a quick cool drink and snack, then hit the road. I drove in front with my car, Corey commanded the big beast, and Abe took up the tail in his vehicle. The first half of what should be a 2.5 hour drive was nearly perfect. Corey just had one stretch where he felt he was running out of gas but we quickly reached the first station on the trek and filled up again. From there, I followed behind and Abe sped ahead to meet us in Superior. This was the stretch with the most incline and decline. The real problems began. The RV started stalling out on a bridge that had already been taken down to one lane because of construction. If Corey hadn't got the engine going again, we would have caused a major disaster, blocking forty or more cars.

Those stalling troubles continued as we approached bigger and bigger hills. On one ascent, he stalled out every few feet, having to start the engine again, make a little progress before it died, and then go all over again. We got out to investigate further. He tried a bunch of things, using his often brilliant mechanical mind to find a solution. We made another attempt and didn't get far before having to pull over again. By this point, Abe called and Corey told him to leave for Phoenix. "Don't wait around for us. Travis can take me home." It was dark now. Corey suggested what sounded nuts to me, "Have you ever seen *Mad Max Fury Road*? You know how the bad guys spit gas into their cars to make them go faster? That's what we need to do. It isn't getting enough fuel!" He filled two of my empty Gatorade bottles with gasoline and cut a hole in the bottle cap. The plan was to spray extra gas into the carburetor as he drove, hopefully giving the engine just enough power to reach the top. I followed, apprehensive. To my surprise, his method worked, though we stopped again at the bottom of the next hill as he stuck his head out the driver's window and called for another empty bottle. He'd sprayed the entire first one just to make it a quarter of a mile or less. We continued with this method and finally overcame the steep part of the journey, coasting down into the town of Superior. But the journey wasn't over. After parking the vehicle, Corey climbed into mine for the trip to Phoenix, dehydrated and overheated from driving the RV with the engine cover off. He slowly began to feel better again. Arriving in Phoenix was surreal. For some reason, being in Southern Arizona for so long, mostly secluded at the ranch and movie set, my old stomping ground feels like a different world, like it belongs in an alternate universe. I plopped down on one of Corey's couches and it didn't take long to fall asleep.

July 11th, 2020

I'm now up at the cabin where we'll film *The New Frontier*. Corey and I hauled the gear with the help of another eccentric mechanic named Terry. Soon after, John arrived and we looked over what needed to be done, feeling confident we can knock it out this weekend without much trouble. We drank a few beers, drove to Roosevelt for dinner, and came back to have a couple glasses of whiskey. The usual conversation ensued during the process: Westerns and women.

I feel behind again. So much of my energy was focused on *Bullets*, *Guide*, and post-production that I have not put the same amount of pre-production work into this film and *Pearl*. With *Frontier*, it isn't as big of a deal since I am approaching it in a loose way. For *Pearl*, I need to get my shit together and start producing asap.

July 12th, 2020

John and Todd South did a majority of the work yesterday, dressing the set to success while I ran for supplies in Globe. On my return, there wasn't much left to do. It shows how effective the decisiveness of men can be. Todd seems like a real good guy. He doesn't drink, smoke, or even consume coffee and I expect he's a "believer" but he seems comfortable around us fuck-saying whiskey consuming fellows.

Our makeup artist and Alyssa will be coming in late, late tonight because they didn't leave Louisiana on time. I'll have to set an alarm to meet them. Jared comes in today too. He and I don't seem to be understanding each other on some aspects of the process. He often asks "Travis, what do you think of how this looks", pointing out a decision I made. "Well, Jared, I did that. So of course I like it." It's like a roundabout energy-wasting way of saying, this isn't working for me. Another thing I hope to overcome with him in the near future is a recurring situation where I like a shot/scene/line of dialog and he doesn't. Then he wants me to come up with another solution. For the *Bastard's Crossing* poster, I came up with a tag line. "What do you think of it, Travis?" "I think it's good, Jared, that's why I wrote it." "Travis, I don't like it. What do you think we should change it to?" "Jared, it works for me. I'm not going to spend energy trying to change something that I think works. If you want something different, find a solution yourself." It's an interesting creative riff we don't seem to be able to repair at the moment.

July 13th, 2020

The ladies' estimated arrival went from 11 to past midnight to 2 to 2:41 as they finally made it past Globe, apparently having stopped to eat and take bathroom breaks every two miles. After hanging with Jared and John on the porch, where John and I both passed out for an hour or so, I set my alarm for 2 and woke up to go meet the incoming members of our team out at the main road. There was no way I'd take a chance on them finding the cabin in the dark. Their ETA came and went as I sat watching the rest of Scorsese's *Italianamerican* and listening to another episode of Bogdanovich's podcast, leaning my head on the window sill and trying not to fall back asleep. Finally, at 3:15am, they rolled up and I led them to our current abode.

Jared expressed concerns about our time to light and shoot these scenes while being as flexible and loose as I want to be. I hope we will find the rhythm as we usually do.

July 14th, 2020

It begins. I did not get as much sleep as I hoped last night in preparation for our first day of filming. Pulled into too many directions and conversations, I felt the time I was supposed to be resting taken away minute by minute.

I am now worried about our makeup artist. Sure enough, she exhibits similar traits to some crew members I've struggled with in the past: disorganized/last minute, an attitude, an energy that makes you want to ask them "if you're not enjoying this, why are you here?" I have only two hopes for her at this point. One, that she is overwhelmed with the good attitudes of the cast and is unable to be a problem because she's outnumbered. Two, that an early heart to heart with her will lead to self awareness and improvement. Seeing these traits again makes me feel that there's a sickness in some people, a disease of negativity and insecurity that destroys them and everything around them. It's way worse than the virus.

On the other hand, I had a great conversation with Jenna, playing Morgan. She came in from Montana for this. John picked her up at the airport and revealed how excited she is when he got back to the cabin. I felt that excitement in a late night conversation with her. She seems like the one who will really understand my work flow for this, a true actress. I am also impressed with Alyssa, playing the young character of Willa. She explodes with enthusiasm. I cast her sight unseen but I am constantly stunned when looking at her at how lucky a choice it was. She appears like a fifteen year old (and is actually 22) in a role that I could never have gotten away with casting a 15 year old in. I actually look forward to digging in with these actors and hope to find a new joy for working with actors that I have not felt in a while.

Finally, more and more, I am trying to abandon old methods with this story and steer away from logic. Instead I want the shots and scenes to be driven by emotion. I want this film to feel female in the sense that it makes sense only in an emotional way.

July 15th, 2020

Our first day was a mixed bag. The one undeniable element of success was the actresses, who I really enjoy working with. They're bringing the energy and commitment I had hoped for.

Jenna was the first to have a nude scene. When we approached it, I told her immediately that our shot for the scene was different than she and I had originally discussed (a kind of far away, looking through a doorway shot with a full frontal view). But now Jared and I wanted to put the camera through the window and closer but leave Jenna partially out of focus. I insisted she look at the shot before with Alyssa standing in. I explained it and how she'd be revealed. She understood and seemed comfortable. "After the take, I want you to watch it and confirm you feel good about it." "I don't need to watch it," she responded. "I trust you." Though I appreciated this, I insisted: "I want you to see it. There should be no surprises." I wanted her to confirm the way her breasts are shown, etc. So we did exactly that and she said it was beautiful. I liked it because the moment feels more free like the European cinema I've always wanted to make.

...

Throughout the day, Jared and I struggled to find a rhythm. He put way more lighting time into the scenes than I thought he would. Even the exteriors. He wants it to look good and so do I but I worry about our pace. Otherwise we worked in unison.

...

The conversation between the makeup artist and I ended up happening in the evening. She again wanted to reiterate how much work she's put in and ask for appreciation. I officially hate when anyone asks for "good job". It reminds me of Howard Hawks pictures and how far our society is from that way of being where you just do your job, don't ask for anything, and you know how good you are. I encouraged her to be confident, to be fulfilled by knowing she's doing well instead of needing someone else's approval. I also told her that if she stops being defensive about everything, maintains a positive attitude, and does her job then she will hear appreciation. She seemed to understand.

July 17th, 2020

This film continues to be one of the most difficult I've made. It's deceptive, simple on the surface and complex as hell beneath. Every day we struggle to stay on time and get our scenes, compared to the last movie we made when we wrapped early every day.

...

Yesterday I grew incredibly frustrated when we left the location to go have lunch at our cabin and I couldn't find Bandit. I spent 10 to 15 minutes looking for him with no luck, finally wondering if he'd jumped in one of the other vehicles. So I returned to the cabin, anxious, and sure enough that's what had happened. Someone had picked him up for no goddamn good reason and taken him back, something that had never happened before or had been discussed. "I hollered for you," was their excuse. Angry, I loaded bandit back up in the car and skipped lunch, wanting to cool down by myself away from humans. I sat on location and read the script. Later that day, one of our actresses Elley said, "You were nice. I would have lost my shit." Of all our team, I knew she'd understood.

...

The ladies are interesting to work with. Jenna is the easiest. I feel we have a true connection. Elley is more stoic but also very professional, prompt in every moment. She's no funny business, a habit she may have developed from years of modeling. I like working with her more each day and feel our connection forming. Alyssa is very good, especially for her age. She feels like a 15 year old though she's 22. When asking for her to express desire in scenes, she often goes straight to technical results, "so should I do this or that with my mouth. Should I make it longer, slower?" I have grown impatient a couple times with these questions, saying "just feel desire. If you feel it, the camera will see it." She looks at me perplexed when I say this. Ultimately though, we have been able to reach the result.

...

It is official. John Sayles has agreed to his voice cameo in *Texas Red*, signed the SAG contract, and even recorded his role. This is one of the most important moments of the 12 Westerns for me, of my filmmaking career. He's one of my heroes.

July 21st, 2020

What a crazy series of days it has been... A few nights ago, we stayed up late to prepare for the fifth day of production which would be a late night shoot. All tired already, we drank whiskey and beer, chatting into the early morning hours in order to reset our internal clocks. By the end of this, it was just Elley, Jared and myself. I told them goodnight and headed for my bedroom only to find someone in my bed! It was the makeup artist, who had drank quite a bit and started saying annoying things as usual. Well, here she was in the master bedroom, tucked under the covers. I didn't know if it was a come on, a move to have sex with me, or just a drunken mistake. Regardless, I called Elley and Jared to attention and informed them of what happened. They found the situation quite humorous. I slept on the couch... not interested in testing a potential compromising situation.

Cut to the morning. I knew the makeup artist would raise the subject at some point. She came over, sheepish, and apologized for what she described as a black out drunk moment where she did not realize at all she was getting in someone else's bed. "Don't worry about it," I said, not believing a word she said, especially considering that her bedroom is upstairs and is nothing like mine. There was some intention and this was proven more true when only an hour later she had returned to my bedroom. Suddenly, I received facebook messages with pictures of her laying in my bed, asking me to come cuddle her for 10 minutes. I was shocked and did not know what to do but it confirmed my growing suspicions that she was looking for a new form of appreciation and reassurance. I ignored her. Elley could tell something was odd. I would explain later, anxious to get out of the house for my return to Globe. Along the drive, I recorded a video asking this person to focus on being positive, focus on the task at hand (something I've consistently requested of her), and that I appreciate her work so far. The message seemed to encourage her and also relieve what physical/sexual thing she needed from me.

Her attitude has become the only problem with this production and its one that plagues us all. To my surprise, I am not the only one she drives crazy and I might actually be the one best at tolerating her irritating behavior. The actresses are so affected by it that they've tried to pull themselves away at any opportunity. John called her a "train wreck". Jared just shakes his head, discouraged that we've run into yet another one of these types. The last night of week one production, I came close to firing her as she asked, "Travis, why do you hate me?" I told her I didn't, that I only want her to do her job and be a positive person on set. Finally, I had to remind her that she is the only one of us having any kind of issues getting along. She refuted this but maybe somewhere deep down inside it sunk in because she was more tolerable the rest of the night. Firing her would be more drama than it is worth. I hope we can survive the last week.

...

Our late night shoot to capture the werewolf scenes was the most challenging of the film so far. I hoped we would wrap at 3am at the latest but we were still filming when the sun rose. With the costume process, playing with rain and lightning effects in darkness, and the difficulty of blocking the shots, it just took much longer than we hoped. Jenna was spent, practically drained of energy between takes but mustering enough to get the moments during them. I can only hope that these scenes will be effective and I feel there is a large burden on the post process, especially the sound design I'll be in charge of, to make sure they are.

To top that night off and the following one (which went till 2am), John's dogs got lost. First, Duke disappeared, giving us all a heart attack. And then the next night Ginger vanished, not returning until 5:30am in the morning. John was a wreck inside, I could tell. Like me, his dogs are his best friends.

July 23rd, 2020

As the production for the *Pearl Hart* film nears, I feel the most unprepared I have felt in this entire process. I got so sucked into battling through COVID to make these summer movies that the fall films were neglected. All I can do is keep chipping away and work as well as I can. Somehow the films will get made or others will in their place.

July 27th, 2020

Another production has come to an end. This one comes with the greatest contrast of feelings I can remember. On one hand, I admire my actresses and already miss them. This sentiment applies most to Elley. I loved her sarcastic wit, her never-failing professionalism. Seeing her ride the horse onto a mark, seeing her help us load gear, seeing her laugh... she's great.

...

On the other hand, our makeup artist ranks in the top five disasters of the 12 Westerns so far, right along the pandemic and suicide. Everyone on the team has grown in increasing frustration towards her. I finally snapped yesterday when she left a bunch of trash on set, claiming she'd finished cleaning up after herself with complete inaccuracy. First she said, "Well I was hoping you'd clean that up for me," still not understanding how any of this process works and then revised her intentions, "I just didn't see it." She continued to pester me, claiming how much she's cleaned up after us in the big cabin till I finally snapped, yelling at her to put down the broom she was using, go clean up her mess on set, and do nothing more. She then went into super pout mode, claiming she would leave late that night with or without Alyssa (actress) who she carpooled with from Louisiana. I spent a good hour of the night arguing with her and saying she would not be paid if she left early. Amazingly enough, she failed to see that she was actually contracted to work today too. She and everyone here is getting off a day early. Just now, after paying her, she suddenly tells me "I need some of that money in cash. My card is cancelled. Oh and I don't have enough gas in my tank to get to the next gas station."

Good god... If one thing changes in my work after the 12 Westerns, it's that I need to work with a small team of reliable people who have been tested and vetted. I'm never going into another production after this journey with anyone whose personality is a mystery.

July 28th, 2020

I feel crazy pressure about my return to Mississippi with currently zero funding for the barrel racing movie. Something needs to happen and happen soon.

Today I'm headed to Tilting H again to scout for *Heart of the Gun* again. It will be nice to see Nick and start sorting out details for that film.

July 29th

When I arrived at Tilting H yesterday, it felt good to see Peter and Carol who have weathered through a couple months of slow business but I was disappointed that they were not quite prepared to show us everything we wanted to see on the property. Their off-roading vehicles were not all running and therefore we couldn't venture to the far stretches of the property where Indian ruins, caves, and more remain a sight unseen. Still, we made progress, roaming around in the near vicinity with Nick to choose some of the locations featured early in the film. It felt good to nail down specifics and know the exact spots where we'll be for several scenes.

We rode out to a scenic creek with high cliff walls, a spot I wanted to see again with fresh eyes. On our return, the Polaris four-wheel drive vehicle broke down. Pete tried to start it with no luck. This happened just as a rain cloud moved over our heads. He told Nick and I to find something to hide under as he headed for higher ground to get cell service and call back to the ranch for transport. Nick and I awkwardly hid over a small rock overhang where the only part of me that stayed dry was my head which I continually bumped on the rocks above. We spoke about the production and plans for making the movie to fill the time as rain poured down. Eventually we saw the ranch manager Kenny driving up in another vehicle. Turns out Pete had given up on cell service and jogged all the way back to the ranch in the pouring rain. We hopped in the back of Kenny's 4x4 and finished the scout.

July 30th

Yesterday was a long one. The first goal was to move out of the cabin and back down to the RV parked in Superior. If I hadn't had help from a friend, there's no way I would have been able to load out all of the things I needed to. My Corolla was packed to the ceiling and still we had to pack things in her truck. By 10am, we'd landed and I could already feel the heat difference, missing the cool air of the mountains immediately. I unloaded everything and then immediately jumped on my first "zoom call" with a person advising better ways to raise money on this new platform we're using. Right after, I called Don Collier, a veteran Western actor, to see if he was interested in playing in *Heart of the Gun*. An old-timer just like Buck Taylor, he wouldn't give me an email address so today I've got to mail him a copy.

Next I spoke with Dallas Sonnier, the head of the production company that made *Bone Tomahawk*, *Brawl*, and *Dragged Across Concrete*. We'd emailed back and forth a month or so ago and he asked me to follow up in late July. The conversation went well. His right wing leanings were definitely clear as he complained about trying and struggling to get movies made for people who don't subscribe to this "globalist, progressive" agenda. I liked talking to him. "You definitely need to work with us," he claimed and spoke of me directing a 400-500k Western for them first. The talk ended with the idea that we needed to find the right script. If he found one, he'd let me know. If I found one, I should let him know.

Suddenly it all seemed a little far-fetched and not as real as it had in other moments of discussion. Nevertheless, I will keep my fingers crossed. Maybe we can work together someday.

...

I got in the car and drove to Florence where we saw the old courtroom, perfect for the *Pearl Hart* movie. It was 115 degrees on the drive there and back and without AC I felt like I was in a traveling toaster. I'm getting that fixed soon. I returned to the RV and Bandit to work some and then hop on yet another call, this time with Henry Parke of True West Magazine. We spoke at length about the 12 Westerns and he says an article could hit sometime in February.

I worked on *Bastard's* the rest of the night until I passed out.

Montana-based actress Jenna Ciralli plays Morgan.

Elley Ringo's bright red hair and the matching red blood never showed up in our B&W images.

Boom operating while directing again with our tiny crew.

Louisiana-based actress Alyssa Dufren plays Willa.
All photographs by Todd South

THE WOMAN WHO ROBBED THE STAGECOACH

The story of Pearl Hart was a tough nut to crack. Though a proper feature film has never been made about her, I could not decide how I wanted to approach her tale. Ultimately, the decision was made to use the iPhone as our filming tool, hoping to give the film a kind of French New Wave realism. Another bold move was made in the casting: a non-actor was chosen for the lead role. Lorraine had never made a film before or even taken an acting class. Again, this relates back

to the New Wave and the Italian Neorealist movement before it in which non-actors were often chosen for the protagonists.

Even if this movie was not as fun to make as The New Frontier and Counting Bullets, I will always be proud of these decisions and feel they've led to a new kind of Western we haven't seen before. The story of Pearl Hart follows a young woman who goes through a series of bad experiences with men, leading her to the life of an outlaw and a partnership with a goofy European drifter named Joe Boot.

Photograph by Todd South

July 31st, 2020

I feel like I'm squatting, close to homeless, like living in my car just with more space. No shower. I have to go to the gas station to take a shit. One day if I ever live in a "comfortable" environment it will be interesting to look back on these times.

...

Made some progress yesterday as John finally got a confirmation from Peter Sherayko (*Tombstone*). He's not a big deal but still brings some notoriety with him which may help us get others. I am interested in offering Bo Hopkins, the last of the *Wild Bunch*, a role. The workload right now, especially with post-production, is enormous. I just have to keep my eyes on the pavement and take one step at a time.

August 1st, 2020

In a little over a week from now I'm supposed to shoot the saloon scenes for the Pearl Hart movie and I have no saloon. The one I wanted seemed available and then suddenly the woman who owns it was going to be out of town. But if I move it a day back, she might be able to do it. So I'm about to get in my car and drive back up the mountain to see it with my own eyes, see if it's worth adjusting the schedule for.

Yuma Prison lowered their fee from 1500 dollars total to $900. It's still a lot and more than I have for this movie but I feel compelled to say yes. With Herzog's philosophy that the money will come somehow, I proceed.

August 2nd, 2020

The other day I very much enjoyed working with Lorraine, the non actress playing Pearl Hart, in our rehearsal outside a coffee shop in Globe. She had lots of questions about the character, some of them good and maybe some a little too much. She seemed to be digging psychiatrist-style into Pearl, not a bad thing, but I reminded her that when filming begins, we can't be in our heads, we just have to feel it and go. She agreed. She was struggling with some of the motivations but I felt like every issue she brought up I responded to with sound reasoning. I didn't see it then but she was fighting the character or at least my direction for the character. This became apparent last night.

She expressed via text that the character never feels sorry for herself. I asked her to explain what she meant and instead she got distracted with other things, sending me wardrobe pictures for hours. Later on, it came up again in a series of three video messages where she thoroughly explained some dialog/scene changes she wanted to make to the script. I was open to hear as always and a couple ideas were either good or acceptable. But the changes started to grow as she went on, eventually altering some pretty significant story moments. I gave her a call as requested after watching. I explained what I liked and what I wanted to stay the same. The debate began. "Analysis is good," I told her, "but I feel like you digging into the character's head has turned into you fighting the character and the script rather than embracing and falling in love with her." She confessed: "I'm trying but I'm struggling with these things and have since I first read it." If she'd made me aware of that before, it's my mistake for not paying attention but I suspect these were dormant thoughts at most till now. She complained about Pearl not seeming strong enough early on (one of her changes removed the section where Pearl is a drug addict). "She's a vulnerable girl who gets used by men over and over. Something is wrong with her that she is drawn to these men who take advantage of her multiple times. She gains strength slowly through the pain of that happening. I've known many women like that." This did not move Lorraine in the slightest: "it's your script and we'll do it your way but from the start I felt this was a script about a woman from a man's perspective." It was here that I made my only faux pas in the conversation. I should have said, "Yes it is." I mean, how do you argue with a statement like that? It comes from this bullshit modern mindset that one person can't make an accurate portrayal of another kind of person's life, something that has been proven wrong through storytelling time and time again. Instead of just accepting that statement, I decided to argue against it, citing my experience with *Silver Slipper* where many female audience members were blown away by how I'd captured the perspective of an 18 year old girl. Mistake. One, I don't think this example meant anything to her. Two, even if she did watch that film now, she'd be looking at it in a tainted way rather than just receiving it freely like those other women.

Ultimately we disagree about aspects of Pearl. At one point she remarked, "Pearl is never shown becoming like her heroes, like Julia Ward Howe." My response: "Well she didn't. That's the truth. Just didn't become some important female leader. Most of her life was a fuck up after a fuck up. She just happened to fuck up once in a way that made her famous but even after that she failed repeatedly to capitalize on her fame, going on the road with a play about her life that did not succeed and disappearing into obscurity." She had nothing to say to this. People want to make something out of Pearl that she isn't. They always have. I of course am making my version of Pearl but I don't believe I've tried to make her into anything. While reading her story, this is what I saw. A life of repeated mistakes. A picaresque tale.

August 3rd, 2020

I've just moved to Miami, to the art collective space where we'll be staying for the first portion of this production. I am so used to staying wherever that it is no big deal for me but I am curious to see how John, Sushila, and Isaac will take to the environment which definitely has a hippie vibe. As I told John just now, it's better than camping.

...

I continue to feel affection for one of the actresses in these Westerns. It's certain that I have fallen for her, though it's a foolish desire. Even if she felt the same, which I doubt, she is attached and happily so from all I can tell. Even more foolish, I have been tempted to tell her, just to get it done and off my chest. However, I decided today to keep it secret and to use it as an acting secret for the character I'm playing in this film. Originally, I thought my natural connection to Lorraine (Pearl) would be enough to fool Joe Boot's bumbling, awkward love for her. Now, in light of her recent struggles with the script and my take on the character, I am not so sure. At the rehearsal the other day, I found myself using that other person I'm fond of. "I see you work. Hard. Strong," I said, looking in Lorraine's eyes but thinking of someone else. Bresson said that film acting was all about hiding so perhaps this secret will help and then when I am finished playing the character I can let it go.

August 5th, 2020

Yesterday, I traveled out with Bandit to rendezvous with Todd South and scout Box Canyon. He showed me a great spot he'd found for the stagecoach robbery. It was good to see him again, another no-nonsense team member. We complained about the media and COVID on the drive in and out, both frustrated with all the contradictions of our society.

...

I wasn't home long before Lorraine (Pearl Hart) came over. We started talking through scenes and then met up with Molly, the person who has set up most of our locations in

Globe and owns the cabin where we shot *Frontier*. She has some wardrobe that might work for Pearl but going through it began to tire me. I'm looking for quick, concrete decisions which is the opposite of Molly's style and Lorraine continues to see things differently than me.

We stood on Molly's balcony, overlooking Globe, unable to come inside because of COVID concerns as Molly brought out one piece at a time to us. Lorraine, continuing to question my take on Pearl, asked, "How much do you know about women anyway?" I answered, "As much as someone can know about a thing without actually being that thing." I started to see (and she even started to admit) that some of the aspects of the character she struggles with most might be the ones that connect most with her own life. She confessed that Pearl's inability to find real success in life reminds her of her own journey or at least the way those around have perceived it. I think Lorraine's relationship with her boyfriend also reminds her of Pearl but not in a way she's comfortable realizing. My first impression of this guy, without having met him, came when she requested to let him visit the *Frontier* set. I asked why, suspecting that she was trying to ease his jealousy/insecurity over the "film thing". Sure enough that was it and I told her that a working set is no place to indulge such insecurities, that I'd be up for grabbing dinner with him instead. She defended him yesterday, calling him "possessive" but stating all his other good qualities, but I couldn't help feeling like she was stretching to justify her relationship. Yet when it comes to Pearl, she is always questioning why the woman hooked up with these men. I believe Lorraine is really questioning herself, her own decisions.

It's not going to be a smooth ride with her. I can tell that. I hope that she falls into the rhythm of filming and that these struggles ease. When all this started, I felt a genuine connection with her. Now that has almost completely faded.

August 6th, 2020

John arrived last night. We grabbed a burger and a beer and caught up on all things. John is taking a position at the manager of Gammons Gulch, the town where we filmed three of the 12. It's a good opportunity for him but only if the owner Joanne can really get out of his way and let him run the place the way it should be run.

We discussed how we're behind on this film, how it caught up to us too quickly. But I think we will sort our way through.

August 8th, 2020

Filming started yesterday with scenes shot at a local inn that served as both the boarding school and Pearl's family home. Working on the iPhone isn't easy. We quickly discovered some of its disadvantages. Because it's a lightweight camera, we had to be very conscious of not making the floor shake while it was on a tripod. At other times, we struggled with its settings, figuring things out as we went. Finally, when reviewing the footage from our first day, we discovered new frustrating issues with how the footage behaves once you put it on the computer and into the editing program. None of these things ruined scenes but were definitely unexpected hurdles. Still, at the end of the day, looking at the footage made me happy that we are making this bold move to shoot a Western this way.

...

Lorraine was a good sport and enthusiastic throughout the day while still frustrating me with her side comments to other people about she and I seeing the character differently. At one point, we were discussing a later scene in the film and she turned to John and said, "I'll need help from my acting coach." What a load of horseshit, I thought. What he's been telling her is exactly the same things I told her but she's receptive to him and not to me. Right in front of the director (who has been giving her notes all along), she establishes him as the go-to. "She just doesn't know better," John said as we discussed it later but I think it's more than that. I think she feels some kind of odd competition with me. She doesn't want to admit I'm right about things. The other day, I told her that all of the photos we have of the real Pearl Hart were staged AFTER she was arrested. Lorraine refused to believe this. Not a half hour later, she showed one of the pictures of Pearl to Molly as an example of Pearl's femine look. Molly said, 'Yes but those were staged after her arrest. They aren't necessarily accurate." There wasn't a peep of defiance from Lorraine's mouth.

All this being said, I have decided to accept her position as long as I'm getting the scenes I want. Can't teach someone to trust me. If she wants to play a game where John is her acting coach, so be it. At least it's John and he would never undermine my vision. But in the end it will be unfortunate that she did not approach all this a different way.

August 9th, 2020

I am the last to fall asleep and the first to wake up on this show, beating even John who is a night owl. Our shoot at the train depot went well and things seemed to be flowing more yesterday, including Lorraine who may be starting to understand how I work, that the scenes continue to evolve on set and improve far beyond what was written on the page.

This local photographer woman showed up on set for the second time. The first day she arrived at the beginning of a take and immediately started snapping pictures. I told her to stop and she got defensive. "I was told I could take pictures!" "Well, not in the middle of the take." I reminded her she needed to not move and be quiet. The very first line of dialog, she busted out in laughter... I stuck my finger back to silence her, keeping my attention on the frame. John told me later that my gesture nearly poked her in the eye and now I wish I had since her behavior on set yesterday was no better. This time she took a picture with flash right in the middle of the take. I wanted to strangle her. Molly, our local liaison, said that she's been reminded many times and says she won't do it but keeps on making these mistakes, unable to control herself. I told Molly, "She hasn't been reminded by the right person." If the lady shows up again, I'm asking her to leave immediately.

August 10th, 2020

Though we wrapped two hours early yesterday, I was as worn out as I've been so far, drinking coffee and struggling to stay awake as I backed up the footage and prepared dailies. It was another good day with only one "Lorraine moment". It seems impossible to get through a day without one expression of her doubt and conflict with my ideas. Nevertheless, she continues to play the scenes well, taking it to a new level yesterday with her sad rendition of Buffalo Gals. It cracks me up that already she has drawn all the credit for this when the song and version of it was my concept and one I've had to insist on over and over this past week while she tried to replace it with something else.

...

Today is my first scene as Joe Boot and probably the most emotional of all my scenes. I explained to John and Michael (actor from California) my struggle to connect with Lorraine for this. They didn't seem to see what I see. I will do my best to think of the other woman instead and play it with all I've got.

...

 John went down to Tombstone, cutting out of our second day early to try and snag Buck Taylor for a small role in *Heart of the Gun*. It seems he accomplished this mission and we now have three Western old timers with good reputations connected to the cast. I hope this leads to more, possibly Bo Hopkins.

August 11th, 2020

We have now reached the end of week one production for the Pearl Hart movie. We wrapped another two hours early again today, sailing through our three scenes. I'm alone at the art collective now and happy to have some private time.

My big scene, first day as Joe Boot, went well. It helped to have John behind the camera watching the takes. Hearing his "That's good" was enough to know I got it. Sushila, our cinematographer, also instilled a lot of confidence in me with her immediate response to the scenes. I did not have to think about the other woman in the moment. I am not sure where the emotion came from... maybe my prep thinking about her? Maybe my original connection to Lorraine? Maybe really just feeling Joe Boot in the moment? Maybe "acting, my boy" as Olivier would say. Either way, my eyes filled with tears and it came alive.

Lorraine spoiled the moments in her usual way, expressing several times throughout the day that she didn't trust we "got it", didn't trust I was pushing her enough, didn't feel it, etc. She compared it with her process in ballet, that the slightest move makes a huge difference. I confessed to her that people who do things over and over and over again I believe to be mostly insecure. I referenced Clint Eastwood, who does a take or two and knows he got it. Today, I tried to have a little heart to heart with her, explaining that one thing I've learned in this process is that directors need an actor's trust as much as actors need a director to trust them. I tried to express that it has hindered me creatively as both a director and fellow actor to feel her constant doubt. Maybe I got through. Probably not. It's who she is.

...

This afternoon after we wrapped, I hoped for a few relaxing hours. They were immediately disrupted by an investor freakout. He's done this to me once before; I wrote about his sudden, irrational behavior before Counting Bullets. Well... it happened again today as he went on an anxious, paranoid trip about his investment in Heart of the Gun, demanding to know where his 10k has gone. It's been sitting in the bank account since he approved that I deposit it. He hounded me, asking for bank statements which I provided, then he accused me of refusing to provide statements. This was followed by accusations that I had "cashed the check" instead of depositing it and that I pocketed the money.

Now this was after I showed several forms of proof that it had been deposited in the bank account for the movie. He continued along these lines, insisting I cashed it. I fought back, trying to speak with reason. Finally, he asked, "You bank with Bank First, right?" I responded, "Wells Fargo." Clearly he may have even been looking at his own books correctly, confusing me with a completely different charge. Regardless, he continued on the attack, nit-picking every single little thing I've done... it was awful honestly. In that hour, I was as stressed as I've been this whole year. My neck tensed up and I felt the pressure of possibly having to get my lawyer involved if the investor decided to back out of our agreement, something he's hinted to in these insane episodes he has. I told one of my collaborators via text and then on the phone, "He's nuts".

August 12th, 2020

I had to lawyer up this morning as the investor continued his psychotic texting, now claiming that I refused to give him the accounting and receipts for the film when I'd clearly said I would show him whatever he needed to see. He demanded his money back once again. I got on the phone with Dorsey, my lawyer and explained the situation. I didn't know it was his birthday. He shrugged it off, asking me to send him what I have and that the investor can reach out to him to talk next week. The rest of the day he forwarded absurd messages the investor sent him which are completely inaccurate representations of the texting/emailing from the last 24 hours. He now claims he only wanted to know about a 1500 dollar charge which I refused to explain (though there's evidence I did explain it). I told Dorsey that I don't feel comfortable communicating with him anymore and want it all to be through my lawyer for now.

Otherwise it was a good day.

August 15th, 2020

I guess I have fallen behind on writing here. The last couple days have been as packed as usual from wake up to lay down with work. I rise around 5am with coffee and sleep at eleven or midnight with whiskey.

...

We started week two of production yesterday with scenes right outside of Superior, the same spot where we shot our ill-fated short *Two Drifters* (something I'd still like to remake one day when we have time). Filming outside in the heat posed new challenges that we did not have during week one. I told Sushila when we arrived, "We need to be careful with the camera. I guarantee you it will overheat." Within an hour, it did and proceeded to do so another 2-3 times throughout the day. We'd take a break and put the phone camera in a cooler of ice to let it return to normal. We had not one but two crew members overheat as well. Around lunch time, Sushila did not feel well and rested in her car for close to an hour with the AC on. When we arrived back at our lodging space, Isaac was even worse. He'd clearly pushed himself too far and John had to eventually get him in a cold shower to cool him down. Scary. Everyone reacts to the heat differently. It has never had these effects on me, not that I am immune to them but it seems that some people more than others can be really hit hard by it. Hopefully they will be more careful today.

...

For the scenes, Lorraine and I were on horseback, the same horse with her holding the reins and me holding her. It was fun and different, a little nerve racking at first as we scaled the rocky terrain, not used to being on one of these animals without a saddle to secure my ass or stirrups to hold my feet. Lorraine kept laughing whenever she took off because my feet would fly up from the momentum. It was quite funny and thankfully was captured in more than one shot. We worked our way up to a gallop for a couple moments which was a lot of fun. She's a good rider, confident and that's what matters most.

We did not have to dirty up for our dialog scenes, covered in horse sweat and our own, looking pretty haggard from the journey. John and Sushila guided us through the moments and John had good direction to help tweak some of my performance. Still, I usually only do a take or two and they're satisfied. I hope they are truly pushing the performance to where it needs to be.

August 17th, 2020

Yesterday was the biggest day of this production and one of the most important this year: filming the scenes of Pearl Hart and Joe Boot robbing the stagecoach. Once again, I was unable to find a local option for the vehicle, resorting to hiring Dan Smith out of Louisiana. The irony of this will never cease to amaze me. I knew this would be a challenging day for multiple reasons: the heat, working in Box Canyon where we should technically have a permit to film, working with horses, managing lots of human beings. As we arrived at our meeting place, I realized my hope of having a small footprint was ruined. There were three or four big trucks with trailers, plus almost every actor brought 1-2 of their entourage. My plan to carpool in was ruined as well as several of them wanted to drive their own cars. Oh well. I tried.

We made our way in on a dusty road, pushing my Corolla once again to its limits as I took my vehicle as far as any other. Lorraine rode with me. We discussed relationships, hers and in general, eventually playing a psychological game of seven questions that are supposed to reveal a lot about you. The questions consist of describing everything from a desert, a cube, a horse, a flower, a storm. When the game is done, the descriptions of what I saw in my mind are interpreted to mean certain things: the desert is how you see life, the cube is you, the horse is your ideal lover, the storm is the way you see problems. No surprise there, my description of the storm was dark clouds on the horizon that I was not afraid of, rather looking forward to their arrival.

...

The day was tough, sorting out all the logistics of getting the stage and people to where they needed to be. Thankfully there was not as much weekend traffic in Box Canyon as we feared and we were able to film in a place where the occasional four-wheeling vehicle could rip roar past us. But the heat... that turned out to be the ultimate enemy. Certain people just can't take it like others. John and I, though exhausted by the end of the day, just don't seem as vulnerable to it. I could have gone another four or five hours. However, Isaac, our sound person, had to break only a couple hours into the production day once again, spending the rest of it in the air conditioned car. Sushila, our cinematographer, struggles to keep her head straight in these conditions, not able to make quick decisions during the take. This is something that caused the biggest mistake of the day. As we set up for the master shot and the last one with most of the talent, I made clear that this needed to be done in one take. The stagecoach would roll off at the end of the shot and ideally not have to come back. However, as we said "cut", John and I were both dismayed to hear Sushila ask for another take. "Why?" We asked with a demanding tone. It turns out that 90 percent of the shot had been out of focus and she hadn't stopped to fix it. I was baffled. She just doesn't understand high stakes scenes where you MUST get the take and as I said before, she does not work well in the heat. I barked at her for the first time, making it very clear that she had made a big mistake. So we called for the stage to come back. The answer on the radio was not good: one of the actors had overheated, almost fainted. Dan, our stage guy, said, "I think we need to take him to the hospital". I was immediately opposed to this, always feeling that people exaggerate such situations and escalate them without reason. As the actor waited in the same car as Isaac, we debated about what to do and I relied on the advice of my peers to make sure I was making a sound decision. I spoke with the actor too and asked if we could see how he was doing in an hour to try and get just one more take. He agreed that an hour might make all the difference.

In the meantime, we stayed busy while the actors ate lunch. picking up my close up and then a shot of Pearl and I riding away. The escape shot was a lot of fun as I mounted awkwardly and hung on for dear life, riding down the canyon. But by the time we returned to our stagecoach robbery location to hopefully pick up that take, we had other bad news. The light had changed considerably. In just an hour, the entire area was now in shade with the sun disappearing over the steep canyon walls. I tried to look for a solution and ultimately decided to accept this as a loss, knowing that we had the whole scene even if we didn't have the master shot. I called to release talent and start packing up. We could also see a storm behind us and began to worry about the possibility of a flash flood.

Nevertheless, Dan still wanted to get a couple shots with no actors of the stage driving fast. I saw the value in this and agreed. I waited with Lorraine while they got the shots up ahead. And then the final unexpected event of the day occurred, one that could have cost lives and thankfully didn't. Dan suggested one more shot before we rode out and as he steered the coach around to get in position, we suddenly saw him catapult off the driver's seat. The front wheels came off too. We hopped out of our vehicles and ran to help him. John, who has good sense with horses, stepped in front of them and I'm thankful that the team of animals are well trained enough to stop because Dan had flown down to the ground, got caught under the wheel and would have been dragged off if they hadn't. What happened was a true freak accident. A welded pin that holds the front wheels to the axel just snapped. It's not something you could ever anticipate. If it had happened in the previous shot, Dan would have been going much faster and Todd would have been riding in the back of the coach. There's a good chance they both would have died. Thankfully, no one was even injured. But we had a dilemma now: how to get the broken stage on a trailer and out of there. The storm roared through the canyon as men put their heads together. Not a mechanical mind, I stood by to help lift and carry as they devised a plan. One step at a time we managed to load this heavy vehicle onto a flatbed. It was a little victory to end the day. In one last crazy moment, two vehicles blasting Mariachi music stopped to watch us load the stage and then suddenly, one of them backed up into the other. Soon enough, our soundtrack was a lot of Mexican voices yelling at each other! It was an insane moment to end a rather crazy but ultimately successful day.

August 18th, 2020

We finished week two of production yesterday, wrapping up the Globe/Miami portion of the production. The scenes took place on Lorraine's property, in a dirt lot where we set up a big canvas tent she has to play as an old mining camp tent where Pearl does laundry and services men with another girl, Mary Allen.

It was hot again as it has been. These scenes are when my character Joe Boot is introduced. We'd decided he would wear a coat when he first meets Pearl, not the most comfortable decision but one that I creatively still agreed with. I think I sweated more than I ever have in my life under that thing throughout our couple scenes together. When I took it off, I was literally soaked, like I'd jumped in a pool. Still, the heat didn't get to me the way it has to Sushila and Isaac. Yes, I know all our bodies are different but I think a lot of it is psychological.

Since overheating, they've really let the heat get to their minds and that has only made their conditions worse whereas it has not effected John, Lorraine, or I. Yes, we get hot but I think we remain mentally determined to get through it, taking care of ourselves but pushing forward. The other two have sunk into defeat. Sushila's not sharp anymore. Isaac is not ready to help like he used to be. I call them "the kids" now and John has adopted it as the term becomes more and more true each day. When we return from filming,

John and I load in most of everything with little assistance. We set and clean up lunch/dinner with no real acknowledgement that we might need some help. It's definitely become a children/parent like relationship. Still, I am grateful for their ongoing commitment to the project. I just hope on these next four days off from filming that they can truly get refreshed going into our week in Yuma.

...

Elizabeth, the actress who played the other "working girl", was easy to work with. She took direction well, adjusted, and clearly took the small part very seriously. I was worried about her simulated sex scene, one that I decided she should do alone under blankets, framing around her non existent "customer". However, she made light of the situation and handled it well. When I tried to find a way to show more of her shoulders by giving her one of Pearl's nightgown tops, she boldly pulled down her shirt, nearly exposing her breasts. John and I responded with shyness that we'd probably rather her wear the nightie... always careful with the current climate of the film industry. I suspect Elizabeth has worked in theater and maybe even experimental theater, environments where nudity is not such a big deal as many actresses in the local film industry make it out to be.

Robert, Lorraine's boyfriend, showed up during our last scene and the mood shifted immediately. He watched as I said these works to her, "I see you work. Hard. Strong. I say to myself, Joe, this is the woman you want," words I mean as the character and outside of the story. I did not flinch or hesitate. I could see it made her nervous.

August 24th, 2020

I am now in Yuma, staying at a hotel with the rest of the crew. I don't know where we would have stayed if it weren't for Mike

Walker, a Yuma local who is playing a part in this and *Heart*. He covered the rooms, something I didn't expect when I asked him, "Could you help us try to find some free or cheap lodging?"

...

We filmed at Castle Dome yesterday, my favorite of all the Western movie sets because it isn't a set, it's a real town. Allen, the eccentric owner, showed us around more, revealing the mining area I hadn't seen on my scout. This place has endless possibilities. "I'd want to make a series here," I told John as I watched him discover the place for the first time with the same wonder I'd felt.

...

We picked a small mining hole and captured five to six scenes within a few hours, working fast but getting some of the best moments we have so far. I love playing Joe Boot, a simple minded sincere man. Lorraine and I were drenched in sweat while performing inside the mining tunnel but other than a short episode with Isaac, our sound person, needing to take a car AC break, we beat the heat. I hope we can expect the same today.

August 26th

The last day at Castle Dome and the first at Yuma prison went as well as they could. At the finish of our filming at the former, we got to explore the Hull mine and see a naturally fluorescent wall that owner Allen says has more colors than any like it in the world.

...

Pearl (Lorraine) was distracted during parts of the day because her "man" Robert was still finding excuses to hang around in Yuma. She expressed her frustration during lunch and I could tell it was pulling her out of some moments on screen. One of those was an alternative ending we decided to pick up, possibly to go after the film's credits, in which a wild theory is proposed that perhaps Pearl did go on to marry a Mr. Bywater but that Bywater was actually Joe Boot! It felt like a fun, clever addition but filming it wasn't easy. She just couldn't get into the moment, phoning in the contentment/peace we asked for with a hollow smile. She reverted to her old ways of questioning the character and my vision for her. As John and I said later watching dailies, she just didn't get there... It's a shame. I feel like in these moments she is questioning Lorraine more than Pearl. Regardless of these moments of friction, I've grown quite fond of her.

...

We split our first day at the prison in half, five hours in the morning, a break, and then five hours at night. Thankfully, we didn't even need the five hours at night. I continue to barely read my own script when approaching these scenes, just approaching the idea of them again and crafting from scratch with the actors, responding to what we've created so far and the environment. I love working this way. So often the actors say "well the script says he does this" and my response of course is "the script doesn't matter anymore". I suppose this could be a dangerous way to work. I could lose track and steer the ship the wrong way. But I feel that it is like navigating by the stars instead of a map.

One of these altered scenes was a nightmare sequence where my character Joe Boot visits Pearl in the prison and asks her to come with him. This foreshadows her receiving news that Joe did in fact escape. As I move through her cell, a darkened dream figure, I say, "Come with me, Pearl. I go." As we crafted the scene, Pearl suggested I say, "Come find me." Take after take, emotions evolved in the scene. In one take, I said at the door to her cell, about to leave, "I love you, Pearl." When she ran out of that shot, she said something like "You son of a bitch," and hid her face on the prison wall. In one of the next takes, she ran into my arms and I confessed in a whisper, "I needed that." In the one right after that, the last one, she ran into them again and said, "I did too."

August 30, 2020

I am now two thirds of the way through this crazy project. Our final day on the Pearl Hart movie was a smooth one with only a few bumps. The management of close to 50 extras went surprisingly well considering John and I were both acting in the scene! We stayed on tasks and wrapped a majority of these people two hours before I'd estimated. The only real issue of the day came at the very beginning when Lorraine decided to completely improvise her court testimony. Prior to the first take, I'd confirmed with her some specific cues the audience needed to react to. She agreed these cues would still be relevant and then said, "Do you trust me?" I said yes and then she walked away with no explanation.

What followed was a first take five times longer than scripted. She basically invented her own monologue, describing Pearl's emotional trajectory from beginning to end. Some of it wasn't bad, definitely natural and true to the character BUT this threw everything off. John didn't know when to come in with his lines as the judge. The audience didn't know when to react because the cues were no longer relevant. To top it off, the camera was set up behind her in a wide master shot! Basically, her improvisation went to waste for an extended and confusing take. After filming with her for a month, you'd think she would have learned a little more about where the camera is and what to do when. She didn't communicate with any of us. After take one, I asked her to return to the shorter, scripted version, leaving her improvisation for the closeup. Here is how the dialog between us went after my suggestion:

Her: "So just cut it down?"
Me: "I mean, give me what the script says."
(Blank stare from her)
Me: "Did you even learn what the script says?"
Her: "No."
Me: "Well, that's what an actor is supposed to do. Have the script prepared even if you're going to improvise."
Her (defiant): "Well, I am Pearl Hart!"
Me: "Don't ever talk to me that way again."

Thankfully the audience was chatting away and none of this could be heard by anyone but the two of us. Later that day, she half-apologized, thanking me for my patience with how the morning went... nevertheless, I am tired of being thanked after the fact for situations that should have been avoided.

Overall, I am still glad I chose her for Pearl. She has had her moments, good and bad. I've been quite fond of her and I've also felt incredible frustration. But the journey is over. Who knows if our paths will continue to cross. She can be incredibly close at times and others, she can be a complete stranger.

...

It's wild and stressful that we start this next one in five days. There is so much to figure out. The trip yesterday produced some possible answers for where we are filming and where we might be staying but nothing solid yet. I hope that today I'll start to get some real confirmations and feel more steady about our progress.

Lorraine Etchell (Pearl Hart) and I (Joe Boot) pose for a poster shot inside Globe's historic jail.

Kyle South horse wrangles for a scene with Lorraine and I in Box Canyon.

Our stagecoach after the freak accident. Thankfully, no one was harmed.

Lorraine and I ride on Lucy South near Superior.

All photographs by Todd South

THE PLEASANT VALLEY WAR

Like Counting Bullets, The Pleasant Valley War was totally conceived during production on the 12 Westerns. Also like that film, John and I teamed up to write and produce. But this was a very different film and we had even less time and money to put it together, not to mention subject matter that would be best suited for a ten hour mini-series. Honestly, we were in over our heads, both reading books on this bloody feud and cobbling together a cohesive story of the most

important events. Somehow with a budget of five thousand dollars and nine days of filming, we pulled it off.

The Pleasant Valley War is a combination of narrative and documentary filmmaking. In scenes and interviews, we tell the story of the Grahams and Tewksburys, two families that turned against each other in what became the bloodiest feud in American history.

Photograph by Todd South

September 1st, 2020

The grind is in full gear right now as I count the few days we have till we start the *Pleasant Valley* movie. Literally writing, casting, and planning with less than a week to go. Somehow though, I think it will be a good production.

September 2nd, 2020

I drove from Superior to Mesa to open two bank accounts and buy hard drives, from there to Payson to pick up the camera from Nick and an investment check, from there to Young where I have settled in to where we'll be staying for this movie.

Arriving here, I hopped right on the computer. There is so much to figure out like who is playing what role just a couple days from now. How am I going to find more money? But it will happen. Somehow it will happen. This is definitely the thinnest I have been spread in all the 12 so far: broke as can be, pulled in multiple directions, at the end of a rope. But I knew this would happen. And I know I will get through it.

September 6th, 2020

We are now two days into our 9th movie. The first two have been successful and also frustrating as hell. Our two shootout scenes were each a challenge to get through. It's that moment on set where the creative energy shifts into survival energy... what do we have to do to make sure this scene is complete and not a disaster? Your mind turns to getting the most basic coverage, you start editing the moments that work in each take, trying to figure out how to work around the ones that don't. I'd love to say we should stop choosing inexperienced actors and especially inexperienced riders but that just isn't realistic. We struggle hard enough to find people willing to participate with the proper wardrobe to start being too picky. The truth is that they need training we don't currently have the time to give them. In both scenes on either day, we couldn't play the way we like to. We resorted to the bare essentials. Ultimately though, we got the scenes and editing may be the final one that saves the day.

...

Being our cinematographer is definitely pushing me to another level, especially in terms of focus. I have always felt confident in my handheld operating skills but my ability to rack focus while operating is definitely a muscle that has not been worked enough. Reviewing dailies, I see my weaknesses. Some of them are passable, either through cutting around them or owning a rougher, less polished aesthetic. I am pushing myself to work with a shallower depth than usual, feeling it appropriate for this story. Also, I've challenged myself to shoot everything at 35mm, not using the zoom but moving in and finding the shot at that length. The one victory so far has been the color grade I chose for the footage, one that everything on and off the team seems to respond well to and that captures that brown/gray *Long Riders* look I was hoping for.

September 10th, 2020

As I write this, I'm sitting in a hotel in Holbrook. Tomorrow, we film our one scene here, a trip we've made to shoot at the location where this gunfight really happened, though the house has now changed and modern things have surrounded it.

...

The past few days have been successful and frustrating. We continue to struggle with our "talent". Some like Mike Walker are amazing but he's done work in the *Walking Dead* and tons of high profile films and shows. Others can't even hold a gun right after being instructed several times. Here are some notable stories from these days:

I got my first body check from a horse. While filming a scene with four horseman passing camera, on the last take I panned to the right to follow one passing rider when another couldn't control his horse and slammed into me. I launched back. John stopped me from falling. The camera was fine. I was fine. Only my toes hurt from the horse stepping on them. After it happened, I had an immediate grin on my face. John was not surprised to see me react this way.

The next day we had our big siege scene and had the most issues with "actors" not performing the most simple actions. One guy was a special case. He wouldn't wipe the half smile off his face as we did take after take of him and the other members of his gang angrily shooting at their enemy's cabin. Worse, no matter how many times we reminded him to hit a certain cue and fire his blank, he missed it. When on the 5th or 6th take, he missed it again, staring like a deer in headlights, I didn't even say "cut", I just walked away. John knew I was about to blow.

The next day we had two inexperienced riders fall off their horses. Or I should say one was bucked off and the other, who happened to be my cousin Phil, kinda launched himself off. Both actors were not harmed but we could not do another take, too risky. A shame. It would have been a cool shot.

Today yet another actor bailed from a horse when he could have stayed on with little effort. This is an odd choice that I see frequently. People throw themselves off a horse, hurting themselves, instead of staying on and trying to control it. And I'm not talking about some bucking horse. Just one that is moving fast or not doing exactly what they thought it would.

We've been lucky. But this is the case whenever you work with horses. They're animals. They're unpredictable. And most of their issues are caused by humans that don't know how to handle them.

I am impressed however with the way some of our people have grown in this experience. Todd, thrown into the deep end of moviemaking, has really figured out a lot about acting just through observation. Bill Carr, who we thrust into a lead role after having only a few lines in *Bullets*, has done a fantastic job. Mike Walker, again super experienced, has proven himself to be not only reliable but inventive in his scenes. It is the most encouraging part of this film to see these improvements.

September 13th, 2020

We did our best to film hard riding/shooting scenes yesterday, like the ones I've always admired in the montage from *Tombstone*. We were limited by my experience as a camera operator and what we could do with the horses but I think we still captured some impressive footage especially because of John, Todd, Troy, and Ben who can all really ride like hell. Unfortunately, Ben crashed into a tree on his first big shot, riding by me as he fired. I'm not sure what happened. Maybe he just wasn't paying attention but a moment later I heard a loud crash. He and the horse ran through a wide tree, colliding with several branches but thankfully not the trunk. He said after that the horse also stepped on him a couple times. To say the least, Ben was a little banged up and down for a while. But he eventually got up and though he said it hurt like hell, he was able to walk around and drink a few beers with us. He's an eager man, truly enthusiastic about making westerns with us and I suspect has found a new family in this little world of ours.

September 15th, 2020

I'm sitting in the warehouse back in Superior, covered in sweat and dirt. The car is mostly loaded with what I'll take to Mississippi, a bare bones selection of all I've accumulated so far. I've stacked up all of Forrest's gear that he rented us the last few months.

...

On my way down from Young, we ran into this lady with a flat tire. She waved me down and asked for help fixing it. The woman said something about not knowing where she was going. "Where are you headed?" I asked. "Yuma." "Yuma?! From where?" "From Tucson," she claimed. "Lady, you're headed the complete opposite direction! Yuma is in the southwest corner of the state." Earlier that morning, I drove halfway to Payson and back to return the camera to Nick. It's been a day on the road and it's not even over.

...

Continuing to tell this story backwards, the last couple days of filming were some of the most fun, especially for John who got to live his childhood dream of riding like hell on a horse in a movie and shooting a whole lot of blanks. I had fun too, capturing these action moments to the best of my ability, feeling that we finally got a good deal of riding/shooting into the 12 Westerns. It was also nice because we were only dealing with our trio and a couple actors who made brief appearances. Frustrating human moments were not as common and the days passed with ease as we approached the finish line for number nine.

September 16th, 2020

This morning while staying in a little cottage in Prescott, my dad called. I could hear his voice breaking immediately and knew something was terribly wrong... my aunt Peggy attempted suicide again and this time succeeded. It was harder to hear my father's voice than it was to think about Peggy. I'd never heard him sound so broken. Tomorrow I will drive up to Colorado to see if I can be any help in this time. As for my own pain from this, I feel only confusion as to why she, the person we knew as the fun loving aunt our whole lives, was so determined to kill herself and anger that she left behind five kids who have already had enough of a hard go.

Todd South, our set photographer, horse wrangler, and actor.

Actor J.D. Pepper plays Tom Graham, one of the main figures in the feud.

Setting up and rehearsing a scene. For this film, I was also the cinematographer.

Texas-based actor Kelly Kidd firing a shotgun blank at camera.
All photographs by Todd South

THE WILDERNESS ROAD and TALES OF THE NATCHEZ TRACE

There's a good argument to be made that in a year of challenging productions, this two punch combo of feature films may have been our most ambitious undertaking and altogether the most difficult. Though less intense than

Deputy's Wife, we faced some incredible obstacles on these two: trying to be accurate to a totally different time period with unique and hard to find wardrobe, locations spread out over four states, the six week long shooting schedule, the continued and progressed battle with COVID, and the sheer size of this epic tale. That doesn't even include the freak accidents you will read about in the coming pages.

The Wilderness Road is the story of three land pirates, infamous outlaws who made their name robbing and killing near the turn of the 19th century. Samuel Mason is a Revolutionary War hero who turns to a life of crime and forms a notorious gang of thieves. Big Harpe and Little Harpe, considered by some to be America's first serial killers, wreak havoc through the Southeast on a killing spree with no end in sight. Their evil paths will soon collide and many more will die.

The Tales of the Natchez Trace, a companion piece to the former film, is a collection of short stories that follow other famous figures from this time and place. From the boisterous Mike Fink to the distrubed Meriwether Lewis and even the dueling Andrew Jackson, the film shares a new look at some of the greatest myths of the American South.

Photograph by Damon Burks

September 21st, 2020

It felt odd coming back to Brookhaven today, like a soldier returning home from war and not knowing if he still belongs there anymore. Bill failed to inform me months ago that our cat went missing... I hope Skip has found a good place to live or died without much pain.

...

I spent the day Saturday mixing and sound editing more than thirty minutes of *Texas Red.* Tomorrow will be the same as I push to finish the rest of the movie.

September 24th, 2020

There isn't much to report since I arrived in Mississippi. It rained more in a few hours than it did the entire time I was in Arizona. I've been stuck to the computer, racing to finish the sound mix for *Texas Red* in time to submit the film to Sundance and Slamdance. It's frustrating as hell hearing how the sound person on that film could have done better with the production audio and even sometimes had a whiny attitude while recording but in the end, I'm thankful the sound is salvageable. Watching the movie finally in a way that I can hear not just the voices but the footsteps, the horses, the water, etc. is a totally different experience. Suddenly, the film is alive and does have the strength I hoped for.

Otherwise, I have been working on plans for the *Wilderness Road*, anxious that production starts in less than three weeks. This will be a tough one, maybe the hardest of them all. I can feel that it's going to be a daily battle to accomplish what we need.

September 27th, 2020

Another three days tied to the computer. Today, I get to step out and scout in Louisiana which feels like a nice reprieve.

On Wednesday, Jennifer came over to straighten my hair for the role of Little Harpe. She gave it a special treatment and the picture I posted seemed to surprise some people about a different look. I love the idea of changing my appearance for roles, much like Russell Crowe did at the height of his career. I've also decided to do every scene barefoot. Apparently the murderous Harpes either wore moccasins or went barefoot.

My brother Big can wear them but I think it will make an immediate statement to the audience if I'm walking around everywhere, inside and out, with no shoes. This man is not right in the head... that's what I hope they'll think.

...

Texas Red is getting closer and closer while we have the usual troubles of exporting the final film. It seems that no matter how many times we do this, it can't go smoothly. Lately, the problems have been on Jared's end: issues getting his color version out of the program, glitches in what he did export, issues downloading or uploading etc. I hope with the next couple movies that we can just have an easy process that doesn't push us right to the deadline. As of now, I have a few days before submitting to Sundance but who the hell knows what could happen between now and then.

...

Nearly two weeks away from the start of a thirty day production (my longest yet), we have no gaffer, no grip, and no one to fill the full time production assistant position. I thought I had the latter figured out and then at the last second the person decided they couldn't do it because we'd be sleeping outside sometimes and they have allergies. Allergies? It's called *The Wilderness Road*. Didn't they think about this a little before talking to me? Same goes for our best contender for gaffer, a guy who was given the pay and dates up front then continued to waste our time for two weeks before finally letting us know the pay wasn't enough. For me, professionalism is deciding when you're given that information if it's going to work or not. You don't waste the employer's time. Is it enough or not? Yes or no? Then you move on to other issues but you don't return to that one.

September 29th, 2020

Oh my god, I am so drained of energy right now. On my way back from Memphis, I got hit with the craziest news torpedo that looked to "sink our battleship" for the *Wilderness Road*. For days, I've been pushing to get the 50,000 and more we raised in investment through WeFunder transferred to my account. Although we're still raising money, the site allows us to pull partial funds if and only if we have 50k in escrow. I thought we did... but it got more complicated. Some people hadn't re-signed their contracts to confirm the investment, others hadn't put in all their info. So we've been hunting them all done, one by one, email after email, trying to get them to sign. Meanwhile, I've been delaying wardrobe orders, waiting to send money to book lodging,etc. Today, I even had to hand our main location a check and shamefully ask them to hold it till our funds are ready. I thought we were hours away from getting the transfer, sure that we finally had enough investors confirm and then on that three hour drive home, I got a devastating email.

You see, somewhere in the process, WeFunder allows investors to "opt out" of having their money (which is already pulled from their accounts and in escrow) disbursed early, electing to wait until our fundraising ends in November. Several chose this option, including one 5k investor! This literally fucked us. With 5850 dollars denied from being transferred, there's no way we could get the money in the next few days. I started to brainstorm solutions. I reached out to my rep at WeFunder, expressing my extreme frustration once again at the confusion, the lack of communication, and the fact that these "opt outs" never showed up on our end at all. I got home, stressed as could be. I started messaging everyone else who had not confirmed their funds, still only a couple thousand dollars but getting us closer was better than nothing. I also emailed that 5000 dollar investor, a person I've never met or heard of, in desperate hope that they might have made a mistake, clicked "opt out" by accident. About an hour ago, I got on the phone with Katie, the rep from WeFunder, to try to solve the issue. She apologized profusely, calling our experience "a shit show". As we discussed all the wildest options for how to resolve this, an email from that 5000 investor came in announcing he'd made a mistake! He did want his funds transferred! A miracle if there ever was one. Katie and I had a big laugh... crisis averted until the next one.

September 30th, 2020

As I finally confirm the filming dates for these next couple months, I lost my first actor because of it. Nicole Dickson was going to play one of the three Harpe women. I wanted to work with her but she just couldn't swing the dates and I couldn't move them. That now left two open seats for the Harpe ladies as I've been trying to fill another for weeks. So I played musical chairs and switched an actress from another role into Nicole's and hit the pavement again trying to find a third lady to complete the trio. I am sure it won't be the last actor who can't do the film because of the schedule.

October 4th, 2020

Casting fun continues as actors keep me on hold for days and then turn down roles, leaving me to start at zero. In my search to find a full time production assistant, my top choice did not work out after days of deliberation. Now, should I hire an unknown, someone whose work ethic and attitude are a mystery, or should I just save the money for other things in the budget and make do with the crew I have? The latter is what I'm currently leaning towards.

October 5th, 2020

Now I feel that I can plunge completely into *Wilderness Road*, the role of Little Harpe and immersing myself into production. As usual, there's more to do than can possibly be done. Tonight, I took my first stab at the side story about Meriwether Lewis' mysterious death. Tomorrow, I'm tackling one about Andrew Jackson's duels.

October 6th, 2020

Some doors are opening and others not at all. I can't seem to find horses in the Memphis area for our first week. I can't seem to find women to play prostitutes then either. All of this is coming up and I am starting to consider just having to shoot without these things, having to compromise big time on the scenes. It's not a good way to start a production.

The power was out for three hours today so I used the time to learn lines. I hope to bring a totally different vocal tone to Little Harpe, speaking fast and with odd changes in volume.

October 8th, 2020

Hit hard by allergies yesterday, wiped out for most of the day. Luckily, it seems to have gone this morning, allowing me to return to focused work. When it happens, I can barely concentrate. There's a big storm coming, headed for the coast, and as usual everyone is worried how it might effect filming. I can't worry about it. What will happen will happen and we will film regardless.

I must start to compromise on some of these scenes: turning a scene of several prostitutes and customers into one with only one lady and one client, losing all of the revivalist preacher's crowd and having him preach to an open field because I can't find the extras, using fake babies when I can't realistically schedule real ones.

October 10th, 2020

I was up till 2 last night receiving Mario from his long drive from Texas. It was a stormy night. As I waited for him under the cover of rain, I watched a fairly large branch, which would have definitely dented my car, fall thirty feet away and instead smack into one of Bill's discarded motorcycles. Mario drove past the house, admittedly hard to see at night. Once he finally turned around and found the driveway, I stood on the roadside discussing where to park his trailer when another car drove off the pavement onto my damn lawn, confused as to where the actual road was. The driver apologized and I thanked the fates that he wasn't drunk or I might be dead. Moments later, a local redneck showed up with his pitbull, on the defense because Mario had turned around in his driveway. He wanted to make sure everything was ok.

...

It appears we have successfully cast Lou Ferrigno in *Heart of the Gun*, our last western. A random casting for this genre, I know, but possibly the only significant recognizable face/name we'll be able to get. John made it happen, knowing Lou from some volunteer police work the Hulk/Hercules did back in the day. I hope this leads to more investment in the film. I still have no firm confirmation that one investor will follow through with his investment, another 20,000 supposed to come our way. The last three months of this project... they feel the most unsure, the most daunting. The world is full of curveballs right now. Which new ones will come my way?

October 11th, 2020
I am not getting the sleep I should, staying up too late talking to my collaborators. Conversation is definitely the best way to

get distracted from my duties and my rest time, even if that's just laying in bed watching a movie. I will have to be better about it on this film if I want to be rigorous with the work, if I want to make serious progress in post-production in the off hours from filming.

Today we leave for the Memphis area. There are a lot of unknowns but also the assurance that we will make whatever it is work.

October 13th, 2020

Day one of production on *The Wilderness Road*, a long one for sure. I left Water Valley in north Mississippi where we spent the night at Damon's place (I slept outside on a porch swing) for a two hour drive to our location near Memphis. I landed, unloaded my packed car, and planned to take advantage of as much pre-call time as I could to shop for groceries, etc. Just as I was about to leave for that, I got distracted, having to deal with where to park the horse trailer. By the time that was handled, the crew was arriving and I needed to facilitate that. By the time I left for those errands, there was limited time. I sent Damon for pizza for the crew's lunch and took off to Kroger, Walmart, Tractor Supply, and even Family Dollar, hitting them all in less than an hour. Frustrated, I was not able to find much of what I needed.

...

The day started fairly well with an outdoor scene. Creek, playing the lead, was able to tone his performance down easily. Once again, on a shot of his character and his son riding away, we struggled with not having experienced riders. I scrapped the shot, saying we'd pick it up tomorrow and we probably will with someone else wearing the character's wardrobe!

...

The night shoot is when we started to face challenges. As always, lighting took much longer than I wanted and I felt my hands tied in terms of blocking/rehearsing as the guys lit the scene. I'm not rehearsing enough, that's for damn sure, and admitted so to Mario as we drank our whiskey at 2am last night. Something to rectify for the coming days.

October 14th, 2020

We caught up a little last night, wrapping before midnight, giving me a chance to get six to seven hours of sleep. However, we did have to push one scene to today, something I hate to do. Fighting time and light, our afternoon went by too quickly and we found ourselves once again rushing to complete a scene. It's a shitty feeling, knowing you don't have the time to dial in the quality. On top of that, our last shot of the sequence involved Creek on horseback naked, a humorous site.

...

A quick note on our sleeping situation so I don't forget months from now. We're "camping inside" a giant wedding hall: cots, air mattresses, sleeping bags, and lots of snoring. Bandit gets on the cot with me even though there's barely enough room for a human body.

October 15th, 2020

The late nights are catching up to me but I'm trying not to show it, waking up earlier than everyone and doing the work I need to before we start filming.

Yesterday had some struggles. I expressed my frustration a couple times that the frame doesn't go up fast enough as

Mario goes ahead with lighting before he's even looked in camera. This, a habit Jared has as well, annoys the shit out of me and leads to wasted time. I've always felt that looking at the shot first and what's naturally happening with the light is important.

Oct. 17th, 2020

On our last day filming near Memphis, I started to feel sick. Of course, the first thought that crossed my mind was, "Shit, this better not be the damn virus." As I write this, not fully recovered, I do not think it is COVID for a couple reasons: 1. I don't have a fever or headache, shortness of breath. 2. No one else around me is sick (yet).

Still, it shows how quickly things can change. If I did get the virus, I couldn't be on set. Would I stop? No. I'd find some way to quarantine for a couple weeks and direct through Zoom. Upon returning home, I got a decent night's sleep and feel a lot better. I hope to do the same the next couple days so that I can hopefully return to week two fully recovered.

...

On the final day of week one, I had my first scenes as Little Harpe. After doing my first take in a moment that happens near the end of the movie, I studied the room for reactions, trying to see if people were cringing at my performance, doubtful, or effected in the right ways. It was hard to tell but I continued and slowly started to get feedback that the voice, mannerisms, and intense attitude was working. The lines flowed and I had a hell of a lot of fun, making me feel more than ever that I may pursue acting in other peoples' films when the 12 Westerns are complete.

October 19th, 2020

Some good things have been happening. I wonder when I look back on this journal if it will read more like a chronicle of bad things or a good balance of both. On Saturday, we went to scout the section of the Natchez Trace where we'll be filming this week. This is government land and comes with a price tag of 250 a day plus 45 an hour if a ranger has to be present. Since we have horses in almost every scene, we'd have to pay for a ranger for all hours of production. In conjunction with this scout, we needed to meet up with Rusty Marks, a man who lives right off the Trace and owns a hunting lodge he offered to let us use as lodging. Not only is the lodge perfect for our purposes but Rusty changed the whole game for us this week. His property around the lodge is good for several scenes and then he took us to a road he has, not quite as sunken and trace-looking as the government's but pretty damn close. I excitedly described a new plan to Mario as we walked along, narrowing our time on federal park land to only one half-day, saving money and filming most of this week on Rusty's property instead. It felt great to find answers to questions and see things fall into place.

In another recent revelation, we've discovered a group in Natchez who portrays this time period and has an upcoming re-enactment. So I'm shuffling scenes to be shot on those days as much as I can. It's kinda wild how much this production is changing and shifting as it goes but all I can do is try to rearrange the pieces and make it work.

...

Overall, I feel like I'm in survival mode for this last quarter of the project. No, not in the sense of just getting by with mediocre scenes, etc. I still want to make the best films possible but with the light at the end of the tunnel and so many unknown factors, I am working on my last boost of strength to make it through. My eyes are set on the finish line and I'll do whatever I have to do to get there even if it gets very rough.

October 25th, 2020

The last five shooting days have been some of the most challenging of the year. We're out at this hunting camp near the Natchez Trace, all bunking up and filming both on Rusty's property and the actual Trace. I have barely any cell service, limiting my ability to do any kind of non-set work and making me incredibly behind on the producing end. It's also why I have not written in this diary since we started week two.

...

On Tuesday we began with scenes of the Harpes wandering around on foot for a montage. It wasn't just the brothers and their three ladies but also two babies. Originally I'd had four babies lined up for the three we needed, thinking I was clever to get an extra in case one of them needed to take a break and could be easily replaced. That got thrown out the window when not one but two mothers flaked on me. I pleaded with the third mother, bringing her two children to not back out, and thankfully she's coming through every day. However filming with babies adds an extra level of intensity to the set. They cried the second they were handed over to the actresses, not something that ruined the scenes but a screaming child isn't the easiest thing to think clearly around. We got through and filmed what I'd consider the most important scene of the movie: Big Harpe killing his brother's child because it is crying by swinging it into a tree. Thankfully we nailed it, moving around from set up to set up without going into the wee hours of the night. We replaced the real child with a baby doll at the right moment and the effect, as far as we could tell on set, worked well. I was happy with the performances, including my own, which unfortunately I could not say the next day.

...

Wednesday we focused on the Brassel brothers scene which involved Big and Little Harpe (me) riding up on and then attacking two innocent travelers. When asked how good of a rider I was by horse wrangler JW Perez, I said "mediocre". We warmed up the horses and they gave tips. I was riding an English saddle for the first time. The balance of riding, acting, and directing, not to mention other duties I have on set may be the most challenging combination I have encountered. We traveled to "Rusty's Trail" and started setting up for coverage of the scene.

Another factor about working with these horses is that they aren't movie trained. I don't know how much difference it would make overall but these are roping or trail horses. Making them ride 100 yards, stop, then turn around and go back to do it all over again isn't what they're used to. Animal or not, they have to be asking, "What the hell is this all about?" especially if they're used to having a semi-logical task to complete. All the horses we've worked with this year also struggle with being "buddy sour" to a degree: if moved away from the other horses they're used to being around on set, they get antsy and harder to control. So from the start, Daulton (Big Harpe) and I had some control issues getting the horses back to our first mark, stopping in place, moving at the right pace, etc. JW said I looked tense. This is always a discouragement to hear when you're trying to be as relaxed as possible. Finally, I took my feet out of the stirrups, finding that riding without them relaxed my legs more and made a huge difference. This of course gave me less balance on the animal, whose name I should mention I suppose, she is called "Yellow."

We started to get the hang of it, the horses feeling a routine of what we wanted them to do. And then we moved onto the moment when Big hits one of the Brassel brothers in the head and I ride after the escaping other brother. He darts up this little hill and I'm supposed to ride up, stop, decide it isn't worth it, and ride back down. I struggled at first to get Yellow to really take off but JW gave me some tips and I started to make some effective turns and rides up the incline. In one shot, I pleased myself big time by riding up, the horse turning before I wanted to go back down, but being able to spin it around back to my mark, having a second gaze just past the camera, and then heading down. It felt like a perfect take. The crew asked for another, unsure if we "got it". I was hesitant, knowing that each take on these horses increases the chance something will go wrong. Back to the saddle I was riding, it was an English saddle with no horn and also an elastic band as best I can describe it. Earlier in the day, the saddle slid to the side during one take. I tried to stay on as best as I could as Tim (the other horse wrangler) watched but ultimately fell off. Well on this final take of the incline, the saddle started to slide again. I overcompensated on my spin to try and stay on again but ultimately tumbled off, hitting the ground, and bouncing up as fast as I could, flashing the crew a thumbs up. They all laughed.

It was very difficult to stay focused on the moments and lines as we did all this and I left the day discouraged that I hadn't really stayed in character. Two things improved my spirits later that day: 1. Watching the footage showed that everything we'd done looked a hell of a lot better than it felt. 2. When I asked Mario if we were better than the other shit-show riders we've worked with in other scenes, he said something to this effect, "From my non-riding eye, I thought you guys totally knew how to ride. You looked like you knew what you were doing. Only compared to the expert horse wranglers can I tell that you're not that experienced." So that was a boost of encouragement after my difficult day on set so far this production.

...

The following one was our only shoot on Natchez Trace federal parkland. We were originally supposed to film there for three days until I discovered Rusty's property and avoided paying 250 a day plus 45 an hour for a park ranger to be there. The park ranger who did show up never got out of his damn car! Supposed to monitor us, he didn't even say hi on arrival, just stayed in his vehicle and played on his phone. I guess I should be thankful that he wasn't breathing down our necks but it felt rude and bizarre, especially after all the hoops we had to jump through to get approval for the location. The morning went well as I returned to director mode and we captured what will be the only shots in the movie of the actual "sunken trace" look, a small path with high walls. We had our good riders at work. But this day carried enormous pressure in terms of time. What we were filming, the sequences that all lead up to and eventually show the death of Big Harpe, are some of the most essential in the film. I knew every minute counted and expressed that to the crew as often as possible. They could tell I was in a different mood when early in the day, Lee Cannon (worked on *Bastard's* and *Texas Red*) kept jumping his line ahead of the others. I warned him two or three times and on the fourth incident I barked, "If you jump your fucking line again, I'll write your character out of the movie." Some of the new crew was a little surprised at this outburst but Shaney, our makeup artist, defended it, reminding them of how many times I warned him.

Going to lunch later than we should have and returning to Rusty's property for the rest of the day's scenes, the pressure of time ramped up. I could feel the day wasting away, pushing the crew and cast to move as fast as they could. It felt like people were moving in slow motion, whether they were or not. For a fairly complex scene, we climbed down a ridge, crossed a creek, and filmed on a sand bank. In this moment, Big Harpe attacks one of our wives right when the posse riders show up on the ridge above and the final chase that leads to his death begins. Juggling all the blocking and timing of the scene, I once again struggled to get my lines the way I wanted them. At least my exit from the scene was good! As the riders arrive, Big takes off into the forest whereas I run across the creek. I moved so fast that the crew joked I looked like I was walking on water.

The sun moved quickly behind the trees as we filmed the riders moving through the forest after Big. Daulton also moved fast as hell. He's a big guy but gave it his all, tripping during one take and rolling onto the ground, getting right back up and going again. I continued to push for speed, knowing we needed to get to his death scene as soon as possible. At one point, when Mario (DP) stopped to take a picture of our resting crew with some prop guns I exploded, "No! No fucking pictures. We don't have a minute to spare. I've said that a hundred times today. This is go time. This is the fucking superbowl."

Sure enough, we found ourselves fighting light in the final sequence but that wasn't our only struggle. Working with period correct flintlock rifles, we were unable to get a good take of the final shot at Big Harpe that puts him down to the ground. JW, on horseback, tried his best take after take but the rifle kept misfiring and the one time it did fire was not quite in frame as the horse moved around erratically, too excited from all the events of the scene. I hope that editing magic will allow us to make the moment work.

The actors did a fantastic job and covered our asses. As Moses Stegall (Nick Murphy) cut off the head of Big Harpe while he's still talking, we were all entranced watching these two incredibly intense performances. It saved us from a special effects makeup gag that unfortunately didn't work as Shaney intended but reinforced that it's good acting that often sells the scene, not the effects. Somehow we finished the day with even enough "blue hour" time to add a scene of me selling Yellow and Blue (Big's horse) to our gaffer Nick, making a cameo in the film. This moment, not in the original script, hopefully will help explain some of the continuity changes of us having horses in one scene, not in another, etc. I don't know if the crew ever fully realized how close we'd come with time. If we'd lost five minutes here and another five minutes there throughout the day, it would not have been possible.

...

Thankfully, the two days that ended our second week were not as challenging, though they were certainly eventful. On Friday, we started the Joseph Thompson Hare side story from *Tales of the Natchez Trace*, the companion piece to *Wilderness Road*. I was super impressed with our talent: Michael Randall who I haven't worked with in years and has clearly grown since then, Hick Cheramie would was super grateful to be in one of the 12 Westerns and continually praised my "machine" work ethic, and two reenactors from Natchez who felt like they'd made plenty of movies. Hick particularly impressed me and I'd work with again any day. At the start of the day, we realized I'd never sent him the revised dialog for the scene so he quickly set upon memorizing the new lines. This is when Shaney mentioned, "Well he has to do an accent so it's not easy to get this new dialog down." Like her, he's cajun. I immediately rejected this idea to cover up his sound. "It's great. I want you to sound like you." He joked, "You're going to need subtitles." I insisted and he claimed I was the second director ever to let him speak in his natural voice!

Even the wagon portion of this scene was a smooth experience. Brad Turner, the life saver wagoner from *Bastard's* and *Guide to Gunfighters*, returned to help us again, bringing with him Denver Mullican's late 1600s antique undertaker's wagon. It was fantastic to showcase this incredible historical vehicle more than we'd been able to in *Bastard's*. Matt, one of the reenactors, did a great job driving it after learning from Brad in only three minutes. Mary LeBlanc brought a "pale white horse" which posed a new challenge: how to get a horse to stand where you want it with zero halter, reins, or rope on it but we pulled it off as Mario filled the scene with fog and we got some truly eerie moments with the animal.

In the afternoon, we moved into yet another chapter of the Trace tales, one that I added to our script only a week ago. It focuses on Murrell, another outlaw who came around in the 1830s and did all kinds of things, including the kidnapping and re-selling of slaves. This was the key to figuring out how to make a short episode about the outlaw, something that had eluded me in previous attempts. The escaped slave would be the lead and Murrell would only appear a couple times. We got some good footage with our two black actors, male and female, during the afternoon and then set upon the chapter's only night scene, once again working with fire out in the elements. The forecast showed a chance of rain but it didn't look too bad. A few shots into the scene, the wind kicked up, lighting flashed around us, and soon enough we were getting poured on. Everyone huddled under a canopy tent. I wanted to wait it out, a tactic that has worked with bad weather time and time again in my previous productions. Thank goodness we did not listen to me because the rain that was supposed to last a half hour ended up coming down for four hours. Once again, the weather forecast is total bullshit. Mario, on the other hand, took the lead in getting our equipment and gear back to the hunting lodge with trip after trip in a four-wheel drive off-roading vehicle the owners let us borrow. It took a while but we were finally all out of the rain, facing a new problem: the power was out. Amazingly enough, we only had two closeups left to adequately cover the scene. The final wide shot we'd filmed when the rain came was usable. It was the only take we got but lucky enough, it would work. Mario had an ambitious but clever idea: film the other two closeups inside, making it as dark as possible and lighting the talent with only fake fire light. After some testing, it proved successful! We drank whiskey and finished the day inside the lodge with a little movie magic.

...

The next day I woke to see we were still out of power and also with no water since the electric pump was not working. We just needed to finish our last scenes and get out of there, I told myself. Thankfully, electricity came back on late in the morning as we started work, making our clean up and load out easier. Returning to Rusty's trail, we filmed the last couple scenes of the Murrel story, completing the chapter. But there was one more incident to get through before the end of our second week... As Mario moved around our location, he must have stepped on a nest of yellow jackets! Suddenly, he was getting stung. None of us realized it was more than one of these little fierce creatures but as he ran back up at us, I suddenly got stung in the face too. We all started to flee the scene, leaving our gear behind. They chased us a good hundred yards. Mario was stung four times and my cheek started to swell. Thank goodness it was no worse. We let the swarm calm down and moved our shots down the trail, all paranoid that we'd get them riled up again. Before nightfall, we were on the way back to Brookhaven, worn out from another week on the *Wilderness Road* and ready for rest.

October 27th, 2020

I'm now in Louisiana in a small town called Franklinton where we'll be filming for two weeks. We're staying at a cabin and house owned by a kind gentleman named Albert Freyder. He's sometimes hard to read. Bandit and I settled into the cabin last night. It will be a comfortable place to spend the next 9-10 days of filming.

...

My main struggle right now is to figure out the rest of our schedule. With four weeks to go, there are a ton of questions of when and where we are filming certain parts of the movie: if we're going to Illinois to film at Cave in Rock or not, if we don't where should we try to fake that, when should we try to film with the flatboat, etc.

...

The one good news is that I had a phone call with the investor who wanted to back out of our last Western. He apologized and said he'd send the check this week. We'll see but at least it's a sign of hope.

October 28th, 2020

Our first day filming down here wasn't a smooth one. Four or five people showed up late for various reasons: Shaney had car issues and went the wrong way, Alexis (our new girl) read the wrong call time, Dunky lost her wallet and couldn't get gas, Thomas was late with the donkeys for who knows what reason. It set us off to a wobbly start and once again showed how little things can effect a whole day.

We struggled with the donkeys (stubborn sons of bitches) and one of the actors on a horse once again, even doing the most basic things. Rain started entering the scene off and on, making one take not match the next. By mid afternoon, I was exhausted and ready to bang my head into one of the wooden doors on set. Somehow we caught up in our night scenes and managed to wrap early.

I felt good about my scenes as Little, not distracted this time and able to stay in the moment. The hurricane is coming but as usual. We're not stopping.

October 29th, 2020

Once again we worked through the weather and once again it was nothing like the forecast expected it to be. Of course you never know... Shaney, our makeup artist, had her house damaged. But the one thing you can count on is that the forecast isn't going to be right.

It took three and a half hours to get our first shot as Mario lit the room. Thankfully there were only minor tweaks to be made for the rest of the day but it was hell waiting, my least favorite thing to do on set. I hate sitting around with nothing to do. Even after rehearsing all our scenes with the actors, we were still hours away from getting the first shot off.

November 2nd, 2020

I'd be lying if I said I wasn't exhausted. Three weeks of production complete and we're only half way down with the *Wilderness Road/Natchez Trace* pair of films, whereas on a normal show we'd be almost finished. The three remaining weeks seem daunting as I have still to answer so many questions about where/when/how I am filming several scenes. Some of the answers are starting to come to light slowly.

November 3rd, 2020

My computer is almost unusable in the cold of this cabin with no heat from the fireplace. It freezes constantly, causing me to reboot and prevent me from any serious progress off set.

...

Last night we sat around an outdoor fire eating jambalaya from a local man named Shane. A few of us smoked cigars. Shane got too drunk and starting making fun of Shaney, our makeup artist, for snorting while she laughs. This turned into him begging, pleading with her to snort more. It suddenly turned into an awkward situation with a slight feeling of backwoods "Deliverance". If he'd gone a step further, all of us were prepared to step in and deal with it, as we could tell Shaney was on the cusp of being freaked out and if he hadn't made us such good food, we wouldn't have tolerated it for a second. Thankfully he chilled out.

...

Running and walking barefoot yesterday on the sandbank gravel was the most challenging physical feat. I anticipated sand and a soft surface but this was all uneven rocks that I had to traverse. My soles were beat up by the time I got home.

November 4th, 2020

We were so efficient yesterday that we were able to pick up the single scene scheduled for tomorrow and thus ensure we won't have to film that day at all, ending our fourth week even earlier. Today will be our final one before we head back to Brookhaven and prepare for the last two weeks of production.

Filming in Franklinton has been a mostly positive and sometimes odd experience. The people here are kind, generous, and don't seem to understand a lot of what we're doing. Our filming schedule has remained a mystery to them as many have shown up on days they weren't needed, having been told by another local person that they should. Miscommunication has been rampant.

November 5th, 2020

I was relieved to return home today to find the check from the one investor for 20,000 dollars in the mail. I could hardly believe it as I signed the check and deposited it on my phone... could this trouble finally be over? I am sure not but at least we got the money.

...

With covid on the rise and our sag paperwork not complete, I continue to worry about the hurdles that lie ahead with finishing the last of the 12. SAG takes about two weeks to respond to even the most simple question and usually that only happens if I call and leave a voicemail. The incompetence of their organization makes me want to say good riddance to SAG projects forever. I don't think they have a clue what we're doing.

...

Week four was a short one, only three days of filming after having only one day off. Thankfully, the crew has yet to show signs of exhaustion. Like no other crew, they have also been drama free thus far, a welcome relief. The acting was good this week two, bringing in two veterans of my work: Scott Alan Warner and Shannon Williams. It makes my life easier to not have to worry about actors being prepared and at least bringing a half-realized performance on take one.

...

We received the most ironic news this morning. After finally giving up on the prospect of filming at the historic Cave in Rock in Illinois for our final week of production and moving on to explore options in Arkansas, producer Damon texted/called/emailed this morning ecstatic that the government had finally approved our request to film at the former location. He assumed I would jump at the opportunity but it may come too late... For one, we now have less than two weeks to prepare a giant company move to a completely different part of the country, something I was hoping to plan weeks ago. Second, the new prospect in Arkansas looks quite attractive, not to mention closer and might fit in nicely with a couple days shooting on an old keelboat in the same area. Major decisions will be made in the 24 hours.

November 7th, 2020

Daulton (Big Harpe) continues to work hard on locations for our last week in Arkansas. I hope he succeeds because I am too tired to take everyone to Illinois at this point.

November 8th, 2020

The first day back for week five certainly was not dull. Upon arrival back at Rusty's hunting camp, we settled back in quickly to prepare for filming at 10am. At five minutes past, Creek had arrived but Dorsey, the other main actor for the day and also my attorney, had not. Now he's been a tad late before but I sensed a call might be needed. So thankfully I had a bit of service and gave him a ring. "Hey Travis. What's up?" He answered. I knew something was wrong. "I'm on my way to church". "Well, Dorsey, your call time is right now." He'd mixed up the dates. Thankfully, he drove the hour and 45 distance in an hour and fifteen minutes. But still, it got the day off to a weird start and it's never good for an actor to arrive flustered, affecting their performances no matter how prepared they are.

We got about the scenes, both talent on horseback, and it went fairly well but was not what I had in mind nor did I have the time to make it so. Much of this film has been that way, demonstrating once again that I need to change my practices if I want to get closer to what I see in my head. More on that soon perhaps. But for now, the other major incident of the day...

In our final day scene, we wanted Creek to cross a small muddy creek so that he could intimidate a group of travelers across the bank. I was just setting up for the shot of the travelers' reactions to him as Creek got stuck in the mud, shin deep. We've gone through this stuff before, traversing it for one of our Harpe scenes, and it's no joke but we were able to get through. As Creek complained of not being able to move and Shaney pleaded to get him out, I gave the actor a sly grin and said "No, he can't wait there while we get this shot."

Creek and I are always fucking with each other and he laughed as I made him stay while we got three or four takes of the others. But my reasoning for doing so wasn't only to continue our pranks on each other, the light was fading and all the traveler actors were only available that day. Wrapping them out was more important however by the time we could focus on Creek, he'd sunk to his knee... this wasn't quicksand but deep, sticky Mississippi mud. There was no life threatening danger but it soon became clear that we were in quite a predicament. The first attempts to drag him out by pulling with sticks etc. did not work. Soon Stephen Huffman and I were deep in the mud ourselves, but remaining safely unstuck, digging by Creek's one trapped leg. We would nearly reach his foot, using all our strength to get that far, only to see the hole fill back up with mud, a formidable enemy. We worked and worked as those on the bank theorized new ways of getting him out.

Finally, Creek insisted that no way we could try would work; a rescue team needed to be called and so we did. His spirits remained high as we joked about the situation while waiting for the sheriff's department and game & fish to show up. "I would have done the same thing as you," he said and laughed. I added: "And if I hadn't then we wouldn't be able to tell this crazy story." The authorities arrived fairly unequipped for such a rescue but were nevertheless able to get Creek loose with the combination of some boards and heavy manpower from William Smith and Tamerius Good, two names I don't want to forget. Creek was free, covered with mud, and clearly exhausted. Stephen and I were hosed off and put on fresh clothes. Shaney was at first surprised that I of course wanted to finish the day, getting our night time scene as well. She shouldn't have been. I will always push to finish the day unless it is absolutely impossible. I did, however, allow the crew to drink while we worked, something I wouldn't condone normally but this was one hell of a day. So we filled our whiskey glasses and went back to work.

November 10th, 2020

Death is a constant companion. The other day our good friend Frank Leggett, who has helped us haul props/wardrobe/gear all over the place and appeared in a couple scenes, lost his wife. Her organs failed and she died not long after. Nick Murphy drove down on a moment's notice to haul the gear from Frank's to our weekly location. Death is always here, waiting, though this year it feels closer than ever.

...

I've been thrown another curveball. Dunky, one of the actresses playing the Harpe women, has been exposed to Covid from her uncle. It's not certain she has it but it is also unlikely she can get test results back in time for filming in two days. I can't take the risk. This means I have to cut all three Harpe women out of the preacher scene. It sucks but there's no other option. We can't risk contamination so close to the end of this show.

November 11th, 2020

Must we have a predicament every day? Once stuck in the mud, now stuck in the sand. Yesterday afternoon, while filming on one of Rusty's sandbanks, the crew decided it would be way easier to drive one of his off roading vehicles down onto the sand rather than haul several loads of firewood by hand and foot. Listening to them, I wanted to veto and it will be the last time I don't when my instincts tell me to. Not far onto their beach drive, the vehicle was stuck. They tried all kinds of methods to get it out and finally I had to call them away from it to shoot a scene before we lost light. As soon as we wrapped that scene, we went back to this effort during our dinner hour, trying to tow it out with the other vehicle Rusty loaned us. After much trial and error, the Polaris was lifted out of its trap. The lesson learned, I asked the guys? Sometimes the hard way is the right way. A short cut isn't always worth it.

November 13th, 2020

A couple days ago I pushed my risk level to the max. It was the scene where Little Harpe is hanged. We planned two shots: one with only my feet dangling while I used the dolly rails to suspend myself and another shot where I stand on boxes with a noose tight around my neck and lean into the rope to make it look like I'm really choking. I would control the amount of leaning into the rope, able to stand back up whenever I needed to.

By all accounts, the first take looked pretty disturbingly real but they did note that I wasn't swinging enough in the beginning. So we went again. Something happened that we had not predicted: I leaned so much into the noose that I made myself pass out. Thankfully the rope was not tied but held and I fell back off the boxes on which I was standing, hit the tree and then the ground. On my end, I had no idea what had happened. I don't remember losing consciousness and felt as if I was in a dream until they shook me awake, having rushed to my side thinking I might be dead. Mario said I twitched on the ground, the most disturbing part of the experience from his perspective. When I opened my eyes, the first thought that crossed my mind was "why did you wake me?" The second was "why am I sleeping on the ground?" Then finally I asked, "Are we in the middle of a take?" Slowly I began to realize what had happened and was laughing to everyone's surprise except those who know me best. I'd lived so why not laugh? And I asked next if it looked good, if we'd gotten the take. We certainly did. What a scary experience, more frightening for the onlookers than myself but certainly the greatest risk I have taken in a long list during these 12 Westerns. Though many would disagree for safety reasons, it was totally worth it, confirmed by watching the footage which is chilling.

...

Yesterday we returned to the re-enactment where we filmed the charlatan preacher scene, another fun one, and started the Jackson duels. Mario was an hour late to location, getting lost again on the country lanes. I was pissed at him for not having a better sense of direction to a place he'd been the day before and it set us up for a stressful afternoon. Working with non actors in the role of Jackson and the other roles involved in the historic duels, I was both impressed at times with their abilities and driven to the point of madness with their inability to follow the most simple directions. They would confuse the entire order of such basic operations as aim, misfire, get angry, cock the gun, fire again. I'd call action and get aim, cock, fire... missing everything in between. All this was happening as the light was truly fading from the sky. We got only the minimum amount of takes to barely edit the story together and literally got our last shot with the last remaining light available. I hate working that way. I look forward to a few "days off" after a few scenes today to wrap up week five.

November 14th, 2020

It feels good to be back in Brookhaven for a few days. Though they will be filled with work, just being here, having the privacy of my bedroom, being able to watch a movie or two, is refreshing. My throat is almost healed from the hanging incident and I can swallow with little pain. My heel still has the splinter in it. Perhaps I will try Jen's epsom salt method again while I'm here.

I feel run ragged and broke. At the back of my mind, while working on these films, I try to figure out how to financially survive the next couple months. It won't be easy. I've literally poured everything into these twelve films and when it's over will be empty.

November 16th, 2020

I've had an unexpected issue with my car, a power steering pump going out that would cause the car to overheat when it does. As I write this, I'm waiting to hear back from the repair shop, who said it shouldn't be a big deal to fix but it still makes me nervous since I need to leave for Arkansas tomorrow and from there, Colorado. The frustration of living in Brookhaven is that I couldn't do anything about this problem on the weekend, all of the repair shops closed as of midday Saturday. I wasn't even able to retrieve my packages from the post office here because everything shuts down by midday Saturday, one of the cons of living in a small town.

...

Saturday night we joined the group of reenactors for their party. As soon as bottles of rum were passed around, I knew it was going to be a drunken night, a prediction that certainly came true. Nick Smith and I got the most intoxicated. But it was a good time with these genuine people and seeds were planted for further historical projects, including one about the Native history in this area.

...

The problem I've been dodging since March, the disease that's changed our living, seems to be on my heels now. This past week, Dunky (one of the Harpe women) had a close call with contracting it but seems to have tested negative. As an extra precaution, I decided to cut the women out of the preacher scene and only bring them back for our upcoming Arkansas scenes. The same day we filmed that preacher scene near Natchez, Daulton (Big Harpe) approached me with a new COVID concern. His mom was infected. He hadn't seen her in the last couple weeks but he had been in close proximity with his brother who could have been infected. We both determined that it was best to wait until his test results came back before alerting the cast/crew to the potential problem since he would have already contaminated us regardless if he was in fact positive. Once again, a negative result was given and we breathed a sigh of relief. But these close calls make me feel that the damn virus is catching up, like a bounty hunter chasing me across the plains. Can I make it to the finish line before he gets me?

November 17th, 2020

What I feared most regarding my car is exactly what happened: it is beyond repair or at least the means I have to repair it and also the logical sense to put that much into an older vehicle. It bounced around from one mechanic shop to another yesterday, ending up at the Toyota dealership where they quoted me 2600 dollars to fix what seems like such a random little problem. A bolt has broken off in the block but apparently this is a major pain in the ass mechanically and would take 20 hours of labor... What a time to lose my wheels. So I'm now hitching a ride with Shaney (makeup artist) to Arkansas and coming back here instead of going to Colorado. When I come back, there will be three options: 1. Somehow we have found a cheaper way to repair my car. This is the most doubtful. 2. I'm able to borrow my landlord Bill's Honda Civic to take out west and return in January. 3. I've found another cheap vehicle to purchase. Mississippi is not the best place to find one because there's no competition for prices. Another hurdle, another curveball thrown in a year of pitches I could never see coming.

November 18th, 2020

I woke up to a gorgeous sunrise in Fairfield Bay, Arkansas. Yesterday's drive was not uneventful with six hours of music and talk from Shaney, another flat tire, and a location scout along the Arkansas river. I am disappointed that my plans to leave from here did not work out. I will have to return to Brookhaven at the end of this week to resolve the car issue and gather more of my things.

...

Today we have a conference call with SAG's rep on COVID. I fear she will grill JD (the person I've chosen to be our "health and safety officer") and I on our practices and preparation for this. I can only hope we will sneak by, able to convince her that we are pulling things together day by day.

November 19th, 2020

This is the last day for many of us acting. I can't say I'm sad to say goodbye to Little Harpe. He's been fun to play but this week, I feel ready to be done, ready to move onto the next character and the next movie. Filming at the cave last night was a pleasure, a refreshing new landscape. I wish we could film a whole week here and add scenes but that just isn't in the cards.

November 22nd, 2020

For two days, we commuted from Fairfield Bay to Little Rock, about a two hour drive on winding roads, to film the last scenes of this six week journey. Our final story of the *Tales of the Natchez Trace* was Mike Fink. I was lucky enough to connect with Ed Williams, the owner of an actual keelboat, time appropriate for our scenes. Filming with this water vessel and his crew was one of my favorite times of this year. The first day, we cast out onto the Arkansas River with a limited crew and shot Fink boasting about his great accomplishments while Davy Crockett, an unrecognized passenger, quietly listened. It was a smooth day. Bandit got aboard for the last couple shots and seemed to be happy to see so much water.

There was another two hour drive home and I waited anxiously for our last day of filming, one with greater challenges. This time, we needed to travel on the boat to a small island in the river, taking two trips to bring all of our cast and crew. The transportation by oar takes time and I could feel our day slipping away before we'd even started. On top of that, the two scenes were not simple ones, nor could they be simplified too much without compromising the story. By the time we had lunch, I knew we'd be fighting light and it wouldn't just be for the camera: it would be illegal to have the boat on the water after dark since it has no headlights.

In the final two hours of this production, the longest film shoot of my career, we choreographed and captured a fist fight scene between Fink and Annie Christmas, a black madame who by legend was his rival. Mario and I were moving at rapid speed, calling out the punches one by one. It was as fast as I've ever worked and behind me I could feel the boat crew getting anxious. With the last bit of light left in the sky, we rolled on the last shot with Annie Christmas walking off into the distance and the keelboat rowed away with the first group of our team. I played with Bandit in the river as we waited for the second haul and gave my best try (a poor performance) at rowing on our way back.

We seemed to be victorious as we packed our things in the parking lot and I got into my new vehicle, a minivan I bought from Daulton. It is the only thing I can realistically afford right now and it also solves other issues of hauling gear around. When things settle down and I can rebuild my life after the war that has been these 12 Westerns, I'll look at getting another affordable ride of my preference.

...

Something happened on our drive home that could not have been predicted by anyone. Within ten minutes of where we are staying, I got a call from Shaney and soon realized that she was no longer in my rear view mirror. "Come back," she said, "My car is smoking and I'm stuck in the middle of the road." I found a place to whip my minivan around and headed back the mile or so to find her. She was not exaggerating. Her little Mini Cooper sat in the middle of Highway 16, smoke pouring from under the hood. As I approached, I could see the inside was filled too as Shaney tried desperately to back her vehicle off the road. Then I saw it... flames from the right side of her hood. "The car's on fire, Shaney. Get out." She grabbed her phone and fled with me to the other side of the street where we watched the car engulfed in flames within less than a minute. We could not believe our eyes. I could not imagine how she felt, having lost a couple vehicles to freak things but this was the wildest yet.

We took a major risk, another passerby and I, approaching the vehicle from behind to try and save some of her belongings. We managed to grab her makeup supplies and bags as the car popped and hissed. He, ironically named Michael Mills, even tried to get her purse out of the front seat. Unfortunately, all of its contents fell out as he did and soon melted with the rest. Our team showed up not long after and we watched the car burn and burn from across the way with some minor explosions as the fire department finally showed up. Shaney is one of those people, like my dad and myself most of the time, who do not freak out in these kind of situations. She kept her cool surprisingly well as she called her husband and family, knowing that her life had suddenly changed. But at least she was okay. Mario commented before he left, that at least our production did not end with a suicide as the one we'd worked on back in March had. Yes, thankfully this is far less of a tragic event than that one. We returned home, cooked burgers, laughed, drank, and went to sleep.

I've worked with Creek Wilson many times. Here, he plays the lead role of Samuel Mason.

My character Little Harpe finally captured for his crimes.

Filming near the Natchez Trace with a wagon from the late 1600s, a historic vehicle we also featured in *Bastard's Crossing*.

Daulton Brewer as Big Harpe. We tragically lost Daulton during 2021.
All photographs by Damon Burks

HEART OF THE GUN

And now we come to the last of the twelve. Originally slated to be shot in June, it ultimately seemed appropriate that this film be the final one of our wild project. It was the script I cared most about, the most personal I've ever written. It had the biggest budget. It gave John his biggest role yet. It has a chance to reteam with Nick Fornwalt, one of my favorite

people to work with. And finally, it was an opportunity to combine everything I'd learned all year, plus all the lessons I've learned the last decade as a filmmaker, and make the best movie I could. If this were my last film ever, I would be content with the work I've done.

Heart of the Gun tells the story of Jack Travers, a bitter man who searches the Arizona territory for his long lost wife. Along the way, he finds a mysterious woman named Sarah, the only survivor from a group of travelers who were massacred. Sarah accompanies Travers along his dark journey, a violent odyssey that may lead them to redemption.

Photograph by Todd South

November 24th, 2020

I am now on the road to Colorado, passing through Texas. Yesterday I took Shaney home, going out of my way to South Louisiana but I did not regret it. Over the last couple days we became very close and I count her as a good friend. I am stressed about the progress and lack there of for this last movie. After the botched scout that was supposed to answer so many questions, I am on edge, Wanting to figure out as much as possible as soon as possible. The people at Tilting H Ranch will promise pictures or answers in a day or two and not deliver for days on end. Our post production process has nearly come to a halt. If I'm not pushing, it feels as if we do not move forward. I am hoping that by the end of my stay at my parents house, I can feel a degree of progress and stand on more solid ground.

November 26th, 2020

I've arrived at my parents' house in Denver. My first day here was hectic as hell as a bomb dropped on us in the morning: apparently the covid testing we were hoping to get for this coming film costs 9,000 dollars a week!

Later in the day, I received a text from our assistant camera person, saying that she's sick and can't work on the film. I was angry at this announcement, especially with a week still to go. Why so hasty to quit? Has she been tested? Couldn't she give it a couple days to see how she feels? She agreed to try and test soon but seemed sure that she can't do it. What the hell... I don't know who we can find to replace this late in the game.

November 27th, 2020

Working in post-production makes you want to travel back in time and kill certain people. Okay, maybe fire them but some of the screw-ups make me feel violently angry. The sound on *Deputy's Wife* is a mess. Some scenes I can salvage through "wild lines", our on-set ADR, but the damn sound guy only recorded a take or two max for each player per scene when I clearly told him to get at least two to three takes. Sometimes I only have one option for a line replacement and if it doesn't match the lips, I'm fucked. Neither he nor the actors kept good track of the changes to their lines... this is something I need to be adamant about as we make this last Western. It can't have these issues and I hope that some of the others in the can don't either. I feel a long road ahead in getting this movie ready for release.

November 28th, 2020

The drama over our assistant camera person quitting escalated yesterday as she suddenly claimed to be negative from her COVID test, feeling better, and back on board. I called the search for a replacement off... a mistake. Here is my exchange of messages with her who I will not hire in any capacity again:

Her: Sorry for the scare. Just wanted to be cautious. Excited to start.

Me: Ok. In the future, please try to remember that warning someone and quitting are very different. Giving me a heads up was a great idea. Saying you're out with a week left was too hasty. Please think about that. You're 100 percent in yes?

Her: Actually, since the experiences of the cast and crew on the last set I've had repeated concerns over the priority of health and safety on these films; and though I'm ill I was going to push myself but no longer feel compelled to do so. I honestly wish you the best and hope for the success of these projects but I feel uncomfortable working on your set at this time and have to put that first.

Me: That is super unprofessional and you should not have signed a deal memo saying you'd work on the film if you had any such concerns.

Her: I'm sorry you feel that way but this has really only confirmed my concerns. In my professional opinion I know I'm doing the right thing for my well-being. I truly wish your project great success; it will have to be without me.

Me: Do not use me or our team as a reference for anything. In no professional world is it okay to sign a deal memo, quit because you're sick a week out, get better and say you're in, then quit again over safety concerns that you never stated before. Goodbye.

Damn her and damn all these weak, sensitive children that we call adults these days. Tough people are an endangered species. Now we're back to scrambling for a replacement... and on the subject of dropouts, one of our actors bailed yesterday because of surgery. A little bit better of an excuse for sure but how many more of these can I expect over the next week or even during production?

Since I always write about the issues, let me briefly state some good things that have nothing to do with the 12 Westerns: watching Bandit play in the snow, seeing my parents gifted a new TV by their international friends (a moment I found so moving it brought me to tears), and watching *Texas Red* with mom and dad last night, during which I felt mostly proud of what we've done.

November 30th, 2020

I'm sitting in a hotel room in Florence, Arizona. As of now, we have still not replaced the assistant camera person.

December 1st, 2020

It appears we may have finally found a replacement for the assistant camera position. Last night I asked Jared if he had any other recommendations. Jared, who can't do it, sent me to Joe who also couldn't do it so Joe sent me to Danyelle who also couldn't do it but sent me to Cole who sounds like he might can do it... I spoke with him today and he seems solid enough, one of those who needs the experience. He sure as hell is going to get it.

December 2nd, 2020

If there's a bad guy this year, a villain in this story, it must be SAG. Not the virus? No. The virus is like the Native tribe stalking me through the desert and it's unsure whether they're going to let me go or attack. SAG on the other hand is like an outlaw that comes into my town and screws things up now and then. They're a thorn in my side, something that was once supposed to protect people and now only causes trouble. Yesterday (and keep in mind this is down to wire for our production to start), their list of demands continued. They take days to get back to me, no doubt taking as much time as they can off while I work around the clock, and then expect me to jump when they say so.

The biggest bullshit they threw at me was AFTER sending the total deposit I needed to wire transfer their way, the SAG rep backtracked, saying that because Lou Ferrigno is traveling two days we owe him an extra 10,000 dollars... I showed John who of course thought it was horseshit too. I wrote the SAG rep back, explaining that our deal with Lou is to do the role for 5000 and that if they insist on paying travel days, I'll go back to Lou to adjust his day rate to equal a total of 5000 for three days. No response. But I anticipate an email fight sometime today about this.

December 3rd, 2020

I've successfully sent off the SAG deposit and also the estimated total of our SAG salaries so that I don't have to worry about making a trip to the bank every week while I'm filming in the middle of nowhere. It's fifteen thousand dollars gone, a huge chunk of the budget. I'm working hard to raise more investment, more money that we need or I won't be able to pay everyone. This isn't the first time I've faced such a situation but I hoped it wouldn't come again. This morning I had to swallow a lot of horseshit from a new investor who I'm courting to put 5,000 into this one (again, a five we desperately need). I had to hear all about his concerns that some are calling this "the John Marrs movie". "Who is in charge?" He asked. I explained to him like a movie child that 1. Producers have producing partners. 2. That I trust John to have authority and that he respects my final decisions. 3. That calling something a "Jimmy Stewart movie" doesn't mean it wasn't directed by John Ford!

From there I had to listen to him about how he's recommended me for the top choice to direct some bigger budget westerns. I flat out told him that I was flattered he recommended me but that things like that don't feel real to me until I see a contract on my desk. He insisted that he and I are on the same level: "We don't need to audition or try out anymore, Travis. We're on the same level now. People know us." I washed the bullshit taste out of my mouth with a third cup of coffee.

December 5th, 2020

I've made it to Cherry Creek Lodge near Young or Pleasant Valley as it used to be called. This of course was not without misadventure. My girlfriend and I loaded up all my gear from Corey's warehouse. I took the brunt of it, weighing down my Mills Mobile probably more than I should have. We took off for the three hour drive. I quickly lost her along the road but didn't think much of it. The van did well most of the drive and then on the steepest and longest incline, I got stuck behind a Winnebago which brought me to a crawl. With no momentum, the van started struggling to regain speed. I switched to lower gears but it did not help any. I could feel it totally losing power. And then... smoke. This of course scared me because of what had recently happened with Shaney's car. I stopped immediately, threw on my hazard lights and after making sure the van wouldn't roll back down the incline (which I was still on), I opened the hood. White smoke poured out but seemingly not from the engine or radiator. Also my temperature gauge had never gone up. The whole thing felt odd.

I had the good fortune to have cell service in this spot, something that is scarce on this entire drive. I contacted my girlfriend and let her know what was happening. Oddly enough, she'd gone a different way and claimed to be 15 miles from our destination. I told her that wasn't possible, thatGPS was clearly leading her wrong. She didn't believe me at the time. I then contacted Corey to start troubleshooting my problems. I checked the oil and found it to be low but Corey said it wasn't dangerously low. I checked my coolant. It seemed good but I added water just in case. Many tried to stop and help me but there wasn't much they could do. I waved them on, waiting for the smoke to completely clear. And then another truck came by. An older gentleman inside was more adamant about diagnosing my problem. He pulled over and got out while his wife waited. Together we theorized about what might have happened. Finally he felt I was safe enough to go another 200 yards or so to a flatter area. I felt good about it too and the van hiccuped a little but made it without much effort. It didn't seem to be smoking again either. Once I arrived there we discovered that we actually know each other in a roundabout way! He and his wife own the house adjacent to the property where we filmed *New Frontier* in July. We joked about them watching us create fake rain and lighting out their windows and they went on their way soon after.

I told my girlfriend I was pushing on, confident that it was the slowing down on that hardest part of the climb and my transmission getting overwhelmed that caused the problem. Apparently she was racing to reach me. The rest of the drive was thankfully effortless. We met up in the town of Young before driving into the property. She still didn't believe me about her first route being the wrong way but she would later after seeing our final destination, a place you can only get to from one road.

...

The crew arrived one by one and it was nice to see all of them. Amber, the lead actress, had arrived too but she'll have her boyfriend with her these first few days, a desire I understand but also one that I feel prevents her from bonding with us until he leaves. The Native American actor had been transported by one of the crew. He felt standoffish, cold and quiet, both upon meeting him and for the rest of the day. My girlfriend defended this as the Native American way, "he doesn't like white people", and I dismissed that as bullshit: "I hired him. I deserve a degree of respect and acknowledgment from him." She apparently bonded with him because he didn't see her as "white". She continued to defend him throughout the day and night, as John and I continued to shrug our shoulders at his unfriendly attitude. Finally, as I tried to sleep in bed, she returned from drinking with John and started a plea for us to understand the native actor: "He wants to do justice to his people. He doesn't want to make them look silly. He showed me images of how he wants to be represented." John, probably five glasses of whiskey in, was the voice of my subconscious, stating confusion and frustration at what she was relaying. Ultimately she said, "He wanted me to tell these things to you guys to make sure you understand." That was it. She'd pulled the trigger. I sat up in bed and with a loud voice proclaimed, "then he can be a man and tell us to our faces. If he's going to be a problem, I will write his character out of the damn movie. I'm tired of hearing you talk about this. I don't want to hear another word about it." I was fed up, annoyed by her insistence, by her pandering to his attitude which has no grounds. If he had concerns, he should have brought them up when reading the script. He should talk directly to me. And she should know better.

She and I have been getting along less and less. I don't know what's happening. I'm certainly stressed but I feel she is not acting like the woman I met. It makes me sad because I feel a growing distance from her... and I did like her.

December 9th, 2020

Day one was a beast as we worked with several complicated elements: moving a wagon, fire, simulated rain. We'd failed to get our wagon transported from Tombstone and to find any other from around this area so we were stuck with only using the one here on this property. The problem with that wagon is who knows how long it had been since the damn thing was moved. The ranch guys, Kenny and Reese, loaded it on a flatbed trailer but on the short, rocky drive to our location, the wheels started to crumble. There was no way we could roll it off. We theorized options but ultimately Kenny went to get the backhoe and lifted the whole wagon in the air, setting it down in our spot.

...

Our afternoon scenes went fairly well, especially for a first day and we broke for dinner prepared for what we knew would be a cold night, not to mention a wet one for some of us with all the fake rain. We've been talking for weeks to Pete at the ranch about their ability to use a water pump to create rain for this scene. Up until even the day of, they were still working to figure it out. A truck came out with the pump and a 300 gallon tank. Within three takes of spraying water on the scene, we'd used up nearly half of those 300 gallons. A refill would take at least 45 minutes, so we knew this wasn't practical. The ranch guys went back to get an even bigger truck that could hold 1500 gallons.

Meanwhile in the first couple shots, we'd encountered another issue. In the darkness of the shot I could see weird bands on the image, what we would call "banding." It can be a problem with some lights, causing the camera to pick up this distracting look. I told Nick about it but we couldn't diagnose what might be causing it other than just low light and the camera needing more. Ultimately we decided to move on, hoping the images would clean up well in post. The guys returned with the bigger truck but we had more trouble to contend with: 1. The spray from the hose wasn't near enough to cover a wide shot of the scene and still be believable. 2. JD and Todd, the actors playing the dead bodies on the ground, were rightfully worried about getting wet and then having to wait while we reset. Over time, much debate, and finally a combination of good ideas from both Nick and I, we found a wide shot that worked by keeping the focus on our hero in the foreground. This allowed the rain, which couldn't nearly cover the scene, to look like it was. It also allowed us to avoid getting the other talent from being soaked.

Suddenly we had victory after victory. In the wide, we also had a risky fire again in which I lit a piece of canvas, which I'd sprayed with a little lighter fluid, hanging off the wagon. I basically ran through the scene doing this after the camera was rolling, ran around the water truck to see if the shot was working while also seeing that the flames had taken off, burning far more of the canvas than we intended. I watched the shot only long enough to know we had enough usable footage and then hurried in to tear the canvas off the wagon and stamp it out on the ground.

All the water was freezing to whatever it hit: the wagon, equipment, my beard. By the end of the night, we had to leave nearly everything there to pick up the next day when it thawed out.

...

The next day we tackled rain again but in a new spot and with thankfully a smaller area to work in. We also developed an interesting new system. With the talent under a big tree, we'd shoot water up into it, soaking the tree, then killing the flow during the shot while drops fell down long enough to get the take. This required us to cover the fire to keep it from going out. So Reese would blast the tree while the team waited out of the way. I stayed near the falling water with my hand on the propane nozzle (this device was controlling the fire), giving it more gas if the water got past the cover and started to douse the flames. I yelled, "Let's go". The water shut off. The team rushed in. Cole, one of our crew, took the cover off the fire. I boosted the flames. Nick and Stephen got camera in place. Forrest landed a bounce to reflect light. John and Amber got on their marks and I called action. Thankfully, take after take, we had enough drops to make the scene work.

...

John and Amber are both great to work with. Of course I knew that about John already but you never know about a new person. She's very practical, all about the work. They are both surprised at the amount of notes I'm giving them take after take, more than I usually do. But John relayed to her that this is my most personal script and also the one I want to be the best of the 12, whatever that means. I guess it means the best to me, regardless of what happens out in the world. I'm also giving them more direction so that they don't miss any of the subtext. They come in real good with usable takes but there are layers missing, especially because in essence this film is a mystery and we have to leave clues for the audience or it won't work. I'm leaving nothing on the table here. I'm giving everything I've got from scene to scene and not settling.

...

Transportation is definitely one of the biggest challenges on this production. Now that we have been filming deeper and deeper into the ranch property, it's impossible to get vehicles back to where we need to be. The ranch has loaned us one Polaris off roading vehicle which is our sole means of transportation for gear and people, other than horses of course. So we'll make a couple runs with that machine to drop off all the gear for the day and then start to run people from the lodge to the location. This takes about 20 minutes or more each time, not a huge time waster but definitely something new to factor into our process. To give you an example, yesterday at the end of day four, I waited behind with Bandit while our actors rode their horses back, Forrest took a Polaris full of people, and then we jam-packed the vehicle on two trips to move all the gear to where we'll be filming later today. So far, I'm impressed at our efficiency to film with very little in a rugged environment.

...

My first scenes were yesterday. Willy, the makeup artist, helped to shave my head again the night before. I put on my bear skin vest and the rest of my outfit. It produced an immediate reaction among the cast and crew. Some found it humorous to see me this way. But when we arrived on set and I rubbed the ash from the previous day's fire on my face, people began to look at me as if I was a maniac. We rehearsed the long scene over and over. I needed to warm up, something I continue to see as a necessity when I'm acting but if I'm ever hired on someone else's movie I'll have to find a way to be ready on take one regardless.

Watching footage at the end of the night, our dailies from the last three days of production, I feel pretty good about what we've gotten. I only hope we can keep this up and reach the end in one piece.

...

Yesterday we applied my scalp makeup for the first time. I'm sure Willy was nervous as she worked on it and received criticism. But she made adjustments and the effect continued to improve. She worked on it all the way through everyone else's coverage in the scene until my shot was up and the hat came off to reveal Dolan's mangled head. I was glad that she pulled it off.

...

At the end of the evening, we had a couple mishaps. After completing what might be the best scene of the movie so far, we'd wrapped an hour or more early and packed up to head back for the bunkhouse. Tom, one of the actors, was going to ride back on one of our character horses but had some trouble and ended up taking a spill. Thank goodness he wasn't hurt bad but he's sore as hell this morning. Another hurdle came when the ranch crew came to bring us our dinner but their Polaris died on them. This left them stranded and their vehicle blocking ours from getting out. We had to push it with a few guys deeper into the rocky ravine to drive through. Finally, after getting back home, having a couple glasses of whiskey and half a cigar, Forrest (gaffer) hit me up, revealing that he never got the memo that it might rain overnight. He still had gear out there which could be ruined. I knew what this meant: I needed to put my boots on and go help him. So a little wobbly from the booze, I set out with Forrest for a cold night ride.

The other big development the last couple days is I think my girlfriend and I are done. Couple nights ago we spoke via text and I tried to explain my thoughts on how she's changed. No surprise, her perspective was that it's me that had changed and been the trigger for our trouble. She wholeheartedly believes that I've become a different person because of the stress of the movie. I explained to her that though all productions are stressful, it's what I do and that the main thing stressing me out is our relationship.

The next day I woke up to a text, not just to me but to John also, telling us she won't be able to pick up Lou Ferrigno as planned. Her excuse was her tires, which are in bad shape and need replacement, but as I texted back and offered to pay for her tires until she can pay me back, it seemed like there was something else going on. That's the feeling John got too and in his very sincere way said simply, "I'm sorry Travis." We both liked her but even he can see how she's changed.

December 11th, 2020

We got thrown yet another major curveball yesterday. As I tried to catch up on my morning emails, I heard murmurs from JD (our COVID officer) and one of our actors about a positive test. Sure enough, minutes later JD was pulling me aside to talk. His face looked grim. Yes, this person had just received his test results from days before and had come up positive with COVID. Fuck. That's what we both said. What now? He'd been in our bunkhouse, eating and working around us for three days. Though none of us showed symptoms, any of us could be infected.

I immediately started thinking of a plan to move forward safely. One stroke of luck was that his scenes were nearly wrapped. He really just had two more shots for the entire movie and we needed to figure out how to re-block the scene in order to get his shots done without having his body needed for the remaining ones with the other actors. I recommended to JD that we do this, wrapping his shots and getting him out of there as soon as possible. From there, we'd finish the day wearing our masks and staying as safe/clean as we could, requiring everyone to get tested the next day (our first day off after finishing week one). This test could show any of us to be positive and depending on how important his or her role (mine, John or Amber's) the production would be dead in the water.

We communicated this plan to the whole team and offered the option to back out now. No one did. JD went to work on finding us a definite location for rapid testing the next day. Nick, Forrest, Willy, and I loaded up into the Polaris with the actor to go film his last two shots. Oh and it was raining this day, something that ultimately saved our asses by providing consistent overcast light but also a difficult element to work in. We figured a way to have this character die away from where the rest of the scenes would take place and wrapped him out in not much more than an hour. I reminded him upon saying goodbye that it was no fault of his, could have happened to any of us which is true enough...

...

Once we got to work with the rest of the cast and crew, it didn't feel too different from a regular shoot day other than the effort to wear our masks and use sanitizer as often as possible. This final day of week one also happened to include some of our most challenging scenes: my character getting his arm chopped off, sticking it in the fire, Timmy (Michael Walker) getting shot, and a lot of big dramatic moments.

As we worked after lunch, it became clear that fighting light was once again going to be our final challenge of the week. The makeup gag for my axed-off arm was a major struggle. Kaylee, or Willy as we like to call her, is a new makeup artist. For the most part she's done good, but there have been a few mistakes. One, she can't keep continuity straight to save her life. After many requests, she still was not using picture references to make sure Sarah's face scars matched and until I insisted over and over, did not notice that my scalp makeup wasn't the same as the day before. I only hope these little mistakes aren't too evident in the final film. The amputated arm was a challenging gag for sure. I hid my forearm and hand up in my shirt and she tried to connect the fake forearm to my elbow. Her first method didn't work at all and I called for gaff tape to help it stay, which it did but posed another problem: making sure the black gaff wasn't seen in the shot. We did a few takes after waiting close to an hour for the makeup to be done and finally dialed in something that could work with some clever edits. By the time we wrapped that scene, we had less than two hours left of light and had to hurry like hell to get the rest of the complicated blocking done. At one point I shouted at John and some of the others who were talking and joking while Nick and I set up a shot, "everyone needs to shut up and listen to every fucking word that's being said. We don't have time to fuck around and repeat things. Now get on your mark!" Some people just don't realize when things are dire on set, that you're literally risking the quality of a scene or the ability to finish it. We did that day as we shot Timmy quickly, faked that my arm was burned in the fire, and then had our hero and heroine part ways. With the last bit of light in the sky, we filmed John riding off while Amber watched. We packed up and went back to the lodge, not knowing if it might be the last production day for *Heart of the Gun* if lab results the next day went the way we feared.

...

This morning we woke up and prepared for that trip to Show Low where six of us would be tested. The rest went separate ways on our days off with the promise they'd be tested and remain as isolated as possible over the weekend. The night before and that morning, some of the cast and crew had asked me if I'd theorized what would happen and how I'd move forward completing the 12 Westerns if someone key to this project was infected. The truth is, I tried not to think too much about it. If it did, I'd go crazy. Rewrite the script? Pause this production and improvise another? The possibilities were endless and all as undesirable. All I want to do is finish this movie and the project but these damn obstacles keep falling in my way.

The test took us a little more than an hour, all tearing up at the probe stuck deep up in each of our nostrils. We then got groceries for the weekend and headed back. When we returned to Young and my phone service came back, I was astounded to see a text from JD announcing that our test results came back... we were all negative!! I had to ask him twice to be sure. It felt like a miracle. Damn lucky bastards we all are. Since then, Nick and Willy (who went home to get their tests) have negative results too. We're just waiting to hear back about two more members of the crew. After that, we'll have to be even more careful than we were before. We dodged a bullet this time but might not the next.

I am tired now but upon returning to the ranch, the good news of the tests was met with bad news from another aspect of production. I will write about this tomorrow...

December 12th, 2020

So as we drove back into Young and stopped to get ice, John looked down at his phone and said, "No..." I knew something was wrong. He showed me. It was a text from Lou Ferrigno, saying something to this effect: "My doctor re-sheduled my surgery a week early. I won't be able to come. Doctor's orders." We were both baffled. John wrote back, "You're not coming to make the movie?" A simple word response came back less than a minute later, "No".

This comes after having him sign a deal memo, ordering his flight, his hotel, arranging his ride with girlfriend (now ex), having her drop out of giving him a ride, arranging a new ride with Daulton (actor), answering a ton of his questions ranging from when he's getting paid to if there's red wine at the lodge and if he can shoot guns in his off time... Basically a whole lot of work for nothing. John was pissed. It was his contact. He trusted Lou. We all did. But there was no point in fighting. Lawyer up? So we can force him to make a movie he clearly doesn't want to make? The night before he bailed on us, John was assaulted with another barrage of questions from the "name talent". I think it was Lou digging for a reason to not come and he didn't find one so he used surgery as an excuse. It is what it is. We lost some money, time, and we won't have his name to help the film. We save money in the long run but it sucks. John and I are brainstorming if it's worth trying to use some of those funds to cast a recognizable face or name later in the production. He reached out to Chris Mitchum last night, who he also has a connection with. In the meantime, we switched Daulton, who was coming from Arkansas to work with Lou, to the Hulk's role (one I created solely for him). It's been a hell of a week that's for sure.

December 13th, 2020

Well, things got more interesting yesterday. On our last "day off", during which I may have taken a break for a total of 30 minutes, John and I planned to scout the big cave, a location Pete (ranch manager) has told me about for months but failed to show us until now. He finally agreed to take us out there so we drove down to the General store in Young to wait for him.

Minutes before he showed up, Forrest (our gaffer) messaged me to say that his test came back positive... the only one of us. Or at least he's the only one of us unless some kind of crazy incubation period thing is going on.

Man down! Forrest is such a key player. It's his gear. He has the knowledge and experience. He's a workhorse. It's like losing the machine gunner on the ship. He has to isolate for 10 days now and will most likely not join us till the end of the shoot.

...

If that wasn't enough, we had another problem on our hands. The rules were that you couldn't come back to set unless you proved a negative test result after our scare with Tom. I followed up with our Native American actor about this yesterday but he'd already been warned that he needed one through several emails. He sent me the picture of a test result in response but I noticed it had no date. "Is this a new test? It has no date?" He saw my message but did not answer. I sent JD what he showed me and asked him to call the actor. You see, in only an hour or two Willy (makeup) and Alexis (Native American actress) were supposed to give this actor a ride to set because he has no car. Suddenly, as I drove out of cell service, I was panicking to warn Alexis not to pick him up unless he proves a negative result or everything would be fucked. "Don't get him until he can prove a new negative test." Thankfully, I had JD to help with this. The actor eventually admitted he was waiting for his results but this also proved that he'd lied with the earlier results, trying to pass a test that may or may not have even been his off to us. Such bullshit! And this was the actor that we'd had the trouble with for being standoffish, for creating the trouble with my ex about his "representation". Now he was lying about the test and potentially tossing our production into the fire.

The next spot of service I got on the mountain road, texts came through from the ladies asking what they should do and some from JD saying the actor could still not prove a negative test. "Leave without him," I told the girls, already formulating a way to revise his pivotal role in the film and make it the Apache woman's instead. John said later, after we'd returned to the bunkhouse, that we'd become experts in adjusting to crazy situations. I joked that we should retire from filmmaking and just do seminars about how to hit curveballs in life. We spent the evening rewriting the script to prepare for filming tomorrow with Alexis instead.

...

The good things from yesterday: the big cave was actually cool, worth the two hour drive. And we had ribeye steaks for lunch, eating better by our own hand than we have so far by the ranch's cooking.

December 14th, 2020

Yesterday, our seventh one on *Heart of the Gun,* was the first during which we haven't had a scare, a surprise, a major hurdle to overcome. It was a regular shoot day with ordinary challenges and therefore, a nice break from the storm.

Alexis, who replaced the Native actor and therefore got boosted from a puny role to a pivotal one, did a fine enough job. It was a challenge to get her to sound like she knew little English but still emote, especially without it verging into cheesiness. I think it was serviceable, not the strongest scenes in the film but also not bad. "Three good scenes and no bad scenes", Howard Hawks said, and that's something I am keeping in mind as I have to adjust the film daily with all these unforeseen developments but try desperately to make sure we retain quality.

December 16th, 2020

I joked once again yesterday morning that the gods don't want me to finish this, that Zeus must be throwing lightning bolts down to see if I'll get back up and keep going. We woke up to no power here at the ranch. Everything is solar powered and when that runs out, there's a generator. Well, the latter wasn't working. It puttered in and out as we tried to make coffee, brewing a cup at a time. I worried breakfast wouldn't be ready because of this issue and delay our travel to the distant cave location. However, the ranch ladies, who have sometimes underperformed on this trip, impressed us with one of the best morning meals we've had, cooked by the light of their cell phones.

We set out in four vehicles for what would be a two hour trip to the cave. Not thirty minutes in, one of these vehicles (a loaner truck the actor Daulton was given by the dealership) wouldn't shift higher than first gear. We waited for him on the steep road, tried to fix the truck, and ended up having to abandon it, piling him and his passengers into the other vehicles. So much for my plan to create more space for the long ride.

We met Corey (my old friend and eccentric collaborator) halfway. He'd driven up in his 1941 Pontiac. I hopped out of John's warm jeep into a Polaris with Corey and we started down the bumpy road to our final destination while he told me stories of his recent adventures.

...

The shoot was not a smooth one. Nick was sick and doubtful of all the frames he set up. When he gets this way, I don't know what to do but have learned better than to fight it. John seemed distracted sometimes, joking around with Amber and I don't blame him: one smile from her and I feel different.

...

We once again barely got our last scene, which ironically turned out to be our best. Corey and I sped back in the Polaris, hands and faces feeling the brunt of the cold air.

December 17th, 2020

My spirit is tired today. I don't even believe in a spirit but that's how I can best describe how I feel. Beat. Worn. I dreamt that all the women I liked wanted John instead of me. A silly dream but one that woke me up melancholy nonetheless.

...

At the end of yesterday's shoot, which was a much needed light reprieve from our challenging days, I rode back on Whiskey. Feeling comfortable at a walk and a trot, I knew the other riders (John, Nick, and Todd) would take off as soon as we neared the ranch. They did and within seconds we were flying. It was fun and scary, the longest time I've galloped so far. I look forward to training more and getting to the point where I can be and look comfortable at any speed on a horse.

December 18th, 2020

Yesterday looked like it might turn into another troubled one as we set out for a long commute to location and John realized he might not have enough gas to get us there. He assumed his less than a quarter of a tank would be fine but somewhere on the curvy roads out of Young his gas light came on. We had a good 13 miles to our meeting spot and then a supposed 3 of rugged terrain down to a remote cabin. Would we make it? It wouldn't have been a question if Forrest and Cole had packed the gas can for the generator but instead they'd chosen to just top off the genny and leave it... I theorized about syphoning gas from another vehicle or the generator into John's but we couldn't find a hose of any kind to allow this. So, we started our way down, scraping the bottom of John's jeep along big rocks as I cringed most of the way to the bottom of this beautiful valley. We'd slipped Kenny and Reese (ranch workers) twenty bucks to fetch up some gas and leave it at the top, hoping by the end of the day that John's vehicle could make it back up and planning if it couldn't that we'd have to make a run with another vehicle to bring the gas back to wherever we were stranded.

Upon arrival at the cabin, which has sadly been vandalized with people's names carved on the exterior, I found a hose! We could siphon the gas after all. But after three attempts (and three mouthfuls of gasoline), I wasn't able to get it to work, even with the generator elevated. Somehow, the laws of physics were against us. So we went back to work and though getting down to location took a good two hours, we were able to get through all our scenes down there without rushing and wrap by 3pm, giving us and the horses enough daylight to climb back out.

...

Our last shot was one of my favorites ever, not just for this film but any film I've made. It started in the reflection of the creek as we see Sarah waiting for Travers. He then appears in the reflection and she raises her head. He says her name, not Sarah, but her real name Gail for the first time in the movie. The camera tilts up out of the reflection as she stands and looks at him. He tells her, "Let's leave this place." She turns back to the camera and breathes a sigh of relief. We went six or seven takes. Nick commented, "You only get this picky when you love a shot." It's probably true. My eyes filled with tears as we got the last two takes.

...

I cringed all the way up too, waiting for the jeep to putter out. Somehow it did not, going the five miles (yes, the ranch boys' estimate of three was quite off target) to the top where we happily refilled. John made his way back to the ranch while I waited for Nick and Amber to complete the journey on horseback. I never feel good about leaving team members behind. It's good to be the last out, knowing we all made it.

On our drive back to the ranch, I suggested to Nick that we wait to have dinner and get the last night scene before eating and breaking for the day. To my surprise, he was up for it. He's become much more flexible with changes and circumstances since we last worked together. So we got back and rounded everyone up, building one more campfire and capturing one of the most emotional scenes of the picture. I had tears running down my cheeks during a few takes but this time not for the performances. There was smoke in my eyes.

December 19th, 2020

The last day of week two went surprisingly well. One of the most lucky things happened this whole production: we couldn't film where we wanted to. Having chosen the ideal place for the final climactic fight, we were dismayed to hear that it was on another rancher's property. Pete, the ranch manager, suggested we check out another spot, further out. I cut Nick's breakfast early and we hopped in the Polaris for a cold ride. Like I said, this might be the luckiest thing that's happened all production as this new location was way better than the first one!

We excitedly hauled our crew and horses out there, plus Jay Pickett who'd come in to play the pivotal role of John White. It was his first day and what a day to start. After setting up the fight, we choreographed his hand to hand battle with John, which was to take place in a cold creek. I stood about thigh deep in this creek, the water right under my balls, for Nick to frame up the shots which we knew had to happen quickly once the actors got wet. The first take, with John tackling Jay into the water, had to go well or it would all be for not since their wardrobe would then be soaked. We worked out all the moves on sand and then went for it. The actors did a wonderful job and what transpired felt real, intense. They were shivering by the time we got all the shots, shedding their coats and getting what warmth they could from a fire we built out of frame.

December 23rd, 2020

The low hit me tonight. It came after my ex broke her two week silence to request I ship her things back and then of course declare that what happened was all my fault, as it has been in my past relationships from all the "research" she's done the last couple weeks. I didn't respond. It wasn't worthy of a response. But it was enough to hurt. Even if I shouldn't be with her and this proves that point all the more, it hurts.

...

Yesterday, our last shoot day at Cherry Creek Lodge, we had our biggest talent group yet with cavalry extras, two Apaches, and several horses. It was a nerve wracking morning as I waited for everyone to arrive, fearing someone essential to our scenes might get lost on the mountain roads, and then waiting even longer for all the horses and riders to get tacked up and ready to roll. We got our first scene close to the lodge and then set out for the creek location, much deeper on the property.

As John mentioned having things to arrange before he joined us and having Todd pony Lucy's horse, I saw an opportunity.

"I've always wanted to ride Lucy," I said and mounted up, electing to ride on horseback out to the next spot instead of taking the Polaris.

...

The scenes went surprisingly well with no horse incidents and cooperative talent, especially the Apaches who were great to work with and JD Pepper who gave his finest performance yet as the Kilgore-like Sergeant Meeker. It was a fine day to end the Cherry Creek lodge journey. Now, the fourth and final week has come.

December 24th, 2020

I am tired in a way that no sleep can cure. My heart is tired.

December 25th, 2020

The only cure is work. Lose myself in one last week of hard work and finish this project. I couldn't even help myself the last couple days and just chill out: John and I started outlining a Western television series... It's called *Contention* and I'm already in love with it.

Today, we go to Yuma. I know this isn't going to be an easy ending to the year but I'm ready to face whatever the next six days have for me.

December 26th, 2020

I wrote a piece about Heart of the Gun that's been brewing inside me the past several days. Here it is:

MY HEART OF THE WEST: THE LAST OF THE TWELVE

You may have heard me mention more than once that HEART OF THE GUN, the last of our 12 Westerns, is my most personal Western, probably my most personal film of any kind to date. Some may have wondered why. I've felt the urge to explore those reasons and as the last week of production on this film and the 12 Westerns begins, it feels like no better time to explain.

Heart of the Gun emerged from the ashes of a breakup back in 2014. It was a brutal relationship, full of passion but also toxic on many levels. It left me broken and full of anger. As I announced the 12 Westerns project for the first time at the end of 2013 and started to write the earliest scripts (Deputy's Wife and Frontier came to life at this time too), a story that channeled those emotions came to be. It was about a man named Travers (the closest name I could use without using my own) who searches for a woman, his long lost wife. But he's not looking for her out of love; he's searching for her in anger, in pain... and if he ever finds her, he may kill her. This woman has red hair, just like the one I dated years ago and along his journey Travers discovers another woman with red hair, a wounded traveler named Sarah. Her face is covered in scars and that's not the only place she's been hurt. Together, they begin a quest of violence and ultimately, redemption. I'd call it a romantic Western. Recently our makeup artist Kaylee remarked at how it wasn't what she thought of as a romance. JD Pepper, one of our crew and cast, called it a "dark romance". I'd argue that it is not dark but real, about the kind of struggle many of us face in love. The script has changed a lot over the years, evolving most when I looked at it in 2019 after taking a break for a few years. By the time we started production on December 5th, I believe we were working with the strongest story I've ever written.

The connections in this Western to my personal life don't end with the protagonist's name and the color of the heroine's hair. The female names are all clues. Sarah was the name of another friend and lover who committed suicide. Gail, another name which recurs through the film, is a play off of the "gale" and therefore an ode to Windy, the stage name for the woman who committed that tragic act. In a final stroke of irony, our lead actress shares the same first name as the woman who inspired all of this...There are more connections I cannot speak of. Not now. Maybe not ever.

Regarding the narrative, no I did not go on some journey to find her. The events of the story are all fiction but the emotions are true. It was written with a raw heart. Sometimes the wounds from those days feel like the scars on Sarah's face: they've healed but will always remind me. Other days, those wounds feel as fresh as they did in 2014. And finally bringing this story to life may have opened a few of them up. It has been a hard month, tough and vulnerable all at once. The moments on and off screen have recalled the best and worth of times. But one thing is for sure, every damn day I've felt like I was making the best film of my career.

I've put my whole heart into this one, saving the last of my breath for this last showdown of the year. It hasn't been a secret to those I work with. John remarked after the first day of filming that I was given far more notes on his performance than ever before. Nick, our cinematographer, knows I'm pushing the scenes as much as I can. Every possible ounce of energy must be put into making this movie as great as it can be.

I will end this year tired, broke, not alone but most likely lonely, and happy because the 12 Westerns will be complete. Today, I am 35 years old and have 26 feature films under my belt. If this is the last movie I ever make, I'd be pleased it was this one. It represents everything I've learned and lived over the last ten years of being a filmmaker. It stands for what I believe about men and women, love and romance, a baptism of fire and blood to find peace and understanding. It has all of me in it and I have given everything I have for it.

December 27th, 2020

Our first day at Castle Dome went better than I predicted. Though it took a while to settle into the new location, bring the gear in, and above all wrangle humans, we completed our scenes and ahead of schedule. A couple of our new talent posed different issues. Lorelei had her first big speaking role in the 12, just an extra before this. She was trying hard but also hard as hell to direct because she's not experienced enough to even know what she's doing with her face, voice, and body. Being aware of how you move, etc and being able to control it is essential to be a reliable actor. We got through the scenes with good enough takes to make it work in the edit.

The afternoon went well but as Peter Sherayko showed up, I could tell it wasn't going to be an easy evening. Peter is now our only "name talent" on the film since Lou bailed on us. He's got a ton of credits, the most famous being *Tombstone*. I knew he was a character from John's stories but oh boy is he a character with a capital C. The cantankerous bastard made it tough on us... resisting camera rehearsal ("let's just shoot it") however not knowing his lines, commenting about doing too many takes ("I guess you're no Clint Eastwood") but being the reason we had to keep going. And all of this came at dusk as we were losing light. Later, Amber asked why I shot the scenes then when they were originally set at night as we laughed in retrospect at Pete's shenanigans. She assumed I might have just been trying to wrap early but I explained that was not usually the case with such decisions. We had a chance to show the story transitioning from day to night, rather than do the movie thing where we magically jump a couple hours into the dark. It's a beautiful thing when you can do it. And even better when everyone is cooperative. Such is rarely the case.

December 29th, 2020

The past two days at Castle Dome have been two of the longest this year. Starting at 3 PM and filming way into the night, I have not gotten more than three or four hours of sleep after each shoot. The first of these two days was challenging with several players, a fight scene, our biggest group of extras for the whole production, and lots of story to tell. I think it was also one of my best moments as a director and producer. I was in the zone. A few people commented that I did not seem like myself but they were missing that I was completely focused and hyper aware of all details. I even skipped dinner, not wanting to lose my focus on the scene.

While the cast and crew ate, I brought in our 20 or so extras and blocked their positions for the scene then cleared them and prepared for rehearsal. I knew that the fight scene would be extra challenging. They always are and it doesn't help when one or more of the actors are difficult to work with. Some don't listen. They don't learn.

Regardless of these frustrations, I would call the night successful. Yes, I think it was 2 AM when we finally wrapped but I was proud of the shots and scenes and the other actors involved. Peter was much better behaved. John theorized that he realized I did not find his schtick to be funny and understood that he needed to be a professional. Elley and John Schile were as reliable as usual. And our background was at their best behavior.

...

Our last day at Castle Dome was much more difficult. So we had less people, the short scenes proved to have mini hurdles we needed to overcome. As John said early this morning, we definitely gave our make-up artist Willy too much to bite off. As she did my scalped head for my final scene, I could tell she was doing it in a way that was not consistent with how it had been done before and figured it would not work for the scene. I'm supposed to get shot in the head twice and was hoping to have a shot showing the scalped head with the wounds. Unfortunately this was not possible and so much time was wasted on our efforts to pull it off. These kinds of disappointments will probably not matter a year from now when we're watching the finished product but it is always discouraging when you really want to see something in a scene and it becomes impossible.

Thankfully, Amber's jump from the second story went far better, however by the time we reached it we were already a couple hours behind schedule. I soon knew that it was going to be the latest night of production. She did an amazing job and was fearless in her jumps onto the bed of cardboard boxes that Charles and Mike set up for her. These scenes are incredibly difficult with our limitations of time and resources, light and how cold it was last night.

Once again, I was trying to edit in my head, piecing together the moments of each take that might work and taking away the ones that didn't. This might be the absolute most stressful place to be in as a director, Trying to live in the editing room while managing the set and ultimately having to make a decision when you have enough footage. We did not stop shooting till around 4 o'clock in the morning and most of us did not get back to the hotel till after five.

The hardest part about this is what we faced the next day, today. Our team has to leave Yuma and travel to our final location in Benson. It's almost a five hour drive and that's a long haul considering how exhausted we all are. I am ashamed to admit it but last night on my drive back to the hotel I was fighting not to fall asleep at the wheel and realized how dangerous it is to push my body and the bodies of my beloved crew this far. I write this on my drive and I can only hope that everyone will arrive safe and then we will have an easy day of filming, though it may be short, and will have a few extra hours of sleep tonight. For that, I shall be grateful.

December 31st, 2020

The end of that long drive from Yuma to Benson did not end as I expected. Concerned that our crew would be totally wiped out by the time of arrival, I anticipated a rough night. However, when I arrived at Gammons, the energy was different. John walked around, playing his new role as the manager of the Western town with pride. Forrest unloaded gear with a pep in his step. Even Nick showed up with a renewed spirit. Perhaps we could all feel it was coming to an end, the final stretch. Regardless, we had the night we needed, capturing our scenes with no major hiccups and wrapping an hour ahead of schedule. We needed it so badly and all went to our respective places to stay, ready for rest.

...

The next day also had an ease to it, like a batter rounding the bases after he hit a home run. I am so thankful to run into home base without worry. Larry Poole arrived from California for his scenes as the Blind Rancher, a gruff actor who was a lot of fun to work with. Lucy, from the Coconut Ranch, astounded me again with how good she was as the Deaf Woman. We moved through our lighting and camera set ups, our refined craft in play. At the end of the day, we left once again a couple hours ahead. I returned to Kim's cabin with the ladies. It is a place with a lot of meaning for me, a home where I hung my hat in the early days of planning these films and it feels right to finish here. I stayed up till 3am cutting a teaser trailer for the 12 Westerns together. Amber kept me company most of the time, sipping whiskey by my side.

Today is our last day of filming. I can't believe we got this far. I didn't think I'd make it. There will certainly be tears in my eyes tonight.

January 1st, 2021

Yesterday, our final day, was one of ease, a simple but powerful scene outside the cabin at Gammons Gulch. As we worked through the shots in no rush, I found myself smiling, unable to contain my joy.

The last shot of the 12 Westerns is an insert on a gun, one that Amber's character Sarah opens and discovers two bullets inside. We set up for this final shot, the culmination of 12 months of everything emotion known to man. She went through the action three times. Waiting to say cut, I looked up at my team, meeting each of their gazes. It was no time for loud cries. I said in a quiet tone, "That's it. We did it." I hugged John first as tears filled both our eyes and then quietly went around to each person with an embrace I imagined might come after getting through a battle. I couldn't say much and admitted so. If I did, my voice would break and I'd fall apart.

We started to bring things down the hill and pack up. As I walked up to the saloon, Bandit came outside. I kneeled down and pressed my face against his, tears falling down my cheeks. I whispered in his ear: "We survived."

John Marrs as Jack Travers, his biggest role to date.

Lead actress Amber Rose Mason riding Kaye South.

Elley Ringo returns to our Westerns as Jodie, a prostitute in scenes we filmed at Castle Dome Museum.

Actors portraying Calvary soldiers and captured Apaches in a scene we filmed near Young, Arizona.

Actor Jay Pickett portraying tracker John White. Sadly, we also lost Jay during 2021. This is one of his last performances.

All photographs by Todd South

This book is dedicated to those of our 12 Westerns family who are no longer with us.

Jay, Daulton, Nate Henning, and Bandit Mills.

Travis Mills was born in Quito, Ecuador. He spent the majority of his early life abroad in Europe and Africa before returning to the United States. He settled in Arizona where he co-founded Running Wild Films in 2010 with playwright Gus Edwards. Since then, they have produced twenty-five feature films and more than 100 short film projects. In 2020, Mills took on his most ambitious project yet: the making of 12 feature-length Western films in 12 months. The project was completed and all 12 films released to the public during 2021. As a writer, Mills has short stories published in several literary journals, many of them included in the collection *A Cowboy in Zambia*.

Made in the USA
Monee, IL
18 January 2024

51078689R10201